CONFESSIONS OF A FAILED SOUTHERN LADY

Florence King

Introduced by Sandi Toksvig

Virago

VIRAGO

This edition published in 2006 by Virago Press
First published in Great Britain in 1985 by Michael Joseph

Copyright © Florence King 1985
Introduction copyright © Sandi Toksvig 2006
The moral right of the author has been asserted.

A CIP catalogue record for this book is available
from the British Library

ISBN-13: 978-1-84408-128-8
ISBN-10: 1-84408-128-1

Typeset in Goudy by M Rules
Printed and bound in Great Britain by Clays Ltd, St Ives plc

Virago Press
An imprint of
Little, Brown Book Group
Brettenham House
Lancaster Place
London WC2E 7EN

A member of the Hachette Livre Group of Companies

www.virago.co.uk

INTRODUCTION

> The witty woman is a tragic figure in American life. Wit destroys eroticism and eroticism destroys wit, so women must choose between taking lovers and taking no prisoners.
>
> – Florence King

Funny women have an uncomfortable place in society. It is as though being amusing is somehow offensive to femininity. In a historical sense, it is as if Eve got Adam's rib and not his funny bone and that when gender roles were divided up at the mouth of the cave it was men who were tasked as mirth makers. Certainly there is hardly a man in the world who thinks he can't tell a joke and there are very few women who will try. There is, however, a quick sociological test anyone can do to disprove this separation of the female from the funny. At any formal function you might attend, go and spend five minutes outside the ladies' facilities. Each time the door opens the sound that will almost certainly emanate is one of laughter. Then, at the risk of an arrestable offence, spend the same amount of time outside the gents. Here the world is almost silent, bar the occasional mutter – usually about golf. Men are too busy literally sizing each other up to waste time on bons mots and amusing observations.

Being funny about life is absolutely ingrained in women but

it is not something generally done for public consumption. One is as unlikely to attend a dinner party that amusingly concludes with a female guest putting a lampshade on her head as one is to hear a risqué joke as the opening gambit to a meeting of the Women's Institute. For most women, finding the humour in life is a secret weapon used to combat the inequities they face and it is utilised daily without too much thought. Gather any three women together and soon they will begin to tell each other stories. Stories that are usually both poignant and comic. This side of humour worries most men in that there is a danger of making some kind of personal revelation that doesn't involve the engine size of their car. Men prefer to engage in something the Americans call a 'joke-off', where they tell one properly formulated gag after another in an attempt to get the biggest laugh. For women humour is a subtler tool that is not about dominating a group through wit, or used to draw attention to oneself. It is not a big leap from the personal to the professional to realise why there are so few women making a living through comedy.

I grew up in the United States in the 1960s and the role models for a fledgling female humorist were slight. If they existed then they tended to base much of their comedy on the fact that they did not fit a traditional woman's mould. There was a sense that stepping outside the bounds of acceptable female behaviour required not a single step but a giant leap. The few comediennes of the time went one of two ways – they either deliberately exaggerated their odd looks for laughs (Phyllis Diller, Lily Tomlin, Ruth Buzzi) or they allowed themselves to be both amusing and pretty by pretending to be stupid (Goldie Hawn, Jo Anne Worley, Judy Carne). Either method had a sort of neutering effect on the comedy and made it all seem much less aggressive.

If there were few funny women at the forefront of comedic performance then there were even fewer in the literary world.

Try as I might, I could not find the female equivalent of the sardonic Mark Twain or the observational James Thurber. There were, of course, female authors with wit – Jane Austen, Dorothy Parker, Stella Gibbon and even Jean Kerr who wrote *Please, Don't Eat the Daisies*, but none, it appeared, with (and here the term always used is interesting) the balls to grab life by the throat and wring a laugh out of it. Then in 1985 the American writer Florence King produced *Confessions of a Failed Southern Lady*. Here, for the first time in my literary experience, was a book written by a woman, that ought to be printed with a mechanism for turning down the volume of the reader. It was, and continues to be, outrageous and laugh-out-loud funny.

It was also proof, if proof were needed, that the greatest gift any parent can provide for the putative comic writer is a dysfunctional childhood. *Confessions* has been called both autobiographical and semi-autobiographical. Either term will do as one way or another most writers are economical with the truth about their past. King was born in 1936 and raised by her grandmother in Tidewater, Virginia. It is in this Deep South setting that the book begins. Florence's family provided material that any comic writer would kill for. Her mother 'was a ninth-generation Virginian, the daughter of a relentless memsahib, yet she shrugged off every tenet of Southern womanhood and turned the air blue every time she opened her mouth.' She had smoked since she was eight, preferred baseball to society balls and had resisted every attempt by her own mother to turn her into a lady. 'Granny tried to put a good face on matters by attending a few games so people would think she approved of girlish sport, but the day she noticed a lump in Mama's cheek and realized it was tobacco, she had to be helped from the bleachers and escorted home.' Despairing of her own child, Granny looked around the family for a suitable female that she could mould into a lady: 'someone delicate and fragile in both body and spirit, a true exemplar of Southern womanhood.

Someone in other words, either sick or crazy.' Granny finds her prize in Evelyn, a nervous young thing whose troubles are blamed entirely on her womb and who convinces herself 'that being delicate down below' is part of her charm. Evelyn takes to carrying an empty pickle jar around in case her womb should fall out in public.

Despite not being the marrying kind, Florence's mother does settle down with Herb, an English ne'er-do-well musician. His lack of prospects does not deter Granny: 'He was English. It was all she cared about. It dropped, like the quality of mercy, into every conversation she had.' When Florence is born Granny comes for the weekend and stays for thirty years in a vain attempt to turn the hapless and hopeless Florence into a lady: 'expecting Granny to stay away from an unformed blob of female material was like expecting a cobra to stay away from a flute.'

The book is full of fabulous one-liners – 'Like charity, schiz-ophrenia begins at home' – and excellent advice for the fledgling Southern belle. We learn that 'Silver is the Southern woman's proudest possession' and that 'every decent woman goes to her husband with twelve "covers," and if the knives have hollow handles he'll be running with other women before the year is out, you wait and see. No man respects a woman with hollow handles.'

It's a book that pulls no punches and it is hard to recall that as late as 1985, King's revelation in it of a lesbian affair at college was considered at best risqué and at worst quite shocking. Here, at last, was a woman who wrote with no holds barred. It was gutsy, daring and great. Whether the book accurately portrays her actual life seems unimportant. What matters is that here is some of the best comic writing ever put down on paper.

When Florence King wrote about her foray into lesbianism there were those in the gay rights movement who longed to claim her for their own. In her subsequent life and writing, King has, however, shown no inclination to take up the pink banner. Her author's biography clearly states 'Florence King has never married' but it gives no indication of what else she might have been up to. Nor did she seem keen to march to the drum of the women's movement. When she wrote her first novel after *Confessions* (*When Sisterhood Was in Flower*) she took careful aim at feminists and shot them down in a barrage of lampooning wit. There is, for example, Grace Garrison-Talbot, president of the Birth Bucket League of America, who bemoans the fact that zoo directors won't enter into a meaningful dialogue about supplying crocodile dung to line the buckets to provide a soft landing for the newborn.

In her writing Florence King has always been her own woman and that woman is a product of the conservative Deep South. She has subsequently written many think-pieces for the American right-wing press, including her long-running column, 'The Misanthrope', where for many years in the *National Review* she professed to hate everyone. One can get a sense of the type of journalism she has plumped for by looking online at another conservative publication that has occupied her time, *The American Enterprise*. The advertisements that frame the copy tell you everything you need to know about the target audience. There is GodLovesSoldiers.com – 'a site for soldiers about Jesus Christ' – or ahuracorp.com who sell chemical detectors to 'immediately identify explosives and chemicals used in terrorist attacks.'

There is a modern penchant for attempting to marry up the personality of the author with the product of their pen, which is not always helpful. Learning that Thomas Hardy was brilliant on the subject of 'man's inhumanity to man' but not awfully nice to his wife should not detract from the writing. The fact that the left-wing, liberal lesbian who wishes to embrace Ms King may find some of her later right-wing associations hard to welcome is unimportant. It is Florence's very refusal to succumb to any social pressures that makes her such a wonderful writer. In her collection of essays, *Reflections in a Jaundiced Eye*, she shows a joyous willingness to have a go at anyone. 'We will never have a nation of cultured and reflective citizens as long as the press keeps printing The Sentence: Neighbours described the gunman as a quiet man who kept to himself.' Her work is that of a woman who can't be pigeon-holed and who doesn't give a damn. Thank God.

Sandi Toksvig, 2006

To the memory of my father,
Herbert Frederick King

'Like most exceptional women, Rosa was not entirely feminine.'

– *The Duchess of Jermyn Street*,
Daphne Fielding

PROLOGUE

There are ladies everywhere, but they enjoy generic recognition only in the South. There is a New England old maid but not a New England lady. There is a Midwestern farm wife but not a Midwestern lady. There is most assuredly a California girl, but if anyone spoke of a California lady, even Phil Donahue and Alan Alda would laugh.

If you wish to understand the American woman, study the Southern woman. The sweetening process that feminists call 'socialization' is simply a less intense version of what goes on in every Southern family. We call it 'rearing.' If the rearing is successful, it results in that perfection of femininity known as a lady.

I was reared. On the day in 1948 that I got my first period, my grandmother gave me a clipping. I suppose it came from the Daughters' magazine since she never read anything else. It said:

When God made the Southern woman, He summoned His angel messengers and He commanded them to go through all the star-strewn vicissitudes of space and gather all there was of beauty, of brightness and sweetness, of enchantment and glamour, and when they returned and laid the golden harvest at His feet, He began in their wondering presence the work of fashioning the Southern girl. He wrought with the golden gleam of the stars, with the changing colors of the rainbow's hues and the pallid silver of the moon. He wrought with the crimson that swoons in the rose's ruby heart, and the snow that gleams on the lily's petal. Then, glancing down deep into His own bosom, He took of the love that gleamed there like pearls beneath the sun-kissed waves of a summer sea, and thrilling that love into the form He had fashioned, all heaven veiled its face, for lo, He had wrought the Southern girl.

That my mother referred to this paean as 'a crock of shit' goes far to explain why Granny worked so hard at my rearing. She was a frustrated ladysmith and I was her last chance. Mama had defeated her but she kept the anvil hot for me and began hammering and firing with a strength born of desperation from the day I entered the world until the day she left it.

This is the story of my years on her anvil. Whether she succeeded in making a lady out of me is for you to decide, but I will say one thing in my own favor before we begin.

No matter which sex I went to bed with, I never smoked on the street.

1

My ladylike adventures have taken me from Seattle to Paris, but last year I was carried back to Tidewater Virginia, which my ancestors helped to unsettle.

A romantic version of my address can be found on the first page of Thackeray's *Henry Esmond*, which kicks off with a description of the Esmond family's royal grant 'in Westmoreland County between the Rappahannock and Potomac rivers.' It was the only book I ever read that Granny did not tell me to get my nose out of. Though she hated 'blue-stockings' – her name for female intellectuals, who could never be ladies – she actually read a few pages of it herself, muttering, 'Esmond . . . Esmond . . . do I know any Esmonds?'

Being an Englishman, my father was singularly unimpressed by Granny's ancestors, so I knew he was getting ready to enjoy himself. I met his dancing eyes and read the message in them: *Don't tell her it's a novel.* We let her go on until she was saying, 'It was Samuel Esmond who married my great-great-grand-father's half-sister.' Preening herself, she added, 'Our royal grant was next to theirs.'

I had heard about our royal grant many times. Granny was always careful to keep it in the same place, but the grantor changed depending upon what monarchical name happened to pop into her head while she was launched on her pipe dreams.

Her boasts were believable as long as she stuck to kings and queens from the pre-1776 era, but when she claimed a royal grant from William IV, my father started laughing so hard he had to leave the table.

'William the Fourth reigned from 1830 to 1837, Granny,' I said.

'Be that as it may,' she replied serenely.

Our ancestors did arrive very early in Virginia – 1672 – but they were not the kind of people Granny said they were, and they rose very little in the social scale in subsequent generations. I would not be at all surprised if I turned out to be a direct descendant of the Spotsylvania hatchetman who relieved Kunta Kinte of his foot.

I began life by letting down the side. Being the first person in my family who was not born in Virginia made the radio quiz shows of the forties a painful experience for me. Crouching like Cinderella beside the huge Philco console, I listened to the wild applause that vibrated through its brocaded sound vents when a contestant named Texas as his home state. Texas always got the biggest hand, but any state seemed to arouse the audience; even Rhode Island got a big sympathy vote.

I looked up at the two adults on the sofa. Granny was crocheting and Mama was reading the *Times-Herald* sports page and chainsmoking Luckies. They looked as if nothing was wrong, and of course, nothing was wrong for them. They had a home state; I did not.

'What would I say?' I asked.

'About what?' Mama muttered abstractedly.

'If I was on the show and they asked me my home state?'

'You're a Virginian,' Granny said with a sublime smile. 'Everyone is.'

'But I wasn't born there. Suppose they asked me where I was born?'

Mama lit a new cigarette from the butt in her yellowed fingers.

'Well, tell 'em the truth, what's wrong with that?'

'Because they wouldn't clap. They only clap for states.'

'If the District isn't good enough for 'em, tell 'em to take their sixty-four dollars and shove it.'

'Oh, Louise!' Granny cried. 'That's no expression to use in front of the child! How do you expect her to grow up to be a lady if you cuss like a trooper?'

'Oh, shit.'

'I don't have a home state,' I mourned.

'Oh, for God's sake! Tell 'em you're from Maryland, then. Washington's really in Maryland anyhow. Washingtonians used to have to put both District and Maryland tags on their cars. Tell 'em *that*.'

Like charity, schizophrenia begins at home. Washington would really have been in Virginia, too, if Virginia had not been what Mama called 'a bunch of goddamn Indian-givers.' In 1789, the Old Dominion donated a section of Fairfax County to make up the South Bank of the District of Columbia; but angered when all the important government buildings were erected on the Maryland side, they took it back. The disputed portion was called Alexandria County until 1920, when it was renamed Arlington County. It was here that Mama was born in 1908.

Arlington is now part of the polyglot Yankee suburb known tactfully as 'Northern Virginia,' but until the end of World War II there was no such place. It was simply part of Virginia, a rural area dotted with small villages whose names survive today as shopping malls or beltline exits: Rosslyn, Clarendon, Ballston, Cherrydale, Tyson's Corner, and Bailey's Crossroads. The people who lived there were not commuters in the modern sense; they might, like my grandfather, have worked for the 'guvment' because the government happened to be close by, but otherwise they looked on the Nation's Capital as a shopping town, the way people in northern Mississippi regard Memphis.

Mama grew up in Ballston on a dirt road in a white frame house bordered by a field of wild strawberries and enhanced by a lacy gazebo in the backyard. She had an older brother, Botetourt (pronounced Bottatot), named for the Virginia Royal Governor from whom Granny claimed descent. Granny, of course, actually called him Botetourt; Mama called him Gottapot and everyone else called him Bud. After my grandfather died in 1921, the worthy Botetourt married and moved to Falls Church, leaving Granny and Mama to fight out alone what was by then a hopeless battle over Mama's image.

She was not pretty but our Indian blood had come out in her and given her face a noble cast. She looked like a blond Duchess of Windsor; the same winglike cheekbones, big tense jaw, and thin clamped mouth. Her stark features and big-boned bonyness were made for devastating compensatory chic, but unlike the Duchess, Mama was not interested in creating illusions.

She started smoking cornsilk at eight. At twelve she taught herself to drive by stealing Botetourt's car and driving all the way to Fairfax Courthouse before they caught her. At fifteen she quit school, applied for a work permit, and got a job as a telephone operator at the Clarendon exchange. With her first pay she bought an infielder's glove and joined the telephone company's softball team as shortstop. Granny tried to put a good face on matters by attending a few games so people would think she approved of girlish sport, but the day she noticed a lump in Mama's cheek and realized it was tobacco, she had to be helped from the bleachers and escorted home.

Scarcely a day passed without an 'Oh, Louise – Oh, shit' argument. The worst crisis erupted over the gazebo. Granny kept telling Mama to 'use' it, so Mama hung a punching bag from the middle of the roof and got one of her good ole boy pals to give her boxing lessons. Needless to say, men felt comfortable around her and frequently took her to ball games and races, but no matter how many times Granny told her to keep her dates waiting, my competitive mother would dress early, lie in wait behind the curtains watching for her escort, and then throw open the door before the first ring and say, 'I beat you!'

Knowing that she could do nothing with Mama, Granny looked around the family for a malleable girl who would heed her advice, a surrogate daughter cast in the traditional mold, someone delicate and fragile in both body and spirit, a true exemplar of Southern womanhood. Someone, in other words, either sick or crazy.

One of the joys of growing up Southern is listening to women argue about whether nervous breakdowns are more feminine than female trouble, or vice versa. They never put it quite that bluntly, but it is precisely what they are arguing about. These two afflictions are the sine qua non of female identity and the Southern woman is not happy unless her family history manifests one or the other. Her preference is dictated by her own personality and physical type. Well-upholstered energetic clubwomen usually opt for female trouble, while languid fine-drawn aristocrats choose nervous breakdowns.

Granny's next-door neighbor in Ballston was Aunt Nana Fairbanks, who made a home for her niece, Evelyn Cunningham. Evelyn was the same age as Mama but famed for a very different sort of double play: on the day she was supposed to be taken to the state mental hospital in Staunton, she had such bad cramps that she missed the ambulance.

Here was an ornament to grace any family tree, so the two dowagers started fighting over her. Picture, if you will, Aunt Nana, *née* Cunningham, moving across her yard in her Mandarin glide to meet Granny, *née* Upton, who is moving across her yard in her Roman matron strut. They meet at a hole in the hedge like two opposing generals in a parley ground and discuss the prize booty both of them are determined to claim.

'Evelyn is having a nervous breakdown,' Aunt Nana said proudly. 'All of the Cunninghams are high-strung.'

'Evelyn doesn't take after the Cunninghams,' Granny replied. 'It's the Upton womb that's causing those spells of hers.'

'I was in the middle of my nervous breakdown when I married Mr Fairbanks,' Aunt Nana recalled with a fond smile. 'I was so run down I only weighed ninety pounds. He had to carry me around in his arms that whole first year.'

'When I married Mr Ruding, the doctor told him I might never be able to carry a child.' Granny smiled. 'I had a descending womb – it runs in the family – and it was just hanging by a thread. I couldn't sleep, I cried all the time – just like Evelyn.'

'I almost lost my mind.' Aunt Nana reminisced. 'Evelyn's mind is going, I can see all the signs.'

'You can just look at Evelyn and tell she's delicate down below,' Granny sighed.

'It's the Cunningham taint.'

'It's the Upton womb.'

Granny got the prize booty. One morning around four she was awakened by a violent pounding at the door. It was Evelyn, her blond hair in rag curlers and her peaches-and-cream complexion streaked with tears.

'Aunt Lura! Aunt Nana said she's going to send me to the *insane* asylum again!'

'There's nothing wrong with your mind, it's your parts. Come in and have a glass of warm milk.'

Evelyn accepted and stayed two years. During this time Granny had the malleable daughter of her dreams. Clay in the hands of a strong personality, Evelyn did everything she was told. There was no need to teach her to be late; her catatonic seizures, when she stood frozen in the middle of her room with silent tears running down her face, were good for at least half an hour. Nor did she have to be reminded to 'make him look for you.' Wandering off was one of her specialties. Ballston parties at this time were enlivened by the many girls who pretended to disappear, and Evelyn, who actually did.

No matter when these spells occurred, Granny always blamed them on premenstrual tension, which she called 'the pip.' Eager to deny Aunt Nana's diagnosis of madness, Evelyn grasped the pelvic straw Granny held out. Soon she forgot all about the Cunningham taint and started talking about the Upton womb, until she convinced herself that being 'delicate down below' was part of her charm.

Choreographed by Granny, she became the most popular hysteric in the Virginia Hump. Men came from as far as Leesburg to gaze into her popping eyes and grasp her trembling hands. The intense femininity that seemed to come so naturally to her held them in sexual thrall. They grew hot with desire when she searched frantically through her pocketbook, shrieking, 'Oh, what am I looking for?' They sighed like furnaces over her habit of breaking into a chorus of 'Jada Jada Jing' and being unable to stop. They could not get enough of her berserk sensuality; the more she shook, the more she gasped, the more their spirits rose, for if she was this way on the porch, what must she be like in bed? Even the man whose car she wrecked came back for more; he bought another one and went on giving her driving lessons just to be near her.

The one man in Ballston who was not in love with Evelyn was Preston Hunt, whose heart belonged to Daddy. If the Jewish boy's problem is the umbilical cord, the Southern boy's is the tail of the spermatozoön. Preston's father was a classic Colonel Portnoy whose favorite word was 'manly.' Preston was not manly enough to suit Daddy. The family hardware store was frequently the scene of screaming debacles whenever Mr Hunt, who saw himself as a hot-tempered *beau sabreur* of the Old

South, lost what little self-control he had and inflicted corporal punishment on his twenty-eight-year-old son.

It was rough-and-ready Mama who met Preston's emotional needs, and so he began courting her. She despised him for being the *garçon manqué* she knew herself to be, but he came along at a time when she needed to show Granny and Evelyn that she, too, could catch a beau. They got together, and to Granny's unanalytical delight, they used the gazebo, where the punching bag swaying gently in the breeze supplied the filip Preston required. He came over every night and sat in the lacy boxing ring talking about his father.

'My daddy whipped me till my nose bled buttermilk,' he confided happily. 'I was late to work this morning and he took an old harness left over from when we sold them, and he just laid it on me something terrible. But I deserved it. Daddy's right to whip me when I need it, I know that. I don't mean to talk against him.' His voice began to tremble. 'You know that, don't you? I love Daddy! Did I sound to you like I was finding fault with him? Tell me the truth, Louise. Do you think I bad-mouthed Daddy just now?'

'You're a sissy, Preston,' Mama snarled in the azalea-scented night. 'I hate sissies! If I were a man, you wouldn't catch me being a sissy! I hate you, Preston! Get out and don't come back!'

Naturally he obeyed but he always came back. He could not keep away from her. A few nights later he would return and they would sit in the moonlit gazebo and whisper another round of sweet nothings.

'I'd like to kill you, Preston. I'd like to get in my car and run right over you. If I were a man, I'd wipe the floor with you! I'd knock you into the middle of next week! Stop doing your mouth that way. You know what way I mean – twisting it down at the corner and making that squirty noise. Why are you sitting with your feet folded one over the other? You always sit like that! I hate the way you sit! *I hate your feet!*'

'I'm sorry, honey—'

'Shut up! Get out!'

In the summer of 1933, he bought season box seats on the first base line at Griffith Stadium and took her to see the Senators play every weekend. As Mama expertly marked her scorecard and squinted through the smoke from her Lucky Strike Greens, Preston gazed at her with plangent expectancy, but she was so intent on the game that she forgot to bully him. Unable to bear the torments of respite, he devised ways to get on her nerves, like eating his hot dogs from the middle, but it drew nothing more than an absent-minded 'Stop that, Preston.'

As the season wore on, he developed several new facial tics, squeezed his blackheads, and even tried wearing one black shoe and one brown one, but Mama was too engrossed in Lou Gehrig to notice. At any other time of the year she would have threatened to cut off his feet and throw them in his face, but not in summer.

By the end of the baseball season Preston was in an advanced state of anxiety. The situation came to a head the night he escorted Mama and Granny to a dinner dance given by the Daughters, at which Granny was scheduled to play the Statue of Liberty in a patriotic tableau.

It was a dressy affair that required all the things tomboys hate, like armpit-length white gloves, so Preston was counting on Mama to be in a bad mood. She was, but there was nothing she could do about it. The hall was crammed with Daughters, and like all Southern girls in the presence of formidable dowagers, she was forced completely out of character. She could not very well bellow threats about running over him while all the old ladies were telling her how sweet she looked, so the abasement Preston craved continued to elude him. He lasted through dinner, but finally the specter of a gentle Mama proved too much for him. Murmuring his excuses, he drifted away. Some moments later when the dancing began he was nowhere to be found.

'Where's that nice boy?' bayed one of the Daughters, and it traveled around the herd. Soon the question was on every wrinkled lip as the dowagers rubbernecked the ballroom, speculating to each other and commiserating with Mama about what a shame it was that she had to miss the grand march.

'I'll split his scalp open!' roared Mr Hunt. But for once, Preston had anticipated his father's desires and beaten him, as it were, to the punch. He was found unconscious in a men's room stall, a shattered bourbon bottle beside him, his stiff white shirtfront saturated with whiskey and blood. Evidently he had slipped while chugalugging and struck his head on the toilet seat. His scalp was split open.

An ambulance came and took him to the hospital.

'Do you want to go to him, Louise?' asked Granny.

Her question turned on the Daughters. Eyes burning with the morbid eroticism of old ladies, they urged Mama to take up a vigil at Preston's bedside.

'A sick man falls in love mighty fast,' said one brightly.

'Men don't care about hugging and kissing,' said another. 'They just want somebody to take care of them.'

'Catch a man when he's flat on his back and he's yours forever,' advised a third.

It was the penis-washing school of femininity. As Mama tried to dream up an excuse they would swallow, a strange voice spoke.

'I say, I found this on the men's room floor. It must have fallen out of that chap's pocket.'

Turning, she saw a tall wiry man in his early thirties with dark red hair the color of black cherries. There was a trombone mouthpiece sticking out of the breast pocket of his tuxedo. He held a cigarette case.

'Oh, yes,' said Granny. 'That's Preston's. We'll keep it for him.'

He handed it to her and was about to turn away when one of the Daughters gazed intently into his face and clawed at his sleeve with her brown-spotted hand.

'Are you here tonight?' she asked.

'I believe so, madam.'

Her egrette danced on her palsied head as she peered closer.

'Have I seen you?'

'That's for you to say, madam.'

'But I must know you,' she quavered. 'I've never met anyone I didn't know.'

'I'm in the band, madam, my name is Herbert King.'

'Oh, the band! Then you're not *here*.' Her head shook harder as she cocked it in the direction of the ballroom and listened carefully. A look of alarm spread over her face.

'But the band isn't playing!' she cried reedily.

'We're on a break, madam.'

'What did you break? I declare, this night is star-crossed.'

Before it could get worse, they were interrupted by ruffles and flourishes from the Ballston Fife and Drum Corps.

'Oh, Law!' Granny exclaimed. 'It's time for the tableau. I've got to get into my costume.'

She and the other Daughters bustled off. My parents were alone together. After a stealthy look around, Herb took a flask from his pocket and poured gin into Mama's punch cup, then served himself a straight shot in the little silver cap. They stood sipping together on the edge of the ballroom as the patriotic tableau began.

As the fifes struck up a shrill rendition of 'Columbia, the Gem of the Ocean,' Granny sailed in, draped in cheesecloth and dignity, a tinfoil-wrapped flashlight in her left hand and a hastily covered 1933 Sears catalogue in the crook of her right arm. Raising the light on high, she began.

'Give me your tard, your poah . . .'

'Who's that old bat?' Herb whispered.

'My mother.'

It was a bad start but the gin helped. After the tableau Mama introduced him to Granny and he offered to drive them home. Granny accepted, charmed by his accent and the nationality it proclaimed. Like all Daughters in their secret hearts, she was such an anglophile that she would have accepted a ride from Jack the Ripper.

They piled into Herb's roadster; Mama in front holding the trombone and clarinet and Granny ensconced in the rumble seat looking like Queen Victoria presiding at a durbar.

She got the shock of her life when she invited him to dinner the following Sunday. He knew nothing about his ancestors and seemed less than awestruck when she told him about hers. Alarmed, she showed him my grandfather's framed copy of the Lancashire Assize Rolls of 1246 containing the name 'Griffin del Ruding,' but all he did was smile politely. Gazing around at the documents and charts that lined the walls of her parlor, he said he felt as if he were in the British Museum, and Granny, whose idea of wit lay somewhere between black-face vaudeville and slippery banana peels, took it as a compliment.

He did, however, expound on the subject of his immediate family because it gave him a golden opportunity to pull Granny's leg. Arranging his face in a deadpan mask, he told her the sad tale of the Kings: his father, a long-shoreman on the Limehouse docks, crushed to death under a bale of machine parts; his mother, dying of the drink in Whitechapel Hospital, his brother Harry, fallen at Ypres and buried in Flanders Fields.

This much was true, but when he got to his sister Daisy he gilded the lily.

'She was a good sort, our Daisy was, but she ran afoul of a heartless seducer. Left her in the family way, he did. After that she took to the streets. Every night she walked up and down, up and down, up and down . . .'

'The poor child!' Granny cried.

'Oh, no mum, she did quite well for herself. She had fifty yards between the station and the church.'

Evelyn fell madly in love with him at first sight. Used to effortless conquests, she simply sat down across from him, smiled her *exaltée* smile, and waited for him to turn to jelly. She met with Herbish impassivity. Challenged by his unflagging disinterest, she started chasing him. When she learned that he liked to attend the National Geographic Society's Sunday night lectures, she got one of her devoted beaux to drive her into Washington so she could stalk her elusive prey.

Herb entered the lobby and found her perched like an epileptic hummingbird on a stone flower urn. There was nothing to do but invite her to join him. Unfortunately, that night's offering was a slide lecture called 'Insects of South America.'

They went into the lecture hall and took seats on folding wooden chairs. Evelyn's poppy eyes widened. 'These are the kind of chairs they have in funeral parlors,' she whimpered. As the room filled up with entomologists, she looked around warily. 'These people depress me. They look like they're a hundred and thirty if they're a day.' She fidgeted and kicked her foot back and forth until the first slide came on.

'The Amazon beetle,' intoned the lecturer.

'Oh, my Lord! Why didn't somebody step on it instead of taking its picture? They ought to cut that old jungle down! I bet they brought back some bug eggs on those old pictures. I itch. Don't you itch? I swear, something's crawling on me. When people go to those old foreign countries they always find things in their clothes afterwards. I bet something crawled in the camera when they weren't looking – *there's something down the back of my dress!*'

The audience was composed of dusty emeritus professor types whose misogyny was easily stirred. Amid barks of 'Get that woman out of here!' Herb led the shaking, sobbing Evelyn outside. As he stood on 16th Street wondering what to do with her, her beau drove up and helped her into the car.

She did not return home that night. Around three A.M. Granny received a phone call from Ellicott City, Maryland, one of the elopement towns of the Upper South. It was Evelyn announcing her marriage to the boy who had helped her stalk Herb. Having caught her in a weak moment, he had begged her to marry him and she, busily scratching, had said yes.

The following week Herb asked Mama out to dinner. I don't know how much his choice was influenced by his bout with Evelyn's full-throttle femininity, but for whatever reason, they started courting. It was a peculiar courtship. They never had a normal Saturday night date like other couples because that was Herb's big work night. They never went dancing; it would have been a busman's holiday for him, and Mama hated to dance. The one baseball game they attended produced a conversation that anticipated Abbott and Costello by ten years, and the bassoon concert left Mama with permanent psychological scars. Herb drank but he didn't smoke; Mama smoked but she didn't drink, so they could not enjoy Repeal. Both liked to take drives in the country but he wouldn't go over thirty and she wouldn't go under sixty, so they could not occupy the same car without giving each other nervous prostration. There was nothing to do except keep on eating dinner, so that's what they did.

What they talked about over their dinner dates is unimaginable because they had absolutely nothing in common. Both had left school at fifteen but Mama quit because she hated school, while Herb's termination was decided for him by the rigid caste system of Edwardian England. Mama never read a book; Herb was a compulsive reader who had educated himself with a library card. Mama hated to be alone; Herb had so many inner resources he could have committed *folie à deux* all by himself. Had he been shipwrecked on a desert island he would have become, like the Birdman of Alcatraz, a self-taught expert in natural history.

They were alike in only one way, and perhaps it was the thing that drew them together. Neither of them had turned out the way they were supposed to. Herb was a product of the East End slums, the son of a slattern who played the piano in a pub for free gin, yet he was a gentleman and a scholar. Mama was a ninth-generation Virginian, the daughter of a relentless memsahib, yet she shrugged off every tenet of Southern womanhood and turned the air blue every time she opened her mouth.

My parents were *sui generis*: they had invented themselves.

Granny was overjoyed by the marriage. Every practicality dear to the hearts of mothers melted in the glow of Herb's sun, which happened to be the one that never set. He was English. It was all she cared about, all she talked about. It dropped, like the quality of mercy, into every conversation she had; the butcher, the baker, the Daughters, the Dames, and the hobo who begged old clothes all heard about 'my son-in-law, he's English, you know.'

That Herb's free-lance income varied, that he worked in an unstable and sometimes unsavory field, that he occasionally hired out as a bartender, that he would never have a pension, that he was, in fact, technically unemployed, mattered not. An Englishman was Granny's version of a doctor.

2

Being a great believer in roots, Granny wanted them to live with her in Ballston, but Herb needed to be near the big downtown hotels and clubs, so they moved to northwest Washington and set up housekeeping in a two-room apartment on Park Road, conveniently located around the corner from the 11th and Monroe streetcar line.

The building was a former townhouse whose owner had been ruined in 1929; unable to afford an architect or a contractor, he had converted the place himself, evidently while still in shock. Mama and Herb had a triangular foyer with the front door on the hypotenuse, an L-shaped kitchen with nothing in the windowless short leg, and a Tudor priest's hole in the bathroom that led to a back porch where Mama kept a wringer washer. To do the laundry, she had to get down on all fours and push the basket through ahead of her. The only convenient feature was a hall that ran down one whole side of the unit, making it possible to reach any room without going through any other. When Herb got home from work at two or three in the morning he could get to the bathroom or kitchen without going through the bedroom and disturbing Mama, who was a morning person. He read until sunrise and went to bed around the time she got up.

Her idea of breakfast was coffee and cigarettes, so Herb

cooked his own bacon and eggs. Her other specialties, culled in bridal haste from Depression-era newspapers, were mock chicken salad, which involved a can of tuna fish; and mock salmon loaf, which involved a can of tuna fish and a bottle of pink vegetable coloring. When Herb, oblique as always, suggested a mockless Friday, she fixed him a hot dog.

She got pregnant shortly before their first anniversary. The news brought Granny to Park Road on wingèd Enna Jettick feet.

'I was worried about you being alone at night, what with the hours Mr King keeps,' she said as she sailed in, 'so I decided to come and stay with you until the baby is born.'

Great believers in roots are seldom great believers in luggage. Granny had never owned a suitcase and looked down on people who did, calling them 'gallivanters.' Hooked over her wrist was an old Lansburgh's shopping bag containing a couple of extra housedresses, six pairs of pink rayon drawers (XL), six pairs of orangy service-weight stockings, an extra set of Shapely Stout corsets, and a curling iron that had to be heated on the stove.

Herb bought a rollaway bed for the living room and adapted to her presence with awesome nonchalance. Their mutual preference for the formal mode of address elevated the situation to an eerily civilized plane. Going into a kitchen filled with the smell of scorched hair to find a two-hundred-pound mother-in-law in a cloud of steam, he merely said, 'Good afternoon, Mrs Ruding,' to which Granny graciously replied, 'Good afternoon, Mr King.'

To everyone's benefit she took over the cooking. Ever solicitous of male comfort and well-being, she fixed all of Herb's favorite dishes: boiled cabbage, boiled potatoes, boiled brussels sprouts, and *boeuf à l'anglaise*, or boiled beef. When he happened to mention that he liked grilled kidneys for breakfast, she put on her hat and went immediately to the store to buy some. In exotic moods she fixed her two gourmet specialties, chili and shrimp curry, omitting the chili powder and the curry powder respectively. Her explanation: 'We don't need any foreigners around here.' Herb agreed: 'There's nothing like good plain food.'

He gained ten needed pounds and the marriage gained a needed buffer. Being home in the daytime had thrown him together with Mama in a Garden of Eden intimacy that neither was equipped to handle. They had never known what to do with themselves in tandem and now there was the problem of entertaining a pregnant tomboy. Washington was full of interesting things to do and Herb had a nose for finding obscure free exhibits and lectures, but Mama would have none of it. The Smithsonian bored her, the Library of Congress was too quiet, and the National Gallery was full of dumb pictures. It was their courtship all over again, with the sobering addition of an embryonic tie-that-binds, so Granny arrived just in time. Now Herb could go off by himself during the day without feeling guilty. He left the apartment after his noon breakfast and threw himself into the most innocent pastimes in the history of husbands. The time slugs on his reading-room slips were his bond.

Mama spent the day eating for two, smoking for six, and listening to Granny's obstetrical lectures. It was the tiny garments subdivision of 'delicate down below.' Descriptions of dilating one, two, three, four fingers; the tragedy of poor Alice Langley who dilated four fingers and stayed that way ('Her husband started chasing other women'); stretch marks, varicose veins, calcium deficiency ('a tooth for every baby'), tubal pregnancies, breeched presentations, ten-month babies that never got born, babies strangled by the cord, the woman who delivered placenta previa, and the woman who delivered a watery mole.

The stygian serial acquired another raconteuse when Granny ran into Jensy Custis on 14th Street. Jensy was a black woman who used to work for Granny in Ballston. Now she was living in Washington and doing free-lance cleaning, so Granny hired her to clean the Park Road place one day a week.

When Jensy saw Mama's swollen ankles, she let out her 'OOOOEEEE!' of fright.

'You got de dropsy, babe?' she asked ominously.

Before Mama could reply, Jensy launched into a story about the time her midwife-mother had officiated at the birth of a sixteen-pound monster born with an exposed backbone, webbed feet, and its face on top of its head.

'Jensy, you remember the watery mole, don't you?' asked Granny.

'Oh, yes'm, I sho does,' Jensy said with a nostalgic sigh. 'I cleaned fo' dat lady's sister fo' years.'

'What's a watery mole?' asked Mama.

'It's a baby that never becomes a baby,' Granny explained. 'The doctor called it a "human deliquescence." It's just lumps of slime held together by stringy bands that would have been the bones and muscles.' She shook her head in wonder. 'It was the only one ever born in Virginia.'

'Ain't been one lak it befo' or since.'

They were like two good ole boys eulogizing a favorite hunting dog.

Granny and Jensy belonged to the babies-are-women's-business school of obstetrics, whose first rule was 'Throw out the men and get to work.' When Mama said she was planning to have the baby in a hospital, they recoiled in horror.

Jensy, a font of puritanism, sucked in her lip and gave Mama a look of heartbroken disillusionment.

'Is dis my sweet pure chile I hear talkin' 'bout goin' to a hospittle? Miss Louise, you doan want *mens* messin' wid you at a time lak dat, does you?'

Granny, more devious, used the excuse of our aristocratic heritage.

'Louise, giving birth at home is the only way to be sure of getting the right baby. Suppose you got some trashy woman's baby by mistake? It wouldn't have any blood. Hospitals get the babies mixed up all the time, you know. Of course, they don't dare admit it, but I have it on good authority. Those nurses are so busy having things to do with doctors that they can't think straight.'

'Dat de truth. Dem nurses is lak de fleshpots of Babylon.'

'Many nurses are insane, you know. They get so jealous from having to take care of other women's babies that their minds go. They get even by deliberately mixing the babies up.'

'Dey lips drip honey but dey's strange womens.'

'As for those identification bracelets,' Granny said scornfully, 'they're so cheap and flimsy they just break and fall right off. Did you know that, Louise?'

She did now. She reached for a pack of Luckies, her fourth that day, and tore off the cellophane strip. She had heard every obstetrical caveat known to science and myth except the one about smoking during pregnancy. For all of Granny's strictures on ladylike behavior, no one ever heard her utter a word against smoking: tobacco, after all, comes from Virginia.

'Louise, promise me you'll have the baby at home. We'll get Tessie Satterfield, and Jensy and I will help her.' Tessie was a retired obstetrical nurse – but never a fleshpot – who lived in Ballston.

'All right, Mother, I'll have it here. Now leave me alone, I want to listen to the World Series.'

Except for taking the sun on the bathroom porch by crawling through the priest's hole, Mama got no fresh air or exercise. Whenever she tried to go out, her keepers set up an outcry. Did she want to miscarry? Suppose she fell down and hit her stomach like Pauline Fairfax when she leaned over to pick up a dime and couldn't stop? Didn't she know that walking during pregnancy put pressure on the bladder? Suppose it burst and the baby drowned? Did she mean to walk past dat firehouse wid all de mens sittin' out front wid dey chairs tilted back an' dem lookin' at her an' *knowin'*?

Her combative instincts dulled by pregnancy, Mama gave in and spent the day lying in bed drinking pot liquor until she was as fat as Granny. Around this time Herb bought another roll-away cot and set it up in the short leg of the kitchen. There, amid his library books and copies of *The National Geographic*, he slept, leaving Mama to her ash-strewn sheets. Granny called his action 'considerate' and told everybody in the Daughters until the telephone wires buzzed with that *ne plus ultra* compliment old ladies bestow on sexually restrained men: 'He never bothers her.'

As the pregnancy neared its end, Granny began casting eager glances at Mama's stomach.

'It's going to be a girl,' she said firmly.

'How the hell do you know?'

'Because you're carrying low. Boys are carried high.'

'I don't have any high or low left. The goddamn thing's all over the place. You're talking through your hat, Mother.'

At the start of the ninth month, she saw a bluish tinge in Mama's navel. From this curio of whelpery she extracted what she wished to believe and manufactured an instant old wives' tale.

'The navel vein,' she intoned sonorously. 'That means it's a girl. You never find a navel vein in a woman who's carrying a boy, but a girl baby always brings one on. You see, when a girl baby turns around inside the mother's stomach, she always pushes up on that vein.'

'With *what*?'

'Miss Louise!'

On New Year's Eve, Mama started to feel certain twinges. It was the biggest night of the year for Herb so Granny told him to go on to work. He returned home the next morning expecting to find a baby in the apartment, but Mama was still in a holding pattern. Four days later her labor began in earnest and Granny called Tessie Satterfield.

Rawboned, crop-haired Tessie arrived amid repeated backfires in her ancient Model A. Mama sent Herb to the drugstore for two cartons of Luckies, but by the time he got back the first big pain had hit and she had bitten a cigarette in two. It was to be six hours before she would be able to smoke another one, a hiatus that goes far to explain why I am an only child.

Around ten P.M. her waters broke and Granny put together another legend.

'Look at all that water! That means it's a girl! You never get that much with a boy!'

'Whatever it is, it sure is big,' Tessie grunted.

After the horror stories Mama had heard, 'whatever' was an unfortunate word. She let out an agonized yell that sent Herb running for the bathroom and me into the world. Nobody who smokes four packs a day can yell very long without coughing. As her gothic ululation changed into a phlegmy rattle, Tessie broke out in triumph.

'I see the head! Keep coughing, Louise!'

'Ack-ack-awwrrrggghhh!'

'Hyeh it come!'

'Ack-ack-awwwrrrggghhh!'

'It's a girl!' Granny cried ecstatically.

'Ack-ack-awwwrrrggghhh!' To some of us, it spells Mother.

Nobody remembered Herb until Jensy ran into the bathroom to get more towels and found him sitting on the edge of the tub with his head between his knees. They scared each other silly.

'OOOOEEEE!'

'Lor' blimey!'

She told him the news and ran back to the bedroom with the towels. It was time for the placenta, a holy relic as far as Granny was concerned. When it came, she gathered it lovingly into a towel.

'Look,' she murmured reverently. 'Nine perfect little sections of blood, one for each month of the lady's missed time.'

'Look at dat.'

Herb emerged from the bathroom during this gynophilic litany, and hearing the word 'Look,' he did.

'Crikey! It's dead!'

'Oh, no, Mr King, this isn't the baby! It's the afterbirth. See? Nine perfect little—'

'Take it away,' he groaned, staggering against the wall. Overcome, he headed for the bathroom again, with Granny and Jensy trailing behind him reciting old wives' tales.

'The afterbirth has to be disposed of in a certain way, Mr King. The husband has to bury it. It's his duty!'

'Flush it down the loo,' he gasped, between heaves.

'Oh, no, Mr King, you can't do that! It's *birth* blood.'

'You spoze to bury it unner a dogwood tree so it bloom in de springtime an' bring de chile good luck.'

They kept following him around with the bloody towel and chanting hex stories until he gave in and agreed to give the placenta a proper burial. After fortifying himself with a shot of whiskey, he borrowed a shovel from the janitor and went out into the alley. He told Granny and Jensy that he dug a suitable grave, but years later he told me that he had thrown the sacred object into a garbage can.

The next day:

'It's a girl,' Granny said tenderly, gazing down at my red wrinkled face.

'Mother, you've said that seven times in the last hour.'

Granny got up and stood at the bottom of the bed and gave Mama an appraising stare.

'Louise, how do you feel?'

'My ass hurts.'

'That's to be expected. I mean how do you *feel*?'

'All right.'

'Well, you don't look all right. You remember Nancy Montgomery? She thought she was all right, too, and then her ankles exploded. I think I'd better stay until the end of January.'

At the end of January:

'I'm worried about your varicose veins. You remember Betsy Winchester? She got so she looked like a road map. I think I'd better stay until the end of February.'

At the end of February, Mama ignored her protests and went out to the store.

'You remember Fanny Wallingford? She died in the A and P.'

'I never heard of Fanny Wallingford and neither did you! I'm sick of being cooped up in this apartment! I feel fine!'

'Be that as it may, I think I'd better stay awhile.'

It was a fatal regional vagary. Southern homes are full of people who are just 'staying awhile.' When Evelyn Cunningham took two years to drink a glass of milk, Granny told everybody that she was just staying awhile. That unparalleled tactile experience of stepping on a human face in the middle of the night lingers like a moist legend on the Southern foot because someone who was just staying awhile was asleep on the floor when you padded slipperless to the bathroom. Sears sells more camp mattresses and foam-rubber pallets in the South than anywhere else in the country. Southerners buy more adhesive tape than anybody else; not to bind our wounds but to make extra name strips for the mailbox so the postman will know who is just staying awhile. The most challenging jobs in America are with the South-eastern Regional Office of the Bureau of the Census, and there's always plenty of overtime.

As Herb would later tell people, the longest-running comedy in the history of the American theater is *The Mother-in-Law Who Came to Dinner*. It opened on Park Road in 1936. Granny never officially moved in with us, she just stayed awhile. Nor did she ever go back to Ballston and pack the rest of her belongings; that would have been an open betrayal of her Virginia roots. Loath to let anyone actually *see* her moving, she announced that she was just staying awhile and asked people to bring things to her.

Each time our relatives and friends visited us they brought over another dress, another pair of Enna Jettick laced oxfords, more rayon drawers, and those crocheted head scarves known in Granny's youth as 'fascinators.' One week Aunt Charlotte and Uncle Botetourt brought over a hat, the next week Dora Madison produced the veil, and the week after that Evelyn Cunningham showed up with the stuffed bird. It went on for more than a year, but nobody ever suggested that Granny had moved. They simply pulled another size 44 from a Lansburgh's shopping bag and said, 'Since you're staying awhile, I thought you might need this.'

Thread by thread, button by button, they put Granny together again. The tactful transfer reached its climax the day Dora brought over her one-eyed fox fur piece and Aunt Charlotte appeared an hour or so later with the creature's missing eye.

Everybody knew what she was up to. Expecting Granny to stay away from an unformed blob of female material was like expecting a cobra to stay away from a flute.

3

The experts of the thirties swore by the bottle but Granny preached femininity, so Mama nursed me for eight months. The immunities I gained were canceled out by the perils of our particular madonna-and-child scenario. My little blankets were full of scorched holes and I developed severe colic from her impassioned shouts of 'Throw him out at third!' as she listened to the radio.

Once I was weaned I passed exclusively into Granny's hands. It was the era of the scientific nursery; women's magazines insisted on strict schedules, fanatic measurements like two-thirds of an ounce, and the absolute need to protect 'Baby' from germs. But Granny, a Southern primitive and a hardy Saxon underneath her genteel veneer, dismissed it all with 'A few germs never hurt anybody.' If I dropped my pacifier on the floor, she picked it up, wiped it off on her apron, and stuck it back in my mouth. She doctored me herself. Intoning, 'Whiskey or salt will cure anything,' she spoon-fed me hot toddies and taught me to gargle before I could talk. I received no vitamins, no cod liver oil, and was never touched by a pediatrician.

She refused to recognize what the magazines called 'tender baby stomachs,' so I acquired all sorts of acquired tastes by the age of three. Raw oysters, pickled pig's feet, and olives were my staples, and coffee was my favorite beverage. 'It won't hurt her,' said Granny, and Mama, who drank twenty cups a day, poured us both a refill.

Whether it was a chemical imbalance or simply a manifestation of the nonconformity that swirled around me, I developed a dislike of sweets that grew into an aversion and thence into what seemed to be an allergy.

'My nose is beating,' I whimpered one day, after eating out of politeness a piece of candy a neighbor gave me. The bridge of my nose was throbbing like an arterial pressure point.

The idea of taking me to a doctor never crossed Granny's mind. She was not one to go all medical as long as genealogy was at hand.

'The Uptons have never had anything like that, neither have the Rudings. Mr King, does beating nose bridge run in your family?'

'No, but we lived for a time at Notting Hill Gate.'

After I outgrew my crib I slept with Granny on the convertible sofa. On any given night our bed contained a hot water bag or an icebag, depending upon her affliction of the moment; tubes of Ben-Gay and Musterol with or without caps; loose Lydia Pinkham pills that felt like buckshot; old mustard plasters that fell off her back and stuck to the sheets; a box of Kleenex; crochet needles; and one or more copies of the Daughters' magazine.

Without her Shapely Stout corsets, she billowed out like a tube of Pillsbury biscuit dough when you press on the dotted line. Each time she turned over, I identified with the characters on comic book covers who were always racing away from collapsing skyscrapers or cresting tidal waves. Her sound effects were out of the Mesozoic Age, an accusation she denied with her usual sublime self-assurance.

'I do not snore. Snoring is unladylike.'

My training for ladyhood began with the duets we sang in

bed. 'They don't write songs the way they used to,' she said darkly, citing 'Body and Soul' as an example of degeneracy. To keep me from 'going bad' when I grew up, she taught me suitable hits from her youth. Propped up on our pillows, she crocheting and I crayoning a coloring book, we gave forth with earnest renditions of 'She's More To Be Pitied Than Censured,' 'She May Have Seen Better Days,' and 'The Picture That's Turned Toward the Wall.'

'Oh, shit,' Mama said from the bedroom.

Mama took care of my outings. Her favorite arena was Meridian Hill Park on 16th Street, which contained an equestrian statue of Joan of Arc that she liked. Gripping the handle of my stroller, she would break into a dead heat and race down the terrace yelling 'Charge!'

Her addiction required a lot of time out but she always observed Granny's ironclad rule – the only one, to my knowledge, that she ever paid any attention to.

'I'm going to have a cigarette while we're sitting on the bench. It's all right to smoke on the street if you're sitting down, as long as you don't do it while you're walking.'

We sat down a lot on our walks. Had we lived anywhere else she would have fallen into a nicotine fit, but Washington, like the Paris that inspired it, has a lot of parks. We had no sooner left one than Mama was hurrying furtively toward another like an espionage courier who can't remember where the rendezvous is supposed to take place.

Herb never returned to Mama's bed. He went on sleeping on his rollaway in the kitchen leg, which became his reading room as well. How chaste a cot it was I do not know. If he occasionally closed his after-work book and crept down the hall to the bedroom, it was for nothing more than a brief conjugal visit. In the mornings he was always asleep in his retreat like a monk in a cell.

I don't know why I called him by his first name; perhaps because Daddy has two syllables, while Herb is a one-syllable sound that falls easily off the childish tongue. A more interesting question is why no one corrected me. Mama was not one to care about such niceties, but Granny was a stickler for good Southern manners and Herb himself held such typically British views on children that he would not even let me refer to Mama and Granny by pronoun. 'She is for she-goats!' he would snap, yet he never made me call him Daddy.

I think their permissiveness sprang from an unconscious wish on all their parts to regard our family group as three siblings with Granny at the matriarchal helm. Mama wanted a buddy instead of a husband, Herb wanted an intellectual companion instead of a wife, and Granny wanted to boss a show, any show. By never saying Daddy, I symbolically eliminated the patriarchal figure that would have spoiled their game.

My unfilial custom caused consternation on Park Road.

'Is he your real father?' a lady asked me.

'Yes, ma'am, but I call him by his first name.'

She shook her head in disapproval but she did not seem very surprised. A man who wears a tuxedo while emptying the garbage at four A.M. is bound to have strange children. His sartorial habits led to a number of puzzled inquiries. The most memorable incident occurred one night when he stopped by the corner drugstore on his way to work and ran into old Mrs McIntyre, the neighborhood Nosy Parker.

'I've been meaning to ask you something,' she squawked in her going-deaf voice. 'Are you an undertaker?'

'No, madam, but I'll be happy to call one for you.'

She didn't hear it but everyone else in the store did.

Now when he went out in the daytime he usually took me with him. We walked up to the Mount Pleasant branch library, I holding his index finger and he talking, patiently explaining what things were and how they worked: streetcars, fire hydrants, the yellow line down the middle of the street. When we entered the library, the stern-faced spinsterish librarians would look up with smiles and carol, 'Oh, here's Mr King!' in a way that made me realize that women liked Herb the way men liked Mama.

While he chose his books I had to sit absolutely still and recite to myself things he had taught me: the alphabet, the Presidents, and the five degrees of peerage (duke, marquess, earl, viscount, and baron). When he had his books he would take me upstairs to the children's room and help me pick out something for myself.

Afterwards we sat in the park outside the library, ostensibly for me to play but really because he could not wait to get at his books. He would open them and do some preliminary scanning, and I, never much for playing, would do the same with mine. One afternoon he uttered a triumphant 'Ah-ha!'

'What?' I said.

He tapped the page. 'Occam's Razor. It's the law of intellectual thrift devised by William of Ockham, a medieval philosopher,' he read aloud. 'He said that hypotheses should never be developed beyond necessity.'

'What's that mean?'

'When your grandmother joined the Daughters, she produced proof of twenty-three qualified ancestors. But she only needed one.'

'. . . Oh. I get it.'

On our way back home we stopped by the arcade market on 14th Street and had a snack. I had coffee which usually involved a struggle with the disapproving counter girl, and Herb, who had a sweet tooth, chose a sundae. A popular concoction at this time was something called an Ethiopian Delight – green pistachio ice cream for Mussolini, chocolate syrup for Haile Selassie, and a cherry for the League of Nations. It was the kind of cue Herb always took advantage of; when we got home, he pointed out Ethiopia on the map and showed me pictures of Mussolini and Haile Selassie in *Life*.

He taught me how to print my name, and devised a way to teach me how to write in script. In the early hours of the morning after he got home from work, he sat at the kitchen table laboriously dotting out my name over and over in a drugstore tablet. I spent the next several days tracing the dots until I was able to sign myself with a fairly respectable flourish.

All went well until he tested my ear with the idea of giving me music lessons.

'Sing this,' he said, playing a note. I complied.

'Now this,' he said, playing another one.

'They're the same,' I protested.

'She's right,' said Mama. 'I'm a witness. Sounded like the same goddamn toot to me.'

He gave us a long studious look, nodded in resignation, and put his clarinet away.

Our apartment gave every evidence of having been decorated by Jekyll and Hyde. 'Herb's alcove,' as it was known, was a model of spartan order, while Mama's bedroom looked at all times as if the Gestapo had just searched it. Granny saw nothing unladylike about this and in fact encouraged slovenliness as a mark of aristocracy. She looked down on good housekeepers, dismissing them as 'scrubbers.' A scrubber, I learned early on, is a Northern woman who substitutes good housekeeping for good blood; knowing that she can never be a lady, she develops a bee in her bonnet (i.e., unfeminine insanity) about being able to 'eat off the floor.'

It was virtually impossible to eat off our table, hidden as it was under skeins of crochet yarn and clippings from the sports page that Mama was saving for her baseball scrapbook. Slut's wool like gone-to-seed dandelions lay undisturbed under our furniture, dishes were piled up to the spigot in the sink, the refrigerator handle stuck to our hands, little pieces of singed food clung to the stove burners, and the oven door had a permanent gummy border of gravy and long rivulets of greasy scum. In *Reflections in a Golden Eye*, describing the stove of the Captain's wife, who was half-Yankee, Carson McCullers wrote: 'Their gas stove was not crusted with generations of dirt as her grandmother's had been, but then it was by no means clean.'

Ours was a pureblooded stove.

Jensy still came once a week, but except for washing the dishes she did little to alleviate the mess. She and Granny spent most of the day sitting at the cluttered table drinking coffee and talking about how wonderful the world would be if only they could run it. When they finished their encyclicals, they polished the silver.

Their silver ritual was supposed to teach me the ladylike art of taking care of my 'things.' Silver is the Southern woman's proudest possession and highest priority as well as the subject of much of her conversation. The night before her daughter's wedding, a Southern mother will sit on the bed and talk intimately about silver. Every decent woman goes to her husband with twelve 'covers,' and if the knives have hollow handles he'll be running with other women before the year is out, you wait and see. No man respects a woman with hollow handles.

A marriage can fall apart if a bride does not choose her silver pattern carefully. A good pattern is known as 'They've been making that one forever.' A bad pattern is known as 'They don't make silver the way they used to.' Bad patterns are the stark modern designs that are easy to keep clean; a good pattern is as busy as a Grecian frieze and manifests what silver company brochures call 'the elegant and highly prized glow of deep patina,' i.e., those black lines made by ground-in dirt that you can't get at no matter how many gauze-wrapped toothpicks you use.

My first household chore was wrapping gauze around toothpicks so Granny and Jensy could sit in the midst of wall-to-wall patina and polish silver. They polished it while it was still shining from their last polishing; they polished it while a mouse gnawed happily through a soggy bag of garbage; they polished it while a flapping window shade gave off a duststorm under their noses. Our silver was the only thing in our home that was ever really clean, which is a sure sign of a Southern home.

Granny's pattern was the goodest of the good, as furrowed as a damaged brain and so full of acorns and rose-buds that our palms ached after every meal. Thanks to its Laocoön intricacies, it frequently served as a salvaging conversation piece for appalled visitors who were trying not to look at the filth, like Mr Van Vrees, the insurance man, who was from Poughkeepsie. Granny always offered him coffee and asked for news of his ailing mother.

'She's having trouble with her knees,' he said. 'They're so sore and swollen she can't stand up.'

'Oh, what a shame,' Granny commiserated. 'Whatever caused it?'

'I . . . er . . . I really don't know . . . The doctor can't – Say! This is beautiful silver. What's it called?'

'Williamsburg Carbuncle,' said Herb.

Something that actually did run in our family was agnosticism. Herb believed in reincarnation, Mama preferred unorthodox home truths like 'When you're dead you're dead,' and Granny's theology had been enervated by her superiority complex. A lifetime of looking down on the Bible Belt South as only a Virginian can had driven her into a bizarre form of heresy: Christianity reminded her of places like Georgia. As usual there was an etiquette factor in her thinking. She objected strenuously to the Baptist habit of referring to 'Jesus' as though he lived down the road and always carefully said 'Our Lord Jesus Christ,' yet her views on his place in the heavenly pecking order were bleak.

'Girls in occupied countries always get in trouble with soldiers,' she said, when I asked her what the Virgin birth was.

She did, however, believe in Heaven because it was a ladylike place with pink clouds, harp music, and a man to open the door, but most of all she believed in that Chivas Regal of Protestantism, the Episcopal Church. About every six weeks or so she became spiritually gravid, awakening on Sunday morning with a smug smile that told us she was in the mood to lord it with the Lord.

'I think it would be nice if we went to church today,' she said modestly.

'I hate hats!' Mama yelled.

Granny always argued her down and plunked one of her own Empress Eugénie numbers on Mama's unwilling head. I donned a sickeningly sweet bonnet with long velvet ribbons bought expressly for these redemptive excursions. We alternated between Grace Church in Georgetown, where I was eventually christened, and St. George's in Arlington. Granny led the way up the aisle trailing fascinators and Djer Kiss dusting powder. After making sure she had everyone's attention, she went into a full genuflection and made the sign of the cross over her jutting bosom, eyes closed in perfect devotion. When the spirit had passed, she signaled Mama and Herb with a flap of her elbows and they stepped forward and hauled her to her feet.

The service was no sooner under way before she went to sleep. Whenever she slumped in one direction, Mama or Herb would give her a shoulder nudge and send her the other way. I kept hoping she would start snoring while I had plenty of witnesses but she had to be on her back to do her best. Upright, all she produced was a rhythmic *poc*! that punctuated our whispers.

'The third soprano from the right is flat.'

'I'm going to be flat on the floor if I don't have a cigarette.'

'Lighten our darkness we beseech Thee, O Lord, and by Thy great mercy defend us from all perils and dangers of this night.'

'What's a snite?' I asked.

After church we always drove over to Congressional Cemetery to visit the family plot. It contained two graves. One belonged to my grandfather, whose stern gray slab contained a Masonic emblem and the dates 1868–1921. The other stone was a tiny white one topped by a reclining lamb and inscribed with the wistful dates 1905–1910. It belonged to Mama's brother Charlie who had died of polio when she was a baby. I loved the lamb and always patted it.

'Why did he have to die, Granny?' I asked one Sunday.

She shifted on the stone bench and sighed. 'It was July, and so hot, the hottest day I ever saw. He went off to play, and when he came home he turned the hose on himself. I always thought that was what did it – President Roosevelt went swimming on a hot day. He took sick that night. The doctor came but there was nothing he could do. The paralysis took his legs and rose up. When it reached his lungs, he was gone.'

She stared for a moment at the wedding ring that was now embedded in the flesh of her finger. 'The undertaker couldn't come right away – Ballston was real country then and he was off somewhere on another call – so we had to have ice. Everybody in town brought us theirs, and Mr Ruding and I took turns sitting beside Charlie and keeping the ice on him.'

She shook her head slowly. 'It's the strangest disease . . . Your mother was a baby in her crib, lying right there in the next room, but she didn't catch it. I wonder if they'll ever figure out what causes it?'

Looking up, I saw Mama watching Granny with an expression of mute pleading. Suddenly, in some instinctive way, I understood something: Charlie had been Granny's favorite child. Mama was too young to remember him, but his ghost must have shaped her life, urging her to become a tomboy to replace the son Granny had lost. I think Herb must have understood it, too, the way he always understood everything about people. It explained why he was the only member of the family who never tried to tone Mama down; he seemed to know that she had to act out her conflicts, and in her own brusque way she was grateful to him.

On most Sundays we visited family in Virginia. 'Our people,' Granny always called them, disliking the word 'family' for its bourgeois implications. Anyone could have a family. She wanted a race all to herself, a breed apart, a private gene pool in which to dunk herself with ponderous grace the way she did at Colonial Beach in her skirted bathing costume.

It boiled down to paying a day-long call on Aunt Nana and sitting in her dim parlor talking about whose mind was going and who was passing clots. Granny and Aunt Nana did all the talking, with Granny eventually dominating the conversation for reasons that were clear to me even at four: however much Aunt Nana might wish otherwise, the fact remained that very few women lost their minds, while all women menstruated, all women had the menopause, and most women gave birth. Long after Aunt Nana had run out of hand-wringing maniacs, Granny still had a full storehouse of pelvic disarray to relate.

Herb called her Sunday monologues 'The Ovariad.' He always retreated to the kitchen to play chess with Billy Bosworth, Evelyn Cunningham's husband. They were not friends – Herb had no male friends – but there was a certain bond between them. Herb had given Evelyn away, so to speak, when he handed her over to Billy in front of the National Geographic Society on the night of the lecture, so Billy regarded him as a kind of father-in-law.

Evelyn, of course, could not get enough of 'The Ovariad.' She sat at Granny's feet and I sat in a corner chair reading my library book while the sanguine saga gushed and flowed around me.

'It just went *splat* and there she was wearing a white dress. She found a lump as big as a golfball in it. She thought it might be a cancer starting so she called the doctor and he told her to bring it over in a jar and let him look at it, but she was so upset she left the jar on the streetcar and had to go down to the car barn and fill out a Lost and Found form before she could get it back. By that time it was all dried up.'

'Oh, shit.'

'Louise, the child can hear you!'

Granny worried constantly that I would be corrupted by Mama's cussing, but she did not care how much of 'The Ovariad' I heard. To her way of thinking, it was part of my training in Southern ladyhood. Thus, by the age of four, I was conversant with wombs, tubes, polyps, cauterized cervixes, curettage, floods, flows, splats, and the change of life. Menstruation was such a commonplace topic that I could not understand why drugstores modestly wrapped Kotex in brown paper before placing them on the shelves. If druggists could have heard what I heard in Aunt Nana's parlor, they would have sold them with full-color photographs of blood-soaked napkins on the front of the box.

Granny continued her Ovariad at the movies whenever the plot gave her the slightest encouragement. She hit pay dirt the day we went to see the Technicolor foxhunt extravaganza *Virginia*, starring Madeleine Carroll and Sterling Hayden. It began with carefree scenes of riding to hounds, but to Granny's delight the healthful outdoor exercise soon stopped. Madeleine fainted on the field and took to her chaise longue, where, fetchingly attired in a black riding habit that emphasized her pallor, she sipped delicately at a medicinal glass of port.

Madeleine actually had TB, but Granny was not interested

in any organ as high up as lungs. She immediately jumped to conclusions.

'Wine makes blood,' she whispered to me. 'She had a miscarriage, only they can't come right out and say it. She had no business bouncing up and down on that old horse – that's bad for a woman's parts.'

Soon Madeleine weakened so much that she had to go away to a sanitarium. Before she left she promised to come back to Virginia, and she did. She returned in a coffin that was deposited at the train station, and Sterling Hayden had to sign for it.

'He knew she was too weak to carry a child. He should have been more considerate! The doctor should have told him not to bother her!'

It was the first of her comments that I did not understand. As voluble as she was about how babies, either whole or liquefied, came *out*, she was remarkably taciturn about how they got *in*. She divided sex into two categories: the unmentionable kind involving men and copulation, and the fun kind.

'Granny,' I said as we walked home from the show, 'how did Sterling Hayden bother Madeleine Carroll to death?'

'Never mind.'

'But I want to know.'

'You're too young.'

'Granny, *please* tell me!'

'Oh, all right,' she said irritably.

I waited breathlessly for the revelation.

'Your grandfather was a perfect gentleman.'

Going to the movies with Mama exposed me to an entirely different kind of running commentary:

They Died With Their Boots On: 'I wish he'd stop kissing her and lead a cavalry charge.'

The Women: 'What this needs is George Raft.'

Anna Karenina: 'Oh boy, here comes the train!'

Back Street: 'That woman ought to have her head examined.'
Madame X: 'She's wasting the taxpayers' money.'
Kings Row: 'How the hell is he going to do her any good? He can't even turn over without help.'

Many years later when my insular life opened up and I met people whose second language was Yiddish, I learned that Mama was what is known as a klutz. There is a comparable Southern word, but never having seen it in print, I am not sure of the spelling. It is either 'slewfoot' or 'sluefoot.' The first is a variant of 'slough' or 'slog' and suggests someone tramping through mudholes or swamps in heavy boots. The second is a nautical word of unknown origin that refers to the violent swing of a ship's spar, or any lurching, veering movement.

However it is spelled, it's a word I grew up hearing. It invariably cropped up whenever Southerners discussed Eleanor Roosevelt, but to me it was my mother's nickname. Granny brought it out on a long sigh whenever Mama did some domestic thing badly or started a fire with her cigarette, and my uncle, undoubtedly to get even for 'Gottapot,' called her 'Slewfoot Lou.'

That slewfootedness affected her mothering is like saying that hemophilia affected the course of the Romanov dynasty. Today I admire her lack of vocation for motherhood, but at four I was convinced that she was trying to murder me. Two things happened, one on top of the other, that made me draw this disturbing conclusion. The first involved the sudden disappearance of most of my teeth.

It was, as Snoopy would say, a dark and stormy night. Herb was at work, and Granny was in Richmond visiting her sister, which meant that Mama was playing without an infield. It also meant that she was in charge of the cooking, so we walked up to the Chinese restaurant on 14th Street to get some carry-out.

'I'm cold,' I said, as we headed back home.

'Walk under my coat,' Mama offered.

It worked fine until we came to the corner of 13th and Park Road. I can still see the curbstone looming up in front of me as I write this, just as it loomed up that night when I tripped and fell and hit my mouth on it. There was a shattering pain, and the terrifying purplish color of my blood in the dirty yellow glow of the streetlamp.

It was not the kind of crisis that brought out Mama's strength. She would have been great on the *Titanic* or in an air raid; at Little Big Horn or Thermopylae she would have stolen the show from Custer and Leonidas, but at 13th and Park Road she fell apart. Moaning 'Oh, Jesus Christ . . . oh, shit!' she slung me over her shoulder like a sack of meal and ran the rest of the way home.

In the kitchen, when she got a good look at me, an expression of helpless terror spread over her face. All of my front teeth were knocked out except one that hung by a thread of flesh, and the inside of my bottom lip felt like the surface of a cheese grater. I was screaming in pain and fear and there was blood everywhere, even on my shoes.

Mama's solution was salt. Grabbing the blue box of Morton's from the stove, she opened the spout, yanked my head back by my hair, and poured the stuff directly into my mouth. Naturally, some of it went up my nose and into my eyes. I won't even try to describe the agony.

'It'll sterilize you!' Mama yelled over my shrieks. 'It's so you won't get lockjaw! Salt's the purest thing there is! That's why they say "the salt of the earth"!'

I struck at her and pulled away and ran down the hall to the bathroom, where I tried futilely to reach the cold water faucet on the basin. Mama turned on the water and lifted me up, and I cupped my hands and splashed water in my mouth and eyes. I rinsed and rinsed, spat and spat, until the pain receded and the bleeding stopped. The loose tooth came out and went down the drain. When we were both calmed down, Mama fixed me an icebag (after dropping one tray of cubes on the floor) and put me into her bed, where I lay whimpering until Herb came home at two A.M.

'Did you take her to the dentist?' he asked, after hearing the story.

Mama exploded. 'If she doesn't have any goddamn teeth, why does she need a goddamn dentist?'

He considered this in his imperturbable way – I suppose it did have a certain awful logic – and then suggested aspirin. He fetched the bottle from the medicine chest and Mama began crushing tablets in a cup. They were adult strength and she used four or five, but when Herb objected to the massive dose she replied, 'Just for good measure.' She dissolved the crushed aspirin in warm water and I managed to swallow it.

'Atta girl,' she said approvingly. 'You'll be all right now. That's enough aspirin to kill a horse.'

That made me burst into renewed sobs. 'I want Granny!'

Mama's mouth tightened and she looked away, but I was too young and too sick to realize that I had hurt her, or to care. After all, wasn't she trying to kill me? That her saline solution to the crisis was a direct outgrowth of Granny's dictum that whiskey or salt will cure anything also eluded me. All I knew was that my mother had done to me what brutal sea captains did to flogging victims in sailing-ship movies: poured salt on open wounds.

The next day they called Granny in Richmond and she hurried home. When the question of taking me to a dentist arose, she said, 'Dentists don't know anything,' and then took me to one. It was always the same: she would consult professionals if she had to, but first she had to run them down. 'Doctors don't know anything,' 'Lawyers don't know anything,' 'CPAs don't know anything' were household chants in the dual service of her ego and her anti-intellectualism.

The dentist performed a mopping-up operation and Granny fed me thick cream and raw oysters until my mouth healed. Not having any teeth was a source of embarrassment to me, but Mama supplied me with a comeback for the curious: 'Tell 'em you got in a fight, and if they think you look funny, they ought to see the other girl.'

'Oh, Louise!'

A few months later, the hand that rocks the cradle struck again. It happened at my uncle's house when Mama decided to teach me how to bat.

'You chop at the ball the way girls do,' she said scornfully. 'You're supposed to put your whole body into it, pull it all the way around in a follow-through swing. Like this! See how—'

I saw stars and crumpled to the ground. Somewhere amid the buzzing and shrilling sounds in my head I heard a voice cry out, 'Oh, Louise! You've killed the child!'

I came to in Aunt Charlotte's bed with an icebag over my fast-swelling lump. Mama stood at the foot of the bed trying manfully to conceal her terror. She held a cigarette lighter; as my eyes opened, she flicked it on and moved it back and forth in front of my face.

'She's not blind!' she yelled. 'See? Her eyes are following it!' Flicking the lighter off, she moved swiftly to the head of the bed and bent over me.

'*Boo!*' she bellowed in my ear. I jumped and started crying.

'See? She's not deaf!'

'She might go crazy,' Aunt Nana said in a voice full of hope. 'Being hit in the head like that . . . You never can tell what it might do to her mind.'

Mama had a test for this, too. 'What's two and two?' she fired at me.

'Four,' I whimpered.

'See? If she was crazy, she'd say five. Which weighs more, a pound of lead or a pound of feathers?'

'Chrissake, Louise,' Uncle Botetourt grumbled, 'leave the poor kid alone. You've done enough for one day.'

'Shut your goddamn mouth! Don't go giving me any orders, you turd-faced son of—'

'*Both* of you shut up,' Aunt Charlotte snapped. 'She's got a bad enough headache as it is.'

They shut up and everyone stood around the bed staring at me. It was like a Russian novel. For the next several weeks I was observed closely for dizzy spells and speech problems, but I never developed either one, or any other physical impairments. Whether or not I went crazy is impossible to say; a maniac could hide in my family as a leaf can hide in the forest. I merely harbored the certainty that Mama was trying to rub me out because I was not a boy.

I knew she had wanted a boy; she was always careful never to say so outright, but her whole stance proclaimed it from the rooftops. I derived no comfort from the knowledge that Granny had wanted me to be a girl and that Herb was a woman's man who disliked male companionship. Of the adults in my life, I loved Granny best and enjoyed Herb's company the most, but these were secondary priorities formed in my conscious mind and based on logical choices. I was concerned with that vital primitive priority: to a small child, especially a female one, it's the mother who counts, even if she comes in third in a race of three.

The conviction that I was marked for infanticide remained with me until the second grade, when Mama proved her love for me with two heroic acts, one of them positively hair-raising.

4

We were evicted from Park Road early in January of 1941 after a building inspector saw the plumbing pipes that the distraught owner had installed all by himself. The structure was condemned and we were given a month to move.

Mama and Herb responded with alarm. Their marriage depended upon old houses that had been cut up into apartments by people who did not know what they were doing. As long as there was an extra piece or an accidental cul de sac, Herb could play St. Jerome in the Desert and Mama could litter in peace, but a logical floor plan would lead to divorce or worse.

It was the only time I ever saw Herb bestir himself. He hurried out with the newspaper and returned an hour later wearing his old serene look. He had signed a lease on a two-bedroom apartment around the corner at 1020 Monroe. We already knew the building. It lay overtop a block of small stores. Some were convenient, like the Chinese laundry and the Greek deli, but the Monroe Bar & Grill was not. Worse, the windows of our new home faced the streetcar tracks, there was no cross-ventilation, and the rent was an exorbitant sixty-five dollars. Never has an apartment boasted so many unwinning features, but Herb insisted that it was a find.

He meant that it had an alcove. Actually it was a dressing

room off the master bedroom and thus more connubial in spirit than his former kitchen hideaway, but even so it was *haut* Herb. Mama took one look at it and started singing 'There'll Always Be an Alcove.'

Since we were moving only around the corner, we did not hire a van. Jensy produced three strong nephews named Booker, Kincaid, and Donald to take the furniture, and the rest of us followed with linens, pictures, and clocks. It looked like an integrated looting.

Granny and the nephews hit it off superbly. Each time they returned from a sprint across the street with a table or a bed, she promised to dance at their weddings. Soon the ambience reached such dizzy heights that they were inspired to make her a bet: they could carry her seated in our heaviest armchair all the way over to Monroe Street without stopping to rest.

They took our huge leather Morris chair out to the sidewalk and Granny sat down. Hefting her aloft, the nephews got a running start and careened down to the corner just as a street-car was approaching. Unable to stop their momentum, they dashed across the tracks in front of it as the astonished motor-man and all the passengers stared. Seeing their interest, Granny smiled graciously and, remembering to keep her wrist stiff like Queen Mary in the newsreels, gave them a perfect imitation of the royal wave.

'The last of the great white goddesses,' Herb said.

She made friends in the new building at once. To her great joy, our immediate neighbors were all women in their forties or fifties whose menopauses were either in progress or fresh in their minds. She was thrilled to learn that 12B contained a bizarre vibratory condition known at quilting bees as a 'singing ovary.' It was the well-nurtured property of Miss Inez Shields, a fluttery, domestically inclined spinster who stayed home and kept house for her capable, efficient sister, Miss Rose Shields, who supported them both with her job at the Bureau of

Engraving. Miss Rose made money and Miss Inez made a buzzing sound. Peeking into their kitchen, I saw Granny holding a rolled-up magazine to Miss Inez's stomach and listening at the other end.

'I'll tell you what's wrong with her ovary,' said Mama. 'Those goddamn streetcars did it. We're all going to have singing brains. They'll have to carry us out of here in rubber bags and take us to St. Elizabeth's.'

The streetcars were the old-fashioned kind with wicker seats and motors front and back. Eleventh and Monroe being the end of the line, the tracks simply stopped at the corner. There was no way to turn the cars around for the trip back downtown, so the motormen made the juice flow in the opposite direction by driving over the switch, which lay directly under our windows. They had to approach it at a certain speed to keep from getting stuck on it; to make sure the tracks were clear of traffic and pedestrians, they rang the bell from Park Road to Monroe Street. When the wheels hit the switch, they exploded with a metallic roar and gave off cascades of sparks, bringing cheers from the drunks leaning up against the Monroe Bar & Grill. The motorman then reversed the seats manually – twenty separate crunching slams – and manned the opposite set of controls. Sometimes, of course, a car got stuck on the switch. When this happened, the motorman had to grind back and forth like someone trying to saw through a knight in full armor, until the car came free.

Anything for an alcove.

Having moved to 1020 in the winter, we did not receive the full impact of this procedure until it was time to sleep with the windows open. By August we were as scrambled as Quasimodo, so we took off for a vacation at Colonial Beach.

Granny always enjoyed the drive down because of all the historical road markers around Fredericksburg. HERE WAS FOUGHT . . . ONCE STOOD THE HOME OF . . . BURIED NEARBY . . .

GRANTED BY KING CHARLES II TO . . . and Herb's favorite, ON THIS SPOT, all filled her with immense pride.

'Think of it,' she said to no one in particular.

When we arrived at the cabin site we found Uncle Botetourt and Aunt Charlotte, Dora Madison with a group of her girl-friends, and the usual assortment of Uptons. These were the people we had expected to find. Also present that year was someone who was destined to make the summer of 1941 a season that would live in imbecility. Charlotte was in the middle of saying 'There's something you should know . . .' when suddenly a cabin door opened and there stood Evelyn Cunningham in a pink seersucker sunsuit.

Seeing us, she sprinted down the cabin steps and threw her-self into Granny's arms.

'Oh, Aunt Lura! Aunt Nana made me go to a new doctor and he's going to hook my head up to a machine and read my brain!'

'If he can find it,' Mama muttered under her breath.

Soap operas at this time were modest radio offerings con-cerned solely with love affairs, so none of us knew what brain waves and electroencephalograms were, but Evelyn was eager to enlighten us. She followed us into our cabin and recited a year's worth of medical history as we unpacked, talking faster and faster, higher and higher, gasping for breath, widening her eyes, licking her lips, until at last she crossed wires and had a chok-ing fit.

'Now you stop this foolishness,' Granny ordered. 'There's nothing wrong with your mind, Aunt Nana's just talking through her hat. It's female trouble that's causing those spells. You've got a descending womb. It runs in the family – I had the same trouble myself and I can see all the signs in you.'

'You think so, Aunt Lura?' Evelyn asked hopefully.

'I don't think it, I know it. You're delicate down below, that's all. All of us Upton women are.' She sighed. 'I've told you this over and over, Evelyn. Why do you let Aunt Nana fill your head with nonsense?'

The answer was easy. Evelyn and Billy had rented Granny's old house, putting Evelyn in dire propinquity to Aunt Nana, who had jumped at the chance to plump for insanity again. If God was on the side of the strongest battalion, Evelyn was on the side of the nearest.

Now Granny was the nearest. As she launched into her lecture on the descending womb (known to medical science by the cold name of prolapsed uterus), Evelyn's strained face relaxed and she returned to the female trouble fold.

'Oh, Aunt Lura, you're smarter than that old doctor any day!' she shrieked, rushing over to give Granny a big hug.

When she scampered out of our cabin, Herb opened a bottle of beer and sank wearily into a chair.

'That woman has a voice like a castrated Irish tenor.'

'She's nuts,' Mama proclaimed flatly.

'Oh, Louise! You sound just like Aunt Nana with her talk of the Cunningham taint. Evelyn has *female trouble*.'

'Mrs Ruding,' Herb sighed, 'Evelyn's problem has nothing to do with either the Upton womb or the Cunningham taint. She's suffering from historical displacement brought on by her unsuccessful struggle to be a Southern belle.'

'Why, she was a belle,' Granny said indignantly. 'Men flocked around her.'

'That's only one small part of being a belle,' Herb replied. 'Many women throughout the world are admired by the opposite sex, but they aren't Southern belles.'

'Then what is a Southern belle?' Granny demanded.

'A state of mind,' Herb said. 'One which Evelyn is geographically incapable of achieving. The belle is a product of the Deep South, which is a product of the nineteenth century and the Age of Romanticism. Virginia is a product of the eighteenth century. It's impossible to extract a belle from the Age of Reason.'

'Do you mean to say that Virginia has no belles?' Granny asked incredulously.

'That is correct.'

'Herb's right,' Charlotte said pensively. 'Look at all those plantation novels and movies about Southern belles. They're never set in Virginia, it's always somewhere 'way down South. Scarlett was from Georgia and Jezebel was from New Orleans.'

Granny scowled at her traitorous daughter-in-law.

'What about Sally Fairfax?' she huffed.

'Her fame rests solely on the fact that George Washington fell in love with her,' Herb replied. 'But she was a married woman when it happened, so she can hardly be considered a belle, especially since she discouraged him firmly and consistently without indulging in coy games.'

'No wonder they never made a movie about it,' Dora Madison said, giggling.

Mama was enjoying Granny's defeat.

'Name another Virginia belle, Mother,' she challenged.

Silence fell. Mama threw Herb a grin and punched him in the ribs. It was her way of saying thank you.

I was to dine out on Herb's theory thirty-six years later when 'Roots' aired on television and a number of non-Southern friends asked me why the Sandy Duncan character seemed oddly 'off.' It's simple: she brought to the Virginia of Thomas Jefferson a giddy flutter that belonged in the Alabama of Jefferson Davis.

At our picnic that afternoon, Dora Madison made a beeline for Herb and they fell to discussing the books they had been reading. Her girlfriends gathered round and gazed at him with an awe that hovered on the edge of romantic titillation. Here was the 'real honest-to-God Englishman' Dora had promised them; a man who did not call them honey, who crossed his legs at the knee, who looked at a woman's face when she talked and actually listened to what she was saying. Seated in a row with their eyes locked on him, they looked as if they were watching a Ronald Colman movie.

After the picnic we all went down to the boardwalk. Granny bustled into the Bingo hall, bought five cards, and settled down to a serious evening of old-lady vice. She always stayed until they closed the doors so we used her as a rallying point to make sure we didn't lose any children. The rule was to report back to her at specified intervals, though whether her glassy gambler's eyes even recognized us remained in doubt.

Herb and Billy Bosworth went off to play darts and I went with Mama while she had her palm read. When Madame Zenia got to the finger sworls, she had to use a magnifying glass to penetrate the nicotine.

'I see a strange man,' she rumbled in her whiskey voice.

'I see him every day.'

Three hours later we were hungry again, so we found Charlotte and Dora and went to the crab shed. As we were about to enter, we heard a shriek behind us. It was Evelyn, waving frantically, pointing to her mouth and running sideways in imitation of a crab. It was her way of telling us that she was hungry, too.

She joined us and we took a big table in the middle of the restaurant. The waitress spread newspapers over it and we ordered a mess of softshell. When they came, we all fell to except Evelyn, who was staring at an empty pickle jar on the table.

'I'm going to steal that jar,' she whispered.

'Why?' asked Charlotte. 'There's nothing in it except juice.'

'I know, that's why I want it. It's *pickle* juice.'

She rolled her popping eyes around the room to make sure no one was watching; then she grabbed the jar, screwed the lid tight, and shoved it in her big straw handbag.

'It's so's I can catch my womb in case it falls out,' she informed us.

'Oh, for Christ's sake!' Mama exploded. 'How the hell can a womb fall out?'

'Aunt Lura said it could!' Evelyn wailed.

'Mother's full of shit!'

Evelyn's answer was a sob. Putting her fingers in her mouth, she emitted a long steady moan that made everyone turn around and stare at us. She sounded like a smoke detector.

'I think we'd better go,' said Aunt Charlotte.

'Bring those crabs,' Mama said to me.

They paid the check and hauled the weeping Evelyn to her feet. She cried all the way down the pier and across the boardwalk, sagging into Charlotte's arms while we followed behind with greasy newspapers full of our uneaten supper.

'Women!' Mama muttered.

The next night I ran into Evelyn at the cotton candy stand. I tried to escape her frantic company by saying that I had to report to Granny at the Bingo hall, but she grabbed my hand in her clammy grip and said she would go with me.

It was Saturday. The boardwalk was packed with Marines from Quantico, sailors from Anacostia, soldiers from Fort Belvoir, and defense workers from the shell factory at nearby Dahlgren. As we inched our way to the door of the Bingo hall, Evelyn screamed.

'Here it comes!'

Wrenching open her pocketbook, she tore madly through its chaotic contents, throwing combs, cosmetics, and old streetcar transfers in all directions until she found her pickle jar.

'Please!' she cried. 'Please give me room! My womb's falling out!'

Her plea was instantly effective. As she squatted down and shoved the jar between her thighs, soldiers, sailors, Marines, brawny workingmen, the whole backbone of our nation moved as if impelled by some primitive religious instinct and formed a circle around her. Terror, disgust, and fascination bounced across their faces like the ball in a sing-along film. Were they Christians shrinking from a succubus, or Dionysian revelers admiring a maenad's cooch dance? Nobody knew. All certainties had vanished; the world was flat again and simple man was teetering on the abyss.

Attracted by the uproar, people poured out of the Bingo hall, among them Granny with a toaster and coffeepot clutched to her Daughterly bosom. She took one look at Evelyn and dropped both.

'Oh, Law!'

A vacationing doctor pushed his way through the crowd.

'Is she in labor?'

'Her womb's falling out! Her womb's falling out!' Granny cried, sounding just like Chicken Little. The doctor gave her an incredulous stare.

A few minutes later the police arrived. At first they thought Evelyn was drunk and exposing herself. Nothing was showing, but her pornographic squat and the position of her hand made one of the cops mutter something about Spanish fly. They called for an ambulance and she was taken to the hospital in Fredericksburg, the rest of us following in several cars. The chief of gynecology examined her and said there was nothing wrong with her womb, but this only made her scream louder. She went on screaming until they had to put her under sedation.

Billy stayed with her and the rest of us drove back to Colonial Beach. The next day everyone was exhausted and Herb was in a foul mood. No one had ever seen him mad before; his equanimity was a family legend, especially to those who had lived with Granny. He spent most of the morning brooding alone on a sandbar. Later in the afternoon he came and got me and said we were going for a walk. It was not an invitation.

We walked nearly to Monroe Bay before he said what was on his mind.

'Don't you ever get like Evelyn.'

'But suppose it runs in the family?'

'Bugger that! I am sick of this pelvic Shintoism.' He pointed a finger in my face. '*You* decide what runs in you. Don't ever let anyone or anything else decide for you. Is that clear?'

I nodded.

'I've made a careful study of this family,' he went on. 'Evelyn is the creation of Aunt Nana and your grandmother, and they have created a Frankenstein. One of them wants her to go barmy and the other wants her crankcase to fall out, all for the sake of some outlandish vision of ideal womanhood the two of them have cooked up. *They are both wrong!* Don't forget that. Naturally you will continue to respect your grandmother and obey her in everyday matters, but *don't listen* to her madcap theories. Is that clear?'

'Yes. What does Shintoism mean?'

'Ancestor worship.'

'What does bugger mean?'

A sheepish look crossed his face.

'It's something like what your mother means when she says "shove it."'

'You mean "bugger" is British for "shove it"?'

'Well, yes, you might say that.'

We walked back to our cabin. Herb lapsed into another silence, his brows puckered in thought as if he wanted to say something else but wasn't sure how to put it. Finally he spoke again.

'Your grandmother and Aunt Nana really aren't the kind of women they would like to be, so they use Evelyn as a doppel-ganger.'

'What's that?'

'German for substitute. You see, as long as Evelyn behaves in a feminine manner, Mrs Ruding and Aunt Nana don't have to. All they need do is claim kinship with her, wait for her to collapse or abandon her wits, diagnose the problem as some quintessentially female plague, and then announce that she inherited it from them. That way, they can go on being autocratic without risking exposure. If Evelyn is weak, it follows that they are weak.'

'What's autocratic?'

'Bossy.'

'What's quin – quinner—'

'The highest example of something. As in, your mother is the quintessential baseball fan.'

'Oh, I get it.'

'You know,' he said slowly, 'this Evelyn business has been hard on your mother. Knowing that Mrs Ruding would prefer Evelyn for a daughter has hurt her more than she lets on. If she seems brusque at times, try to understand her. Imagine how you would feel if you had a sister that everyone liked best.'

'I don't want any goddamn sister.'

'I believe you have taken the point,' Herb said dryly.

I had. I was still half-afraid Mama would murder me, but I began, in a childish way, to grasp the basic family picture. And a small relief, like a single bead of sweat, rolled down my mind: I did not have to grow up to be like Evelyn.

When we got home from the beach it was time for me to start school. I was enrolled in Kindergarten B, or beginning kindergarten, which met from one to three.

Mama and I walked down a crooked little street called Rock Creek Church Road to Raymond Elementary. The kindergarten classroom was on the ground floor. It had its own toilet, a piano, a bird in a gilded cage, and bulletin boards full of cheery paper cut-outs. Glassfront cabinets containing building blocks, pots of paste, and stacks of construction paper lined the walls.

At one o'clock the teacher clapped her hands, announced

that school was in session, and dismissed the mothers with a gracious but pointed nod. They gathered themselves up reluctantly and moved toward the door. That's when it started. A little boy near me opened his mouth and bawled, and it traveled around the room like a virus. Each time another child broke down, its mother came catapulting through the door with arms outstretched and features shattered. It was a mass engulfment. One child threw up, another held his breath, another hurled himself on the floor and kicked, and one little girl simply collapsed and curled up like a bean. Her mother knelt beside her and burst into tears.

Mine was standing in the doorway looking disgusted. She caught my eye and mouthed *Are you all right?* I nodded. It was a lie, I was miserable: I wasn't used to children and they were getting on my nerves. Worse, it appeared that I was a child, too. I hadn't known that before; I thought I was just short. Who were these watery moles anyhow? Were they always this noisy? I waved to Mama and she left.

The janitor came in and mopped up the vomit and the bean was carried out in maternal arms. The rest of the mothers stood outside the door pressing their faces into distorted shapes against the glass and making mist with their heated breaths. I felt proud of Mama for being such a brick. The teacher, less tactful now, shooed them away with a desperate two-handed gesture like someone flapping a towel at a clutch of rioting hens, and they departed at last.

Once they were gone, the class calmed down and grew quiet except for the sounds made by a vigorous thumbsucker. I was dying for a cup of coffee. The teacher seated us at long worktables, passed out drawing paper and crayons, and told us to draw a picture of anything we liked. I picked the *Titanic* because Herb had just told me about it and shown me photographs from his ship book. I drew an ocean liner and colored it in. Depicting an iceberg on white paper stumped me until I remembered Herb saying that icebergs look blue. When I finished, I printed R.M.S. *Titanic* on the bow and signed my name in script in the lower right-hand corner, pulling the tail of the *g* around to underline the whole business the way ancestors did in documents.

When I handed the drawing to the teacher, she stared at it for a very long time.

'R.M.S. *Titanic*,' she said at last. 'Do you know what that means?'

'Yes, ma'am. Royal Mail Steamer.'

'Why did you make the smokestacks yellow? They're supposed to be red.'

'No, ma'am, the *Titanic* was White Star Line. They had yellow ones. Red is for Cunard.'

'I see.'

She reached for a sheet of paper and began writing. A misunderstood feeling stirred in me, destined to be the first of many in a lifetime dappled with this sort of thing. I throbbed with alarm when she folded the note and pinned it to the shoulder of my dress with one of the emergency safety pins she kept on the lapel of her suit.

'When your mother comes to get you, make sure she reads that.'

'What did I do?'

'Nothing. Just tell your mother to read the note.'

I don't know why she didn't wait and tell Mama herself. Maybe her teachers' college had taught her never to discuss a child with a parent when the child is present. More likely, she simply couldn't take any more mothers that day.

The note said: *Florence is too advanced for Kindergarten B. Please bring her to Kindergarten A beginning tomorrow at nine o'clock.*

Translated into Mama it said: 'She was the only one that didn't cry! You should have heard all those goddamn sissies! I swear, they reminded me of Preston Hunt and his "daddy," except they were carrying on over their mothers.'

'It was the picture, Louise, and the fact that she signed her name to it,' Herb argued, gazing proudly at my artwork. 'That's what "advanced" means. It was knowledge, not behavior.'

'No, it was because she was brave!'

'She's in school, not the Coldstream Guards.'

'Be that as it may, she got promoted the first day. That's what worries me,' Granny said darkly. 'It doesn't do for a girl to be too bright. She might never come unwell – all her blood will go to her brain. She reads too much now. There's something unrefined about a reading woman, they always reek of the lamp. How can she grow up to be a lady if she's always got her nose in a book?'

Herb winced. As much of an anglophile as Granny was, she did not appreciate certain finer points of usage as practiced on the other side of the Big Water.

'Mrs Ruding,' he chided, 'I am not a duke, a marquess, or an earl. Therefore, Florence can't be a lady. What you mean is "gentlewoman."'

'Oh, I don't like that,' Granny said, wrinkling her nose in distaste. 'It sounds masculine.'

'Oh, shit.'

Granny took my kindergarten coup as a personal challenge to her ladysmithery. Casting around for an antidote to my burgeoning intellectualism, she forced me to submit to knitting lessons. Under her tutelage I grasped the basic knit-and-purl easily enough, but my needles refused to click or flash or lend themselves to any of the verbs associated with dexterous womanhood. They scraped.

'You will make your father a scarf for his birthday,' Granny ordered.

Herb liked conservative colors so I began with slate gray, but I soon tired of looking at it and switched to dark blue. The blue bored me after a few rows so I chose a ball of light gray and knitted on. Pleased by my show of industry, Granny left me to my own devices and went off to Richmond to visit her sister. I had to have the scarf finished by the time she got back. To make the task more bearable I changed colors every day, using maroon, royal blue, magenta, vermilion, yellow, orange, red, and purple. By the time Granny came home, the scarf was four feet long and contained every shade in her knitting basket. She and Jensy were horrified when they saw it.

'It look lak Joseph's coat.'

'It'll go with anything.' Mama chuckled.

I had knitted in the privacy of the room Granny and I now shared, so Herb had not seen the insane rainbow that would soon be his. Granny took it off the needle and blocked it, and I wrapped it in conservative dark green paper.

Granny gave him the usual pajamas and socks. Mama's gift was even less of a surprise: she took five dollars out of the housekeeping money he had just given her, stuck it in an envelope, and handed it back to him saying, 'Happy birthday, buy yourself a book.'

He opened my gift last. Only an English face could have resisted a double take on seeing what was inside, but fortunately he had one. Holding up my garish handiwork, he wrapped it around his hand the way a man fashions a mock knot in a tie to see how it will look on.

'I say, that's a handsome scarf. I'll be proud to wear this. Thank you, little one.'

And he did wear it. That night he stood before the mirror in his tuxedo and wrapped my lumpy gift around his neck as though it were the finest evening silk. When he put on his overcoat, the wool puffed out around his collar like a goiter but the master mold of fashion did not seem to notice. When he came home, he wrapped it carefully in tissue paper and put it away in his bureau with the same care he gave to all his possessions. He wore the scarf all that winter; never in the history of haberdashery was anything so awful so cherished.

After the scarf birthday I noticed a change in Jensy. Up till then she had always walked a wide circle around Herb. She dealt in stock characters where white people were concerned, and he did not fit any of the stereotypes she felt comfortable with. She knew how to handle good ole boys and Big Daddies, but Herb was neither, nor even a Southerner. Lacking Granny's reverence for all things English, she knew only that he was a foreigner. This meant what she called 'dark-complected,' which Herb was not, and 'heathen,' which, technically at least, he wasn't, either. But what had always disturbed her the most was the way he fell between the slats of her Bible-drenched certainties. To Jensy's way of thinking, he should have been a sinner: he worked at night, he aided and abetted dancing, and he handled hard liquor when he tended bar, yet he spent his free time reading books. In Jensy's world, people either came to ruin or they didn't; being neither Saved nor Damned was not only impossible but intolerable. For years she had been waiting for Herb to go one way or the other; the longer he remained in his incomprehensible limbo, the more her spiritual equilibrium suffered. It was like waiting for someone to drop the other shoe.

The tact and sensitivity he showed over my birthday gift enlarged her moral scope. 'He done right,' she proclaimed, and proceeded to tell the scarf story all over Washington's black community, using it as the subject of her Sunday School lesson on the Golden Rule and as a parable on The Family Man when she went with her church ladies to harangue the habitués of the Florida Avenue billiard parlors.

5

Herb's thirty-ninth birthday fell on December 1, 1941. Flat feet and weak eyesight from years of reading made him safely 4-F, so Mama took up arms in his place.

She went into a frenzy of patriotism, buying war stamps, saving newspapers, returning empty toothpaste tubes to the drugstore's 'victory counter,' and smashing anything stamped MADE IN JAPAN. She bought a pack of airplane-spotting cards and sat at the window on blackout nights peering through a crack in the shade and hissing, 'Bang! Vrroom! Ak-ak-ak-ak-ak! Wouldn't it be fun if we got invaded? We could take field rations and water canteens and go up in the hills and fight just like Churchill said.'

'Oh, Louise!'

We went to the movies every time the picture changed so she could snap to attention when they played 'The Star-Spangled Banner,' and took the Marshall Hall ferry so she could salute Mount Vernon. But what really fascinated her were the bullet-proof Bibles. Designed to fit the breast pocket of a GI's battle jacket, Bibles with metal covers were guaranteed to deflect bullets aimed at the heart. According to the newspapers, several of them did just that. From time to time the *Daily News* ran photos of soldiers holding shattered copies of the Holy Writ sent to them by their loved ones that had reputedly saved their lives.

'The War Department probably assigned an expert marksman to shoot Bibles,' Herb said.

'You know what your trouble is?' Mama yelled. 'You're a clinic!'

She bought herself a bulletproof Bible and wore it in her suit pocket. It was the only Bible we had.

Though she had ignored the mother-daughter dress craze, it delighted her that I now had 'my' war to go with 1917–18, which she called 'her' war. She favored me with off-key renditions of 'We Don't Want the Bacon We Just Want a Piece of the Rhine,' and made me memorize a bloodthirsty anti-Kaiser poem called 'The Spike on Willy's Hat' that she had recited in school; but when she referred to my book bag as my 'kit' and tried to get me to wear it on my back, Granny demanded an immediate cease-fire.

'Louise! The child will grow up warped!'

Granny's idea of an unwarped female was one who comforted the sick and afflicted, so to counter Mama's bellicose influence she made me accompany her and Jensy on their temporal acts of mercy.

Jensy had a strongly developed sense of Christian charity. Granny had a strongly developed sense of Granny; her good works sprang from a desire to win for herself that Holy Grail of Southern accolades, '*great* lady.' Her quest took her down paths of righteousness strewn with bedpans and rubber fingers into any sickroom she could lay her hands on. The more necrotic they were, the better she liked it, for the greatest lady is the one who gets somebody who shits through a hole in his stomach or blows snot from a hole in his throat. If she gets somebody who merely has the flu, she might as well smoke on the street.

Jensy found her projects through her church, which kept a list of people born in slavery who needed nursing care. Granny found her projects through the Daughters, but otherwise they were the Bobsy twins of coprophilia. Their cases were well into their eighties and nineties and all were known as 'poor souls.'

We traveled by streetcar and I was the Gunga Din, toting urinals, enema bags, shopping bags full of old clothes, and Thermos jars full of sloshing broth. When we reached our destination, I had to stay out of the way but not too far, and think good thoughts while listening to the squirty cascades of impacted bowels coming loose. The first time it happened I threw up out the window. After that I sneaked a book along and read with my fingers stuck in my ears, turning the pages with an elbow.

They also called on shut-ins who were trying to support themselves with cottage industries, like old Mrs Ramsey, who crocheted rugs. Granny and Jensy raffled them off for her, which is how it came to pass that we almost got arrested in the zoo.

Armed with a chance card, Granny buttonholed prospects in the Saturday crowds while Jensy and I followed behind and held up the dubious prize. Things were going well until a policeman stopped her.

'Ma'am, you can't do this. No gambling allowed here, it's federal property, you know.'

I looked fearfully at Jensy but she shook her head. 'Uh-uh,' she grunted. 'Let yo' big momma do the talkin'.' She pulled me over by the fence and we watched the legal battle from the sidelines.

A new Granny crystallized before me. As she gazed up into the policeman's face, I saw her lashes flutter behind her bifocals. Her gray head tossed with sprightly promise and her wrinkled mouth took on a pert simper, until she seemed all aquiver with gentle girlish passion. This stage of the counterattack lasted several minutes, then her face fell into tragic lines. Stepping closer, I heard snatches of the conversation. 'Poor soul . . . the doctor cut . . . eaten up with . . . going all through her system . . . she lost her . . . no one in the world . . . only a matter of time.'

The next thing I knew, the policeman was digging into his pocket for a dime while Granny removed a hairpin and punched out his choice.

And then there were the funerals. Death has no sting to a child who sees old ladies listening eagerly for the thump of a newspaper at the door so they can 'find out who died.' The high priestess of Granny's circle of necrophiles was a Mrs Bell, whose favorite expression was, 'She doesn't look like herself.' No final display was good enough for Mrs Bell; either the embalming was faulty ('She started to *go*') or else the cosmetician had compromised someone's postmortem reputation. The latter was on her mind the day she met us at the door of the funeral parlor in a mood of high dudgeon.

'Miz Ruding, I want you to see this.' She dragged us into a viewing room and pointed into the open coffin. 'Now *you* know and *I* know that she never wore anything except a little powder on her forehead and nose. Now look, just *look* at what they've done to her! Lipstick, rouge, eye paint! *Eye* paint, Miz Ruding!'

'Oh, that's terrible, truly it is. She'd have a fit if she could see herself.'

'They've got her all gussied up like a lady of the evening. I told them and told them but they wouldn't listen. They don't lay people out the way they used to, let me tell you. They've got the prayer book up too high – why, it's almost under her chin! And look at the way they've got her turned to the right. She's almost on her *side!*'

'They do that nowadays.' Granny sighed. 'It's supposed to make them look more lifelike but I don't like it one bit.'

'We've got to wipe that paint off and straighten her out, Miz Ruding. She'd never forgive us if we let her cross over looking like this.'

'You're absolutely right, Miz Bell.' Granny put down her

handbag and gave me a nudge toward the door. 'You go over there and stand where you can see if anybody's coming.'

As I took up my sentry duty, an organ somewhere in the establishment began playing 'Whispering Hope.' I tried to figure out why standing guard over this covert operation was different from playing war games with Mama. The answer came to me when I glanced back at Granny and Mrs Bell pulling and tugging at the helpless corpse like a couple of ghouls: this was 'feminine.'

Our do-gooding involved complex streetcar rides all over town. Fortunately Washington's public transit was not segregated, so we could all sit together, but Jensy still worried that we would get separated at some crowded transfer point and I would get lost. To make sure I realized the seriousness of the matter, she told me a story.

'I knowed dis l'il gal dat strayed off from home an' fell in a ditch. She didden have nothin' to eat, so she ate her arm, den she ate d'other arm, den she ate her laig, den d'other laig. 'Fore long, she ate herself all up an' dey didden find nothin' left 'cept a pile of bones in de ditch.'

'I'm glad,' I said. 'I hate children.'

Granny's mouth fell open.

Watery moles have no gender. Mama and Herb scorned their own sex and got on famously with the opposite one, but I transcended such earthling bigotries and dwelled in that 14th Amendment of the human spirit known as 'Everybody stinks.'

Recess was the bane of my existence because I had to play – yes, *play* – with the watery moles; otherwise one of the Life Adjustment teachers would spray me with friendly fire. It was a transitional period in education: the traditionalists were on their way out and the huggybears were on their way in. Huggybears loved playground duty because it gave them a golden opportunity to smoke out introverts. When they saw one, they came bounding up like lovelorn fascists, shrilling, 'What are you doing here all alone?'

I wasn't always alone. Like Jonathan Swift, I found something to like in the occasional Tom, Dick, or Harry. My exceptions were named Peg Jennings and Helen Koustopolous; both lived in 1020 and Helen's father ran the Greek deli downstairs. I spent a fair amount of time in their company but the grand viziers of other-direction had trouble counting in small numbers. They were not happy unless everybody was engaged in an activity big enough to require what they called 'give and take,' like marching on the Tuileries with equal parts of the Princesse de Lamballe's dismembered corpse on our pikes.

My nemesis was my 2B teacher, Miss Tanner, who always squatted down when she talked to her students so we would feel she was one of us. It was like conversing with a troll on a heath.

'Don't you *want* to be popular, Florence?'

'No, ma'am.'

'Now, I just don't believe that. I bet you can be the nicest, friendliest little girl ever! Aren't there times when you feel warm and friendly toward people?'

'Yes, ma'am, there's one time.'

'Will you tell me about it?' she whispered. 'It'll be our secret.'

'When we go out to the country to visit my uncle . . .'

'Yes? Go on.'

'When the train goes through, and the men who work on the train wave to people.'

'And you wave back?'

'Yes, ma'am.'

'And give them a big friendly smile?'

'Yes, ma'am.'

'And you feel all happy inside?'

'Yes, ma'am.'

'There! I told you so! Now if you can be warm and friendly

with the train men, why can't you be warm and friendly with the other children?'

'Because the train men keep on going.'

Miss Tanner's favorite way of teaching history was a game she invented called 'My Name Is . . .' We had to pretend to be a famous person from the past and recite our life stories as if we were on radio's popular problem show, 'Help Me, Mr Anthony.'

Mr Anthony chose for his raconteurs the members of his studio audience who led the most hellish lives. Stiff upper lips were out. Announcing, 'I have a broken home in the balcony,' he drew forth abysmal, tear-drenched tales of infidelity, beatings, knife fights, drunkenness, wages lost to gambling, desertions, and wondrous rare diseases that held Granny and Jensy spellbound. Herb called the show 'the common man's Agamemnon.'

Miss Tanner had a grand time on 'My Name Is' day. Seated in a little chair just like ours, she frowned, shook her head, and winced in disgust as a little Magellan told of having to eat rats and boiled leather on his world cruise, and beamed with delight when a little Martha Washington detailed the housekeeping tasks at Mount Vernon.

Then my turn came.

'My name is Lizzie Borden—'

'Stop!'

I tried to explain that I had chosen Lizzie because her domestic problems were more suited to Mr Anthony's show than the exalted cares of kings and queens, but she refused to listen.

'Where did you learn about Lizzie Borden?'

'My father told me about her.'

'Your *father*?'

I saw her point, but it had not occurred to me before. Herb told stories with such dry detachment that no one would have guessed that he shared paternal status with the minced Andrew Borden.

Miss Tanner did not believe in punishment so she reasoned with me instead.

'There are so many *nice* women you could pretend to be. Why don't you put on your thinking cap and see how many you can come up with?' Here she pantomimed putting on a cap, and then held her finger to her temple in the thinking position. Brightening, she held it aloft in the eureka position. 'I know one! I'll give you a hint: her first name was the same as yours. Do you know who I mean? Florence Nightingale!'

The watery moles thought that was funny and laughed. I wanted to drain their blood like the medieval Hungarian countess Herb had told me about.

'Do you know who Florence Nightingale was?' Miss Tanner prompted.

'Yes, ma'am. She was a nurse in the Crimean War. The English soldiers called her "the lady with the lamp."'

Something passed across her eyes, swimmingly at first, before it found its focus and hardened. I knew then that she disliked me. Not the normal feeling teachers have for troublesome students, but a full-blown adult dislike.

After that she had it in for me, but not in the classroom. Her natural habitat being the playground she tried to make it mine, too. She forced me into the co-ed baseball game between the boys and the tomboys who both jeered, 'You bat like a girl!' It was an academic point; I jumped rope like a paraplegic. It was more than just being unathletic. I had such a visceral hatred of groups that it caused a kind of paralysis that struck during recess. Resistance to team play seemed to pour like wet cement through my bones, displacing supple marrow, until I was ballasted with my own contempt.

My ineptness made me the last hired, first fired on the playground, and hence more than ever likely to be alone. Miss Tanner's genial hounding continued, so I conceived the idea of 'taking an end for good' in jumprope. This way I could seem to be participating while remaining outside the fray. The girls who liked – yes, *liked* – to jump rope hated having to take their turn at turning, so for a while I was popular in a windmillish sort of way. While I turned I fantasised murdering watery moles and huggybears by walking into their midst with a hand grenade concealed in my undershirt, like Veronica Lake blowing the Japs to bits with her loaded bra in *So Proudly We Hail*. It did not help. The thought of dying in a group only made me feel worse.

I learned the futility of appeasement when I tried to cope with Miss Tanner according to the rules for honeymoon etiquette that Granny issued when Dora Madison got married: 'Be as pleasant and cheerful as possible, and remember to exclaim over special treats.' It didn't work. I was as maladroit an actress as I was an athlete; my exclamations turned to ashes in my mouth and my face invariably gave me away.

I sensed that my face was part of the problem. I didn't look like a loner; I looked like a straight-haired Shirley Temple, or more sickeningly, a blond Margaret O'Brien. Strangers on the street murmured, 'What a *sweet* little girl,' to each other as I went by, which always made Jensy hoot, 'Babe, you sho can pass.' Something told me that if I had been plug-ugly or a boy, no one would have cared what I was like, but a pretty girl was supposed to be a melody, not a misanthrope.

Miss Tanner carried her Life Adjustment campaign over into my next report card: *Florence displays an unfriendly attitude and does not mix with her peer group.*

'Her *what?*' Mama said.

Herb defined the word.

'Oh. Well, that's a crock of shit. What the hell do they think they're running, a popularity contest? I poured ink all over Irene Upton when I was in the second grade and there wasn't a word on my report card about it – and she was my cousin, not my peer. You remember that, Mother?' she asked proudly.

'I do indeed.' Granny sighed.

Usually vocal in all matters concerning me, Granny said little during the peer-problem controversy. Unable to conceive of a human being who did not want to 'know everybody,' she was simply and plainly at a loss for words. Mama was not.

'Do the other kids pick on you? Don't let 'em get away with it – wipe the floor with 'em! Knock 'em into the middle of next week! Break their goddamn—'

'Hold yo' hosses, Miss Louise! It ain't a question of fightin' wid 'em. Sound to me lak she doan eben know 'em.'

'Jensy's right,' I said. 'Nobody picked on me like you mean. I just don't like them.'

'Why not?' Granny asked incredulously.

'I don't know . . . just because. Anyhow,' I added, 'I do like Peg and Helen.'

But liking Peg and Helen was not enough for Miss Tanner, or perhaps it was too much. Her next written report said: *Florence sets up exclusive cliques and makes it clear to the other children that they are not welcome to join.*

'That bitch doesn't know her ass from titwillow!'

Plucking Herb's fountain pen from his pocket, Mama turned the report card sideways in the southpaw manner and wrote in her backhand script: *What do you want, egg in your beer? Everybody's friend is everybody's fool. You're a Friday turd at a Saturday market. Yours truly, Mrs King.*

Mama's note came to the attention of the principal, Miss Ballinger, a tall, lanky spinster whose pince-nez took the dimmest of views on Life Adjustment. All of the teachers, traditionalist and huggybear alike, were terrified of her. She phoned Mama and talked glowingly of my reading and spelling. Very little was said about my peer problems, and when Herb took his turn at the phone, even less. In fact, they did not discuss me at all. The moment Miss Ballinger heard his accent, all pedagogical thoughts flew out of her head. 'Why, you're English!' we heard her carol as we clustered around with our ears cocked.

Somehow they got on the subject of the Celtic burial cairns she had seen on a long-ago walking tour through Scotland. When Herb said, 'They buried them standing up in their chariots, you know,' Mama walked away waving her hands in the air. Granny left when the subject turned to Druids. I stuck it out to the end but my name was never mentioned.

Granny nearly had a stroke when Miss Ballinger announced her decision: I was to skip the 3A.

'She's going to be an old maid!'

I liked the 3B and got along famously with my new teacher, Mrs Otter, who gave off a weary cynicism that inspired trust. She did not care who played with whom and confined her written reports to serious breaches of discipline.

It made me happy that it was Mama instead of Granny who rescued me from Miss Tanner. I took Granny's love for granted because I had won it at birth merely by being a girl, but Mama's love was more precious because my sex had been a disappointment to her. But it was precisely because I was a girl that there had been a Tanner affair at all. Miss Tanner would never have hounded a boy in the same openly gleeful way, and Mama would not have sprung to a boy's defense; she would have delivered a philippic on sissies and told him to fight his own battles. For that matter, no son of Mama's would have been in school in the first place; he would have been in the children's ward at St. Elizabeth's, confined in a plastic bubble and hooked up to a twenty-four-hour phenobarbitol dispenser. Having a daughter, on the other hand, brought out the best in her, and at last she seemed to realize it.

She surpassed herself a few months later when I became the focal point in a family fight over our plot in Congressional Cemetery.

'Botetourt phoned me today,' Granny said one night at dinner. 'He wants to replace the old tombstones with one big marker.'

'No!' I screamed.

Everyone jumped. I looked wildly into their eyes and burst into tears. 'He can't take Charlie's lamb! Don't let him!'

Granny stirred uncomfortably. This was my uncle's decision, and imperious as she was in all other ways, she did not believe women should contradict men or try to dominate them – at least not openly. A true woman, she frequently said, got her way by using indirection and feminine wiles. She called Uncle Bud and essayed a few simpering cajoleries on my behalf, but they had no effect on him.

Mama shot out of her chair and grabbed the phone.

'Listen, you goddamn sonofabitch, Florence loves that lamb! You lay a finger on it and I'll put *you* in the plot!'

'It's Mother's decision,' Uncle Bud said confidently, 'and she just told me to go ahead.' He hung up.

I was so upset I stayed home from school the next day. There were several more phone calls and Mama did all the talking at our end. Granny was reduced to wringing her hands.

'Charlie's marker isn't marble, Louise,' she pleaded. 'Just porous stone. The caretaker told Botetourt that the lamb could break off at any time. The stone is so old that it's beginning to come loose from the ground because of all the moisture and shifting. Porous stone does that, Louise.'

'To hell with the pores! They can fix whatever's wrong with it and hammer it back down again.'

Just then the phone rang. It was Aunt Charlotte with a peace offering.

'I just talked to Bud,' she said, 'and he's willing to give you the lamb.' She giggled. 'I pretended to cry and he gave in,' she explained proudly. 'We'll pay to have the lamb taken off the stone and Florence can keep it.'

'Oh, Louise,' Granny said happily, putting her hand over the mouthpiece, 'it's all settled. Botetourt is going to give us the lamb.'

'*Give!*' Mama bellowed. 'Who the hell does that shitass bastard think he is? He's not giving us anything – I'm going to *take* it!'

She stormed over to the hall closet, yanked her coat off a hanger, and tossed mine to me.

'Louise, what are you going to do?' Granny cried.

'He's not going to chop that lamb off and toss it to Florence like some old bone you give a dog. I'm going over to that goddamn graveyard and take the whole friggin' slab!'

'Louise—'

'Don't Louise me! Get out of the way!'

She borrowed a pickax and shovel from the janitor and tossed them in the back of the car. It was eleven in the morning on a rainy February weekday; the cemetery was deserted. I carried four Lansburgh's shopping bags, one inside the other, and Mama brought the tools.

The little tombstone moved when she leaned hard against it. She grunted with satisfaction. After about ten minutes of hacking and digging she got it out. We shoved it into the shopping bags and hurried back to the car, looking for all the world like Burke and Hare. When we got home Granny was lying on the sofa with an icebag on her head. She looked at the muddy shopping bags and groaned.

'Louise, how could you? You *stole* it! How *could* you?'

'It runs in the family,' Mama replied. 'All those ancestors you're always bragging about were nothing but a bunch of thieves – that's why they were sent here.'

My parfit ungentil knight-mother . . . How I wish Chaucer could have known her. Years later when I read *This Side of Paradise*, I underlined a passage that reminded me of her: 'She had that coarse streak usually found in natures that are both fine and big.'

6

My first adult book was *Gone With the Wind*, which I read when I was eight. My favorite character was Ashley because he reminded me of Herb. I saw Melanie through a bedpan, darkly, and Scarlett disappointed me when I came to the sentence: *She had not willingly opened a book since leaving the Fayetteville Female Academy the year before.* Thanks to Granny's fallen woman songs, my favorite female character was Belle Watling.

A book that proved to be a great comfort to me was plugged inadvertently during Traffic Safety Week assembly when Washington's chief of police came to our school to give us a lecture on how to cross the street.

'The red light means STOP!' he boomed congenially, tapping his chart smartly with his pointer. 'The green light means GO, and the amber—'

The audience dissolved in hysteria. Girls shrieked, boys yelled 'hubba-hubba,' and the teachers blushed furiously as they ran up and down the aisles trying to quiet us down.

Herb was probably the only person in America who bought a copy of *Forever Amber* for its descriptions of Restoration London. Amber was an illegitimate daughter of the nobility who was farmed out to rustics and raised among people who sensed something 'different' about her. The adults disliked her, the village girls envied her, the boys were afraid of her, and everybody called her stuck up. She had peer problems long before she met Lord Carleton, so I identified with her at once.

I did not understand the sex scenes so I asked Peg for clarification. As the youngest in a large family, she was in a position to receive a wealth of trickle-down information not available to an only child. We had the 'intercourse is when' conversation that passed for dirty talk in 1944. Her description of the beast with two backs puzzled me.

'Where does the lady put her feet?'

'In the air.'

There was no air in *Anthony Adverse*. Compared to Hervey Allen's water symbolism, Granny's sexual euphemisms were models of clarity. Anthony copulated in oceans, whirlpools, waterfalls, and once, I was certain, in a giant copper vat. I could not understand what kept him from drowning, or, given the logistics of the missionary position as described by Peg, why the lady didn't drown first.

'Get your nose out of that book!' Granny cried. 'That's the biggest book I ever saw! I don't know how you can pick it up, much less read it. I have told you and told you that a lady is accomplished but *never* bookish.'

'Be that as it may,' I replied.

Granny wasn't the only person nagging on this subject now. The moment the war ended, GIs came home singing the praises of the European woman's perfect femininity.

'Bullshit, they said that the last time,' Mama snorted.

She seemed to be the only person in the entire country willing to stand up for the home team. Newspapers and magazines picked up the scent and inundated the reading public with articles on 'What's Wrong With the American Woman?'

'This fellow Henry Adams answered that at the turn of the century,' said Herb. Opening *The Dynamo and the Virgin*, he read aloud: 'An American Virgin would never dare command; an American Venus would never dare exist.'

'What the hell does that mean?' asked Mama.

'America is a Protestant country and a puritanical country. There's no female ideal in America, never has been. Therefore, it's culturally impossible for the American woman to be feminine because she has no defining goddesses.'

'What about all those Catholic foreigners we've let in?' Granny demanded. 'Seems to me like they're trying to Mary us to death.'

Herb shook his head.

'Their chief ambition has been to Americanize themselves. And to that end,' he added ruefully, 'they've weakened their goddess heritage. The American Catholic doesn't see the Virgin as the figure of commanding womanliness that the medieval world worshipped. She's been turned into a long-suffering Irish mother. American women who copy that kind of femininity will end up as martyrs.'

Granny looked discomfited. I wondered if she was thinking about her missions of mercy. Though she would never consciously pattern herself on a Catholic figure, she had opted for goodness instead of badness.

'The soldiers in that article were talking about Dutch women,' I countered. 'Holland is a Protestant country.'

'Yeah,' Mama agreed. 'How come they're such goody-goodies?'

'European countries that are Protestant now were Catholic for many centuries, and pagan before that. The Protestant women of Europe have race memory on their side,' Herb replied.

'What's race memory?' I asked.

'An instinct that remains in people from something their ancestors did.'

'Race memory runs in our family,' Granny said with a pleased smile.

Mama squared her shoulders and lifted her head.

'We don't need any goddamn goddesses from over there. They called Jean Harlow the American Venus and now they're saying the same thing about Jane Russell. Americans can invent anything,' she said proudly.

'Ah, you've hit on the key to all this, Louise,' Herb said eagerly. 'American women *do* have to invent their own female ideals – that's why there are so many counterfeit versions of femininity, like the Southern belle.'

'This is the silliest conversation I ever did hear,' Granny huffed. 'American womanhood is as constant as the tides. That Henry Adams is just some old foreigner who doesn't understand our ways.'

For once Herb's poker face deserted him.

'Mrs Ruding, he was the great-grandson of President John Adams and the grandson of President John Quincy Adams.'

'Be that as it may.'

The articles got worse when the Japanese occupation began. Writers poured invective on American women for not washing men's backs. A few desperate women took up back-washing; 'Why I Washed My Husband's Back' appeared, but the practice did not catch on. Another one did. Rosie the Riveter succumbed to journalistic bullying, quit her job, and scurried back to the home. Pleased by her obedience, the magazines called off their dogs and began praising American women for their good sense. The feminine mystique had begun.

Characteristically, Mama picked this time to drop her bomb.

'I'm going back to work.'

'Oh, Louise!' Granny cried. 'You're a married woman with a child!'

'The child is ten going on forty and I'm going back to work.'

'I wish Mr King would keep his theories to himself,' Granny sighed. 'He's put ideas in your head, and he's going to put them in that child's head, you wait and see,' she added ominously.

'It doesn't have anything to do with that John Quincy Shitass stuff,' Mama said quickly. 'It's because I don't have a goddamn thing to do around here. You do the cooking, Jensy does the cleaning – all I do is go to the friggin' grocery store! I'll be as crazy as Evelyn if I don't get out of this apartment.'

She would not be dissuaded. Granny gave in, but before turning Mama loose she delivered a lecture on the proper way to apprise a husband of such unwarranted intentions.

'Mr King is very sensitive. You must make him think that your getting a job is *his* idea.'

They rehearsed, with Granny playing Herb's part, until she felt Mama had it all down pat. The performance opened at the dinner table after Granny had served the coffee (her motto was 'Feed him first'). She gave the cue and it began.

'A full nest knows no rest till fledglings take to wing,' Mama recited rotely.

Herb's spoon stopped in mid-stir.

'Time hangs heavy on empty hands. Cares grow . . . days grow long when cares grow short.'

It was vintage Granny, but Herb was too agape to be concerned with sources. He must have thought she wanted to have another baby.

After waiting through a trenchant pause, which I'm certain she was counting, Mama gave him a look of such determined submissiveness that he flinched.

'I was thinking of going back to work,' she murmured with unprecedented equivocation. 'Do you mind?'

He recommenced his stirring.

'It's up to you, Louise.'

'Okay, that's what I wanted to hear. I'm going back to work.'

Granny shook her head in despair. Later on after Herb had left, she took Mama to task.

'Louise, I've told you and told you that you must think of male pride. Men have to be—'

'Oh, Mother, I can't fart around with that Southern stuff, it takes too long. I gave it a try like I promised, now stop fussing.'

She returned to her old job as a telephone operator. Some of the seniority she had collected before she married was still good, so she advanced quickly. The murderous pace and tension of the work suited her temperament perfectly and even seemed to relax her; forbidden to smoke on the job, she got used to fewer cigarettes and managed to cut down to two packs a day with no trouble.

However vehemently she might deny it, her decision to go back to work had everything to do with that John Quincy Shitass stuff. In his quiet, sardonic way Herb had saved me from the destructive aspects of Granny's ladysmithery, and now he had saved Mama from herself.

Granny was right about one thing: his Henry Adams theory did put ideas in my head. The approach of puberty was beginning to add another dimension to my peer problems, making me wonder what kind of a woman I would be and what my adult life would be like. At ten my powers of speculation were still extremely limited, but I had a feeling that I was destined for the kind of tumultuous situation that Mama called a 'beaut.' Seeking some sort of answer, I read *The Dynamo and the Virgin* and turned Henry Adams into a household oracle. Ignoring Granny's laments ('If I hear that name one more time . . .'), I pursued the subject of America's goddess shortage with Herb.

'Take, for example, the Southern woman's obsession with maiden names,' he said. 'Have you ever heard anyone refer to Evelyn Bosworth?'

'No, it's always Evelyn Cunningham.'

He nodded. 'What other examples can you think of?'

'When we go to see Aunt Nana, all the old ladies call me "Louise Ruding's girl." Some of them call Mama "Lura Upton's girl."'

'Quite right. You probably don't remember this, but there used to be a very old lady of ninety-five or so who remembered Mrs Ruding's mother. I actually heard your grandmother referred to as "Mary Codrick's girl."'

'Aunt Nana even does it with her own name!' I said, warming to the subject. 'Like when she says, "Never let it be said that Nana Cunningham deserted a friend in need."'

Herb crossed his legs and smiled an almost catlike smile of immense intellectual satisfaction.

'Genealogy in the service of perpetual virginity,' he purred. 'The land of the clinging vine is actually the land of the clinging maiden name, isn't it?'

I graduated from elementary school that spring. Near the end of the sixth grade we were given an IQ test without being told what it was. The teacher, a huggybear, became so unhinged by the mere thought of a sabot being tossed into her leveling machine that she spent most of the morning praising the forthcoming test in an Aeschylean speech that sounded like Clytemnestra compulsively telling everyone who would listen that she had never, no never, committed adultery.

'I have some good news! You're going to take the most wonderful test tomorrow. It's going to be *fun*! I'll bet you think that's too good to be true, don't you? Well, it is true – how about that? Now, it's a *leetle* bit different from what you're used to. You have to use a special pencil, and you'll be timed. But it has lots of pictures of things like, oh, slices of pie and circles and squares and such. And best of all – oh, I know you'll be happy to hear this – you won't get a grade on it!'

'Then why are we taking it?' I asked.

I got the look all Cassandras get. 'To help you get used to grownup tests,' the huggybear replied, forcing a laugh. 'You're growing up and going to junior high.'

After the test, Peg and I compared notes. Considering our

long-standing mutual aid pact wherein I copied her math and she copied my spelling, our reactions were not surprising.

'I finished the pies way ahead of time,' she said, 'but I only got halfway through the part with the story and the list of words.'

'I was the other way around. The story and words were easy but the pies got on my nerves.'

'You were supposed to figure out which pieces made a whole circle and which were the extra ones that didn't fit.'

'I know. That's why they got on my nerves.'

'I bet they're trying to find out what we're good at.'

'But they already know.'

A voice behind us spoke.

'They're trying to find out who's smart and who's dumb so they'll know what track to put us in when we get to junior high.'

It was Ann Hopkins, the only girl in the sixth grade able to wear a skirt without suspenders to hold it up. She was what Granny called 'overdeveloped.'

'What's a track?' I asked.

'There's 7A1, 7A2, 7A3, and 7A4. Four is smartest, three is next-to-smartest, two is average, and one is dumb. I want to be in 7A2 so I can be popular. Average kids are always the most popular.' Her eyes widened. 'It's even more important for girls to be average. Boys don't like smart girls but you have to be smart enough to ask the right questions when a boy is explaining something to you, so that's why I want to be average. You get the most dates.'

On a hot rainy September morning, Peg, Helen, and I walked to Powell Junior High just above 14th and Park Road. My New Look transparent plastic raincoat, the last word in postwar fashion, was so long that water dripped off the hem directly into the top of my socks. We squished into the building and followed the signs to the auditorium and took seats. At nine the principal entered, followed by four women teachers. He mounted the podium and unfolded some papers.

'I will call the names of those of you assigned to 7A4. When you hear your name, rise and stand by the wall until the group is complete.'

Our three names were not among the ones he called. When the intellectual plutocrats had left with their new homeroom teacher, the principal began on the 7A3s. We were in it, and so was Ann Hopkins. As we made our way to the wall, Peg and I exchanged a resigned glance.

'Words,' she said.

'Pies,' I replied.

Ann groaned at the thought of being next-to-smartest instead of average.

A pretty blond teacher named Miss Ogilvy beckoned us to follow her. As I squished moistly behind her I admired the way her New Look skirt swirled glamorously in undulating waves near her ankles. It also stayed up on her hips, while mine was pinned to my undershirt. To complete the contrast, she looked as fresh as a daisy and I was beginning to smell. It was the plastic raincoat. Some amazing new synthetic chemical, as yet unperfected, was wafting from it like vapor from a cesspool. I sniffed at my forearm and nearly gagged. Whatever it was, it had clung tenaciously to me.

In homeroom, Miss Ogilvy arranged us alphabetically, made a seating chart, assigned lockers, gave us our class schedules, and asked for someone to act as class chaplain for the daily Bible reading. I scrunched down and concealed my face in my stinking arms, terrified that she would pick me because I looked – yes, *looked* – like a class chaplain. Ann Hopkins volunteered for the job and I breathed again.

When the first period bell rang we remained seated because our first class was English and Miss Ogilvy was also our English teacher. After issuing us our books, she passed out composition paper and told us to write a theme on one of the topics she listed on the blackboard. They were: 'What I Did This Summer,' 'What I Want To Be When I Grow Up,' and 'My Family.'

I had no idea what I wanted to be when I grew up. Ann Hopkins did. I glanced over and saw her scrawling 'Wife and mother' in her purple ink and circling the dot over the *i* in her customary way. She and I had already clashed over her ambitions. For all I had heard about ancestors, I had no wish to be one. The idea of having children so they could have children so *they* could have children frightened me. It seemed so pointless, like that blissful measure of time in Heaven that so comforted the devout: 'If a bird transferred every grain of sand on every beach, grain by grain, and dropped them in the ocean, that is the beginning of eternity.'

I derived comfort from what I called 'overness,' possibly because Herb's Socratic dialogues always ended in such neat, inescapable conclusions. Thinking of him, I decided to write on 'My Family.'

My grandmother lives with us. She is my mother's mother, but new people moving into our building always guess it wrong. They think my father is her son instead of her son-in-law because he's so polite to her. When I didn't catch a mother-in-law joke on the radio, Aunt Charlotte said it was because I never saw the kind of stuff that usually goes on between a man and his mother-in-law. Granny's friends like my father, too. They are all Daughters. When they come to see her, he always tells them little things about history that they like. Tessie Satterfield, who brought me into this world, calls my father a prince among men. Jensy, the colored woman who works for us, says they broke the mold when they made my father. The librarians at Mount Pleasant all like him, too. All women like my father but he doesn't have any men friends. I guess that's because he's so nice.

I felt I could have done better if only I had not smelled. My arms had absorbed most of the chemical and reeked at the slightest movement; trying to contain it had affected my penmanship as well as my thoughts. When the bell rang I rushed into the girls' room and washed myself wherever the raincoat had touched me, but the smell remained, at least in my imagination.

I could not afford a lapse like this. I was used to being a pariah for flattering reasons, but now I was a real pariah and it made me feel vulnerable. Dimly I sensed that a female with a personality like mine has to make sure that she looks and smells good at all times, or as Henry Adams put it: 'Those who study Greek must take pains with their dress.' So far I had kept the watery moles in a state of resentful awe, but if I stank, their mood would change to scorn and I would be powerless. Nobody cared how a loner boy smelled, but a girl who is a misanthrope must be nice to be near.

The raincoat fiasco traumatized me so much that I did something completely out of character: I took Granny's long-ignored advice on ladylike graciousness and tried to be friendly.

The object of my sudden warmth was a late enrollee named Harriet Mudd, who stalked into homeroom the next morning and thrust her card at Miss Ogilvy. She had muscular shoulders, thick glasses, and tiny black eyes with an odd bright shine. Her complexion was taupe and her demeanor grim.

'I'm afraid all the lockers have been assigned, Harriet,' said Miss Ogilvy, 'but I'm sure one of the girls would be happy to share hers with you.' She turned to us. 'Do I have a volunteer?'

Every female hand in the room shot up. All the Virginless American dynamos were eager to practice goodness without clout. It felt strange not being the only one with my hand down, but this sort of thing happens to the best of us. Ann Hopkins was waving her arm frantically and I nearly tore mine out of its socket as I hacked desperately at the air near Miss Ogilvy's face.

'All right, Florence, thank you. Please take Harriet out in the hall and show her your combination.'

I rose triumphantly and gave Harriet a bright smile. Her face remained immobile. I told myself she was just shy. As I worked the combination lock, she seemed to be listening for a click like safecrackers in the movies; her eyes, minuscule to begin with, turned into mere pinpoints. She reached into her sacklike purse for a small black notebook, wrote down the combination, then replaced the notebook with a swift, secretive gesture. She uttered not a word the whole time but I looked on her silence as a challenge to my newly acquired charm. I would soon have those taupe toes curling.

She spoke her first sentence to me at three-fifteen that afternoon when I tried to put a book on the locker shelf.

'You touch this locker again and I'll kill you.'

I looked around; she couldn't possibly be talking to me – this sort of thing never happened to gracious ladies who made everybody happy. But there was no one else in the hall; I was alone with my new friend. She grabbed my books off the shelf and threw them at me.

'My Pop was a war hero,' she growled. 'He drove a tank for Patton. He killed lots of people and he showed me and my brother how to do it. You smear axle grease on an icepick and stick it straight in their heart. When you pull it back out, the grease seals the hole so it don't show and the doctor thinks you died of something natural.'

She dipped into her haversack and pulled out an evil-looking instrument and a can stamped WESTERN AUTO STORES.

'That's for you if you don't stay away from this locker.'

She slammed the door shut and jerked her head toward the

stairs, taking no chances that I would sneak back and open it after she was gone. I decided not to argue with her. A girl who called her father Pop was capable of anything. I descended the stairs, my spine crawling at the sound of her ponderous tread behind me.

Peg and Helen were waiting for me outside.

'Why are you taking all those books home?'

'Er, I have a lot of homework.'

'Already? It's only the second day of school.'

I almost told them about the death threat but I hated to publicize my defeats, especially one I had volunteered for. How would it look if I admitted to a falling out with my new locker-mate after only five hours? Even the chronically unpopular took longer than that to get a feud going, and this was more than a feud. Needing time to think, I brushed off their questions and changed the subject to one guaranteed to absorb us all the way home: pubic hair.

I spent the evening with the story on the tip of my tongue. Each time I almost told it, I considered the consequences and stopped. I could not tell Granny. An uncomprehending veteran of my social wars, she would only say, 'What did you *do* to the poor child to upset her so?' I could not tell Herb. He was for good news, like report cards. There was something almost sacrilegious about the idea of going to Herb for help in this sort of crisis; it would have been a travesty, like using a fine linen napkin to wash a car. Herb was a luxury, like Ashley, and the situation clearly called for a necessity.

That meant Mama, but I did not see how she could rescue me this time. Harriet was not a teacher or a tombstone but a girl my age, and Mama could not move in on a kid, even a monster kid. Besides, in a funny way I was afraid that if she met Harriet they would take a liking to each other. After all, they were both loaded for bear; I had a fleeting fantasy of the two of them going out on a rampage together and having a grand old time. The knowledge that they were sisters under the skin was painful, like having a brother whom Mama loved better than me. While Harriet was not a boy, she was much closer to being one than I was, so she loomed in my mind as the son Mama had wanted.

That night I lay in bed reviewing my options. The most direct solution, guaranteed to please Mama, was to beat Harriet up. There were two holes in this approach that no amount of axle grease could close. First, although I was taller, Harriet was much stronger; it would be no exaggeration to describe her figure as burly. Second, how could I, with my long history of peer problems, walk into junior high on the third day of school and start slamming the new girl around for no apparent reason? When the dust settled I would, of course, reveal my reason, but how would it sound? 'She threatened to stick an icepick in my heart.' Who would believe it? Harriet would only deny it. A search of her haversack would bear me out, but that solution was flawed, too. Violent people invariably have an animal shrewdness that I knew I lacked. Somewhere between the fray and the principal's office Harriet, like Lizzie Borden, would find some way to get rid of her incriminating weapon leaving me holding the icepickless and greaseless bag.

A quieter solution was to tell Miss Ogilvy in private, but that would bring me up against the same credibility problem. Teachers are old hands at childish hyperbole. 'She threatened to stick an *icepick* in your *heart*?' 'Yes, ma'am.' If I had known Miss Ogilvy better she might – I say *might* – have believed me, but after only three days? No. Not in 1947. Schools were peaceful places in those days.

My third option was to call Harriet's bluff, but having looked into those glittering peppercorns that passed for eyes, I didn't dare risk it. She *might* stab me. I was afraid of her but more afraid of what she represented. Like all members of the shabby genteel class, I hated low-class people. Being a shabby genteel

Southerner only intensified this prejudice; we are bottomless wells of aristocratic disdain and empty thimbles of aristocratic power. All we can do is badmouth poor white trash.

For the remaining days of that week I carried my books everywhere. Nobody paid any attention; I was always carrying books. As long as the weather stayed warm I could count on not being noticed, but what would happen if I started carrying a coat around I did not know.

By happy chance I never found out. My problem was solved suddenly and permanently on Saturday morning when Granny opened the newspaper and uttered a cry of despair.

'Oh, the poor little soul! Did you know a girl named Harriet Mudd? It says she went to your school.'

Her past tenses were music to my ears. I jumped up and read over her shoulder.

BRONZE STAR WINNER AND FAMILY
KILLED IN COLLISION WITH TRAIN;
SUICIDE RULED

Cumberland, Md. – A speeding B&O freight train took the lives of Albert J. Mudd, his wife, and their two children Friday night when the decorated 3rd Army veteran drove onto the tracks here. Witnesses said Mudd, who had been under psychiatric care at Walter Reed Hospital, shouted 'Here I come, Georgie!' and crashed through a lowered signal bar in an apparently deliberate attempt to end his life.

The story went on to list the names and schools of Harriet and her brother. It was true. Somebody Up There liked me.

'Did you know her?' Granny asked sorrowfully.

'Just a little,' I said, struggling to keep a grievous expression on my face.

'Mudd . . .' she said pensively. 'That's an old Maryland name. Was she descended from that doctor who was involved in the Lincoln assassination?'

'She could have been.'

In homeroom on Monday morning, Ann Hopkins, who had already lectured me on the need to show boys how deep the waters of womanly emotion ran, burst into tears and simulated a fainting spell. That the boys looked distinctly uncomfortable escaped her notice. Miss Ogilvy, no believer in letting students verbalize their finer feelings, insisted on an immediate end to the display and called for a constructive response.

'Flowers!' Ann sobbed. 'We have to send flowers!'

'That would be appropriate,' said Miss Ogilvy. She looked around in that way teachers have when they are getting ready to appoint a volunteer. My hand was down but now there was a clear logic to her choice.

'Florence, since you were Harriet's lockermate would you take up a collection and stop by the florist's this afternoon?'

I went up and down the aisles gathering nickels and dimes, my smile muscles aching from suppression. When I had all the money together, we voted on what kind of flowers to send. It should have been over then but Ann Hopkins still had some more womanly feeling to let out.

'Miss Ogilvy, I think Florence should lead us in prayer.'

Miss Ogilvy handed me the Bible and I read the Twenty-third Psalm, all the while thinking that the death of the Mudd family was the greatest event in the history of genetics since Mendel crossed his peas. I was in a state of delirious joy the whole day, but I had to hide it. All the girls went round with dolorous faces and spent lunch hour talking in hushed tones about what a wonderful person Harriet had been. None of them chose to remember that they had known her for only four days, and that during this time she had not even said hello to them. They competed with each other to deliver the most moving testimonial to her basic sweetness; what she was *really* like, 'deep down' and 'inside' and 'in her heart.' Each girl *knew* how warm and friendly Harriet had been, and I, who did know, had to keep quiet.

By lunch hour the next day, the Legend of Harriet Mudd had sprung up like a Nashville hit. It was the human comedy, female version; being unable to find the essential goodness in Harriet was an admission that there was no goodness in oneself, so all the girls in our homeroom related tender little stories about her: some thoughtful favor she had done them, something sweet she had said to them, a cute joke she had told. And I, to whom she had spoken as Cato to Carthage, had to keep quiet.

Do you think that's all I had to endure? Read on with me, the best is yet to be. When I got home that afternoon, Granny was wearing her good black hat.

'Change into your church dress, we're going to pay a call at the funeral parlor. I've invited Mrs Bell to go with us.'

The caskets were closed, of course, so Mrs Bell did not have a very good time. It was a shame, because she would have been the ideal person to help me realize my fantasy of folding Harriet's taupe fingers around an icepick. Picturing the scene in my mind, I doubled over and Granny patted my shaking shoulders, so I had to pretend I was crying.

The other mourners were extremely fat women with mean mouths and red-faced men with little pieces of toilet paper stuck on razor nicks. Granny gave them a dubious glance.

'These people look right trashy to me but we must pay our respects.'

'We're all equal in death,' said Mrs Bell.

Granny was so pleased by my show of womanly grief that she added an extra dollar to her share of my allowance that week. Of far greater value was the lesson I learned from the whole ungodly mess: I never again tried to make myself liked.

7

I spent only a year at Powell. District of Columbia schools were segregated and the city's black population was growing, so in the spring of 1948 when I was finishing the seventh grade, the school board transferred Powell to the black system. The white Powellites were assigned to Central High, which was renamed Central Junior – Senior High. It was at 11th and Clifton, so Peg, Helen, and I rode the streetcar down.

I started French in the eighth grade. It came as easily to me as math came hard, and salved my Henry Adams complex by providing me with an automatic femininity. Merely by adding an *e* to adjectives and reflexive verbs, I could establish myself as female without following any of Granny's rules.

Herb was delighted with my prowess.

'I knew you had a good ear. It was just destined to come out in a non-musical way.'

'*Tu es gentil de me dire cela.*'

'We don't need any foreigners around here,' Granny said.

'Hinky-dinky parlay-voo,' Mama sang.

It was in French class that I noticed a dull ache in the small of my back. When the bell rang and I stood up, I was aware of a moisture that told me Nature had added an *e* to the seat of my pants. I told Granny when I got home and her eyes lit in ecstasy. I knew what she was thinking: now I would stop reading books and win my Evelyn Cunningham spurs. She was dying to inspect my first production, so into the bathroom we went.

She had been waiting for it all that year and had sanitary belt and Junior Kotex warming up under the sink like a gangster's getaway car in front of a bank. She produced them now with a join-the-club eagerness that filled me with a sense of defeat. I did not want this kind of femininity; effluvia might be Granny's womanly signature but French was mine.

I developed bad cramps, so she put me to bed and gave me a hot water bottle and a hot toddy. Her favorite Southern scenario was complete. I had taken to my bed of pain with female trouble.

'I have something for you to read,' she said softly.

Half-drunk, I looked at her in disbelief. That's when she gave me the clipping. Herb read it the next day.

'Mrs Ruding, I fear this is blasphemous. Adam began as dust, Eve as a rib, but you are a star-strewn vicissitude.'

'Be that as it may.'

I won the French medal at ninth-grade graduation the following year, but my triumph passed unnoticed because Central had by that time become the eye of a racial storm. It was the Powell business all over again. In the spring of 1950 the school board turned Central over to the black system, causing that foremost native Washingtonian and Central alumnus J. Edgar Hoover to go up in smoke. Other Central alumni, including several very prominent men, joined the fray and the fight was on. The city became what is now known as 'racially tense' and rumors flew – the white boys were arming, the colored boys were arming, the Southern congressmen on the District Committee were 'in touch' with the Klans in their home states. Finally a radio station received an anonymous phone call from someone who threatened to dynamite the school rather than let the blacks have it.

'What do you think of it?' the streetcar driver asked me.

'I don't think of it,' I replied coldly.

I was reading *The Fountainhead* while a race riot brewed. The awkward age is the worst time to read Ayn Rand. She liked people to be tall, slim, and beautiful, and I was now slouched, dumpy, and pustular, but I took up Objectivism anyway. Dominique Francon seemed like the perfect solution to the Henry Adams goddess shortage. The purity of her vision made her a Virgin, yet she was undeniably the Venus of the granite quarry, so I looked for ways to imitate her.

I stopped walking and started striding, taking care to turn my flat feet inward so I would look like an egoist instead of a duck. I kept my eyes locked straight ahead, causing myself a number of collisions and falls. I forced my jaw into a rational clamp, which broke the rubber bands on my braces and made me dribble down my front. In the name of individualism I quit *Le Cercle Français*. I longed to quit organizations right and left, but unfortunately, French Club was the only one I had ever joined. I gave some thought to ending my friendships, but having only two, it did not seem worthwhile. The architect who had designed Central was dead, so I could not help him blow up the school, and there was no way to locate the mad bomber, who in any case was probably not an idealist in the Howard Roark mold.

How, then, could I be like Dominique?

One hot spring night while the city seethed, I lay on my bed rereading the scene in which Dominique throws a marble statue out of her window because she cannot bear the thought that unworthy people might gaze upon it. A thrill coursed through my fat-slabbed body. Maybe if *I* threw something out of *my* window . . .

I looked around the room. I did not have a marble statue but I did have a Shmoo, an armless blob of a doll popular at the time that bore a striking resemblance to me. Granny had won it in a raffle. I picked it up and went to the window.

'I do this as an act of scorn,' I intoned, and let fly the Shmoo.

A few minutes later I heard an uproar in the hallway, followed by a violent knocking at our door. Peeking out of the bedroom, I saw a hysterical Miss Inez hurl herself into Granny's arms.

'The colored are dropping bombs!'

Seconds later Mr Koustopolous lumbered in bearing the incriminating Shmoo.

'Say, dissa fell out your winda,' he said, offering it to Granny while his puzzled eyes took in the distraught Miss Inez. When she saw the Shmoo she let out a scream.

'Don't touch it! It'll go off!'

'Hah? Dissa litt'l doll. My Helen, she got one same ding.' He wiped the dirt off the Shmoo with his apron and smiled. 'I see litt'l girl here atta winda. She droppa doll.'

'*What?*' Mama yelled in her crest-the-ridge voice. 'Florence, come here!'

I made the fatal error of trying to explain too much. The sensible thing to have done was to hide behind a semi-lie; own up to it, but say that I had accidentally knocked the Shmoo off the windowsill. Mr Koustopolous had set it up for me by using 'fell' and 'drop.' There was no need to bring up the subject of *throwing* the Shmoo out the window, and God knows it was no time to go into the philosophy of Ayn Rand. Nonetheless, I panicked and did precisely that.

'I had to do it because Dominique did it! She had to destroy everything she loved in case she felt herself weakening and getting like the others! They were secondhanders but she was an individual! So was Howard Roark! That's why he refused to build Greek columns!'

'Hah?'

'What is that child talking about?' Granny asked querulously.

'Dominique and Howard are the only two people they've ever met who blend exaltation with degradation! She hates him because she loves him!'

'Who the hell wrote that book, Evelyn Cunningham?'

Miss Inez was still sobbing, Granny was still patting her, and Mr Koustopolous was still holding the Shmoo. He turned it over and looked at it as though seeking the key to my free-form book report in its batty smile. We were posed in this tableau when Herb walked in.

When he found out what had happened, he chided me gently for frightening Miss Inez.

'She was acting out a scene in a novel,' he apologized for me. 'It's quite simple, actually. You see, the egoist and the compromiser—'

'Don't *you* start!' Mama yelled.

The Central transfer went through despite J. Edgar Hoover. As a consolation prize the graduating ninth graders were given the choice of attending any Washington high school we wanted without regard to the zoning rules. I was on the verge of choosing Western, the alma mater of Helen Hayes, when something happened that rezoned our whole family.

One of the poor souls died and left Granny a house.

It was located far up 14th Street near the Colorado Avenue car barn in what Washingtonians call the 'second alphabet.' It means out toward the Maryland line. It was a row house with three bedrooms, two baths, a glassed-in back porch, and a small bachelor apartment with shower bath and pullman kitchen in the cellar. The deed called this the maid's room.

The house alone was windfall enough in our modest experience, but we didn't get the house alone. Mrs Dabney's will said 'house and contents.'

'It's just a few things,' Granny said.

'Jesus Christ!' said Mama when we walked in.

It was a Victorian parlor maid's nightmare, marked by the kind of decor involving the word 'throw.' Throw pillows, throw covers, throw cloths; fringes, tassels, filigrees, fretwork, beaded curtains, silk screens, and a shredding tapestry illustrating the progress of a Japanese beheading from the victim's farewell to his mistress to the dangling of the headless corpse from a palace window. Next to throw, the operative word was 'occasional.' Occasional tables, occasional chairs, occasional lamps; footstools, hassocks, stacked trays, wheeled teacarts, and enough card tables to start a gambling den.

There was a five-foot mirror over the dining room sideboard but it was virtually hidden by that frondish extra touch no Christian old lady can resist: sheaves of Palm Sunday palm, enough to build a hut, were stuck behind the gilded frame. The magnificent black walnut sideboard was covered with souvenir cups and saucers, elephants in descending sizes, pug dogs, monkeys in sets of three, paperweights with snow scenes, and tiny glass artifacts – shoes, baskets, fans, swans – that could be held on a fingertip.

'She was so feminine,' Granny sighed.

Mama gave her a disgusted look. 'I bet she was one of those women who goes around saying, "I like *little* things."'

The worst clutter was in the glassed back porch. It goes without saying that Mrs Dabney had been the plant type. She had turned the porch into a jungle; the air was dank, heavy with rot and death and the yellowing white suits of Somerset Maugham's remittance men. Herb took one look at it and said, 'Gin and tonic.'

The attic contained seventeen clocks: chime-and-pendulum-stemwinders, a Seth Thomas banjo clock, some Swiss cuckoos, a Louis Quinze with enameled pictures of Fragonard swishes, and three or four of the kind with naked mechanisms enclosed in a glass bubble.

'They don't any of them work,' said Granny. 'She had to dial time-of-day to make sure she didn't miss "Stella Dallas."'

'It figures,' said Mama.

'I'll have a look at them and see if I can fix them,' said Herb. It took us three weeks to clear the place out so we could move in. Now that we had a whole house, Mama and Herb gave up all pretense of being married and took separate rooms. That left one bedroom for Granny and the basement apartment for me – or so I thought.

'I want that apartment for Jensy,' Granny said. She tugged on her corset, a sure sign that a moral absolute was coming. 'The way I see it, this is Jensy's house as much as mine. She helped me nurse Mrs Dabney.'

'Won't it cause trouble in the neighborhood?' asked Mama.

'Why should it? The deed says "maid's room." Now, whoever heard of a white maid?'

We had all heard about Jensy's housing problem. Sometimes it was hard to take her complaints seriously because her standards were so high that only a host of angels would have passed muster as neighbors. She was always telling us about the 'trashy niggers' she had to live amongst. A product of the Booker T. Washington era when 'Be a credit to your race' was the Eleventh Commandment, she found fault with everything black people did. Her tirades could have been lifted from Klan literature. To her, a 'nigger' was any black person who owned a deck of cards, drank a beer on a hot day, or lingered on a street corner longer than it took a traffic light to change. She refused to stop and chat with anyone lest some white person see her and think she was lazing in the sun. She walked so fast it was almost impossible to keep up with her.

She was now alone in the world, having disowned all her relatives. She threw her husband out when Mama was a child, and both daughters a few years before I was born. One of them wrote to her from Chicago but she marked the letter *Return to Sinner* and dropped it back in the box. Now she had only about four or five friends, all hard-core members of her Lily of the Valley church group, known along U Street as the 'witchwomens' for their ceaseless efforts to purify the neighborhood.

'I'm afraid she's going to get hurt,' said Granny. 'She runs around with those Biblebacks preaching to drunks and singing hymns in men's ears while they're trying to play poker. Last Sunday she kicked a checkerboard off some man's lap. One of these days some dope fiend is going to cut her to ribbons if we don't get her out of there.'

Granny was an arch-segregationist but she was also an elitist. The two skeins came together in the Marian Anderson–Constitution Hall controversy. She felt that since some people are better than others, and since Marian Anderson was clearly one of the elect, she should be allowed to sing in Constitution Hall. As for the audience, any colored people who wanted to hear a superior person sing must themselves be superior, so it would be all right to sell them tickets provided the center aisle was used to segregate the entire hall down the middle

Something that used to happen regularly in Washington brought out another aspect of her tangled credo. An African diplomat in a daishiki would try to buy a ticket to a first-run movie on F Street, be refused admission, and end up on the front page of the newspaper. Since the diplomat's ancestresses had been at a safe remove from Southern gentlemen, he was always much darker than most American blacks, but to Granny it made no nevermind.

'They ought to sell him a ticket,' she ruled.

'But he's colored,' said Mama.

'Yes, but he's not *really* colored because he's a foreigner.'

'Mother, sometimes I think you're a little touched.'

'Be that as it may.'

Granny decided not to say anything to Jensy about the apartment until she was sure she was on solid legal ground. It would have been a clear-cut matter in any other part of the South in 1950, but Washington's system of segregation was as full of contradictions as Granny herself, a crazy quilt of law and custom complicated by the fact that the city was Federal territory. Concerts at the National Gallery of Art were integrated because it was a Federal building; otherwise the rule was 'Where there's a roof, there's segregation.' Thus public parks and the drinking fountains therein were open to all.

Some District buildings came under the roof rule and some did not. Public libraries were integrated and Granny the book-hater approved.

'Only nice colored people would want to spend their time in the library, so they won't cause any trouble.'

'Karl Marx invented communism in the reading room of the British Museum,' Herb cautioned.

'That's different, he was a foreigner.'

D.C. public transit was integrated, but any black making a transfer trip to Virginia had to get off an integrated city vehicle and board a segregated Virginia bus at the Old Post Office building on Pennsylvania Avenue. Blacks who wished to make a point were technically free to sit anywhere they liked as long as the Virginia bus was traveling through Washington, but since this would only mean having to change seats when it crossed the Potomac, black passengers seated themselves in the back at the start of the trip.

Some of this mess was straightened out in 1948 when theaters and restaurants were integrated, but schools remained segregated until 1954. The big puzzle was housing. Classified ads listed rentals under 'White' and 'Colored,' but property ownership was somewhat different. There was a black family in one of the houses on Park Road when I was a toddler. If a black person able to buy could find a white person willing to sell, the deal could go through providing there were no restrictive covenants in the deed.

It was all so byzantine that Granny decided to consult a lawyer. Mrs Halloway of the Daughters had a niece who had a fiancé whose uncle practiced law in an old established family firm in Fairfax. The uncle's name was Richard Pinckney Farnsworth, Jr, or as Mrs Halloway called him, 'Little Dick.'

She arranged an appointment for Granny and off we went.

'You want a lawyer who's been called Little Dick all his life?' Mama asked as we drove across the Key Bridge. 'I bet he doesn't have any self-confidence.'

'Louise, the child is listening.'

Mama read the situation perfectly. We never met Little Dick. When we arrived at the eighteenth-century mews that housed the Farnsworth legal practice, we were greeted by none other than Big Dick, still hale and hearty and very much alive at eighty.

'I'm retired from practice,' he explained, 'but I come down to the office every day to make sure that damn fool son of mine doesn't do anything simpleminded. When I heard about your problem, I told him I'd take care of it. I sent him down to the drugstore to buy himself a soda. 'Sides, be a shame to waste such a bevy of feminine pulchritude on him. That's a veritable flower garden of a hat, Mrs Ruding, never saw anything so fetching. You are Primavera! How you, little lady? You grow up to be half as pretty as your mama and grandma and you'll be the belle of the ball. Come on in my office – no, not that one, that's Little Dick's. I gave him the one without any windows 'cause he stares at the wall anyhow. Mine's over here.'

'Preston and Daddy,' Mama murmured under her breath.

Big Dick's office looked like a Shinto temple. A huge oil portrait of the first Farnsworth in America covered most of one wall; except for the Restoration wig and the Van Dyke beard, the Ancestor was the very spit of Big Dick. The rest of the wall space was taken up by membership scrolls in genealogical orders. Big Dick was Jamestown Society, First Families of Virginia, Sons of the American Revolution, and Society of the Cincinnati, i.e., descendants of George Washington's officers. In a corner of the room well away from the sunlight stood a glass case containing a faded and torn Confederate flag and a daguerrotype of another Big Dick look-alike in a gray uniform.

This was the man Granny turned to for help in installing

Jensy in a white neighborhood. She could not have made a wiser choice. As he listened to her story, it was obvious that he had had a Jensy in his life, too. There was no need for Granny to explain her labyrinthine prejudices; he shared them. There was no need for her to explain the many exceptions to her many ironclad rules; he made the same exceptions. He and she were so much alike that they did not even have to converse in a conventional fashion. They spoke in a verbal shorthand that is impossible to reproduce in print. It was a classic example of what psychologists call 'consciousness of kind.'

The actual advice Big Dick gave us was nothing much more than a confirmation of Granny's commonsense analysis of the deed's wording, but he put it in such a gallant way that I could almost hear her toes curling inside her Enna Jetticks.

'You are a veritable Portia, Mrs Ruding! I couldn't have put it better myself! Yes, indeed, Portia walks among us again.'

I could also hear Mama thinking 'Portia Who?' I could straighten that out on the drive home, but they would have to consult Herb on Primavera.

Big Dick walked us to the door and out to the car, holding Granny's arm like the flower of chivalry. As we were about to drive off, he stuck his head in the window for a last bit of Southern chitchat.

'Next time you're out this way, be sure and come by the house and I'll show you the rope one of my ancestors was hanged with. It's silk,' he said proudly. 'He was a viscount. Privilege of the nobility to be hanged with a silk rope.'

Granny's attitude about the apartment and the visit to Big Dick stayed with me. Never had she made it clearer what being a lady meant. She fought for civil rights differently, but she fought.

There was no trouble in the neighborhood about Jensy, but having another member of his fan club in residence did nothing to spur Herb's flagging ambition.

He had been drifting for several years. Since the end of the war, his engagements, whether music or bartending, had become fewer and seedier and his income had shrunk accordingly. If Granny had not had what ladies of her vintage called 'a little something,' we would have been on our uppers.

One of the reasons for his lack of drive came out when Granny suggested a way to improve his sagging career.

'Why don't you organize your own band, Mr King? Play for the rich crowd and the higher-ups in government. You'd fit in so well with people like that. Get a copy of the Washington Social Register and solicit engagements from it. Once you play at one of those parties, the hostess spreads the word to all of her friends. Those women don't want the trashy type of musician in their homes. As refined as you are, you'd be a great success, I know it.'

Granny knew nothing about music but she was on the right track. In a field that all too often runs to greasy-haired gum-chewers and worse, Herb stood out like a rose among thorns. Now that his black-cherry hair had grayed at the temples, he looked more like a casting office Englishman than ever. He could have been another Lester Lanin.

'That's good of you, Mrs Ruding, but I couldn't put myself forward to people like that. It would be . . .' He trailed off, shaking his head.

'Why not?' Mama demanded. 'You're as good as they are.'

He winced. 'Oh, Louise . . .'

There was an ocean between them – literally. Although he had been an American citizen for almost thirty years, he was still the psychological property of Edwardian England. His self-improvement contained no trace of status seeking; he had remained acutely aware of the uncrossable line between himself and his 'betters.' The idea of thumbing through the Social Register for likely prospects filled him with horror.

The other reason for his lack of drive was his American experience. Unlike other immigrants, the Englishman is sublimely unaware of the existence of those privileged beings known as 'real' Americans. Anglo-Saxon blood and easily pronounced names have no power to intimidate him, and so he never develops the inferiority complex that spurs other immigrants to pursue success. When he arrives in America he is neither tired nor poor nor huddled, but simply here. Not only is he excused from proving himself, but the 'real' Americans look up to him.

Herb had met with this attitude from the start and then went on to acquire a live-in mother-in-law who exemplified it. Granny could have turned the Duke of Wellington into a beachcomber, so Herb's subversion was a foregone conclusion. All those years of 'my son-in-law the Englishman' had done their burrowing work. Somewhere along the line he had thrown in the towel and adopted as his motto '*Britannicus, ergo sum.*'

Now that we lived in a paid-for house there was no longer any need to worry about getting the rent together every month, so Herb simply took the entire summer off. He bought himself a jeweler's eye and began the task of repairing Mrs Dabney's seventeen broken clocks.

Clocks, of course, are symbols of woman's monthly rhythms. Having been forced to listen to Granny's 'Ovariad' for so many years, Herb now discovered a way to get even. One morning around three, his delicate instruments with their complex interior mechanisms all started chiming at once:

Bong! Bling! Screee! Eeep! Eeep! Brrrrrrrr! Gloinnnggg! Cuckoo! Cuckoo!

'Goddamnit!'

'Oh, Mr King, you left the alarms on.'

'Y'all be awright up dere? What all dat commotion?'

'Sonofabitch!'

When we turned on the hall light, Herb was standing in the

doorway of his room, wearing his jeweler's eye and grinning from ear to ear.

'You did it on purpose!' Mama yelled.

The clock incident marked a turning point in his life. Not long afterwards he got a Saturday job at a music supply store and spent the rest of his time reading. He never played professionally or tended bar again.

I don't know whether Granny realized the part her anglophilism had played in his early retirement, but she backed him to the hilt, telling curious neighbors, 'Mr King is deep,' when they asked her why he did not work; until he acquired a reputation as a mysterious sage. The people next door spread the rumor that he had helped invent the atomic bomb and had to stick close to home because he was 'on call' at the Pentagon. Someone else, misinterpreting Jensy's statement that he was a prince, took him for an Oxford-educated Mittel Europa émigré who had slipped under the Iron Curtain just before it slammed down. The neighborhood being solidly pro-McCarthy, he was looked on as a hero.

Always the Daughters' pet, he now became their consultant, helping them with their papers on eighteenth-century pewter, and researching the maiden name of the wife of the nephew of Thomas Jefferson's bricklayer's brother so that Mrs Garrison, who was looking for another ancestor, could add a Monticello pin to her sash. Sitting amid the shards of his broken mold dispensing cultural roots to the Shapely Stout sisterhood, he achieved a kind of Herbish patriarchal dominance.

At the end of the Summer of the Clocks, Mama received a merit bonus and was promoted to supervisor. To celebrate, she bought herself three new fall suits. One of them was gray flannel.

8

By the time I entered high school my sex education resembled a bureaucratic snafu. Mama thought Granny had taken care of it and Granny thought Mama had.

In 1950, girls of fourteen were divided into two groups: those who knew a little something and Those Who Knew Too Much. My historical novels had taught me that women *always* enjoy sex, but the authors were maddeningly vague about what it was that felt so good. I wanted technical facts, not psychological states. I already knew that 'ecstasy covered her like the waters of a magic pool.' What I did not know was what exactly happened on all the fictional wedding nights I had devoured.

All I knew about wedding nights was that 'he snuffed out the candle' or 'blew out the lamp' or 'turned down the gas jet.' These thrifty actions were usually followed by three dots to indicate that something else happened . . . No matter how nervous the bride was, she never had to go to the bathroom – just as well, since there wasn't any – and as soon as the bedchamber was 'flooded in blackness' or 'bathed in darkness,' she did not surface again until 'the next morning.'

These novels created an entire generation of American women who cannot have a sexual fantasy without getting bogged down in details about lights and bathrooms. Our problems started in high school when, saturated in wedding nights but knowing nothing whatsoever about them, we discussed them anyway. Like Franz Josef designing a new button for the Austrian Hussar's uniform while the Empire crumbled, we did the best we could.

'Who uses the bathroom first?'

'The bride. That way, she can come floating out in a white negligée while he's opening the champagne.'

'But if she uses the bathroom first, she'll be left alone while he uses it. That doesn't seem right.'

'Yes, but if he uses it first, he'll be undressed before she is, and that's not right either.'

'Why would he open the champagne and then turn around and go in the bathroom?'

'They drink one glass together and *then* he goes into the bathroom.'

'Where are his robe and pajamas?'

'And the ascot. Don't forget the ascot.'

'They're already unpacked. He did that before he opened the champagne so he could just pick everything up and go into the bathroom.'

'When he comes out, he picks her up and carries her to the bed and throws her down on it.'

'How can he turn out the light if he's holding her?'

'She reaches out while she's in his arms and switches it off.'

'That doesn't seem right. He should do it.'

'But then he'd have to put her down, turn out the light, and pick her up again so he can throw her on the bed.'

'But if he turns it out *before* he picks her up and throws her on the bed, he might miss.'

'He leaves one light on so he can see.'

'That doesn't seem right.'

The information Peg had imparted to me when we were eight was: 'The man gets on top of the lady and puts his thing on her thing.' It was still just about all I knew. I remained unaware of erection, penetration, and ejaculation; I thought that a dangling participle was placed on a split infinitive and that was that. While this certainly sounded like what the newspapers called 'intimate with,' it did not explain the furor over virginity and the tragedies that awaited brides who were not intact.

'Men can tell,' everyone said darkly. Tell what? That I had been wiping myself all these years? What caused the terrible pain suffered by Frank Yerby's heroine Denise in *The Vixens* when she bit through her lip? I asked Granny.

'Your grandfather was a perfect gentleman.'

I finally got the word 'maidenhead' out of her before she balked. I thought it sounded like one of those peaceful English villages in murder mysteries. Ann Hopkins came up with 'hymen' and Helen told us it was Greek for 'membrane.' I knew that hymens were connected somehow with the emotional question of who could and could not use Tampax, so I sneaked the brochure out of Mama's box and read it. I had just gotten to the good part when Jensy snatched it out of my hand and told me to keep myself pure for Jesus, who wanted me for a sunbeam.

I locked myself in the bathroom with a hand mirror and tried to find my hymen without ruining myself for marriage. I sort of wanted to get married; having just read Turgenev's *On the Eve*, I wanted to marry a Bulgarian revolutionary if I could find one who hated children.

I examined myself. I knew where I menstruated from, but since that was an area concerned with female trouble I did not see what it could possibly have to do with men. I looked elsewhere and found the clitoris. I did not know it was a clitoris; I called it the 'bump.' As I studied it, the light dawned. This was the famous maidenhead. It had to be – it was the only thing I could find that looked like a head.

It was all clear now. Intercourse is when a man presses on the bump until it falls off. When that happens, you aren't a virgin anymore.

There was only one thing that bothered me. What did you do with the bump after it fell off? Was there a Bump Fairy?

A few months later I was deflowered in the doctor's office. My menstrual cramps had been getting steadily worse since I got my first period. I had already been examined anally by Granny's doctor, who was the sweet-heart of the Daughters, to see if I had any of the exotic maladies that ran in our family, but he had pronounced me 'normal down below.' I didn't feel normal; I was spending the first day of every period curled up in a knot in the high school infirmary, so Granny took me back to him.

'I can do a regular examination,' he told her, 'but I'll have to break through.'

Her hand fluttered to her bosom. 'What will she say when she gets married?'

He patted her shoulder. It was his medical specialty.

'Don't worry, I'll give her a certificate of virginity. She can show it to her husband and he'll know he didn't get damaged goods.'

I climbed into the stirrups expecting a clitorodectomy. He froze the vaginal area with a local anaesthetic and began snipping. I couldn't imagine what he was doing way down there in female trouble land when he was supposed to be cutting off the bump.

'That's got it,' he said, and inserted his finger.

The second, correct, light dawned.

He could find no reason for my cramps, so he patted my foot, told me to use a heating pad and avoid rain.

'There's one thing that really cures cramps and that's having a baby,' he said fondly. 'Now you stay as sweet as you are, you hear? Here's your certificate, honey.'

It was terribly impressive. It began with *To Whom It May*

Concern and bore a notary's seal from his nurse. As I read it, I pictured myself floating out of a bathroom in a white negligée saying, 'I have something for you to read.' I handed it to Granny, who sighed raggedly and put it in her purse. When we got home she showed it to Mama.

'He should have put "Now hear this." Then she could show it to the whole goddamn Navy.'

'Oh, Louise!'

Usually Mama was profane rather than bawdy. While she would say anything to shock Granny, in her own way she was sexually restrained. I think the reason she never talked to me about sex was that she felt girl talk was sissy. This probably explains the unique turn her one sex lecture took.

It happened at the sink while we were washing dishes. Suddenly, out of the blue, she said:

'If a man ever asks you to do something funny to him, you tell him to go to hell, you hear?'

'What do you mean?'

'Never mind. Just promise me.'

Mystified, I promised. We washed a few more dishes, then she spoke again.

'That's why the French can't win a war without our help. It saps their strength. They spend all their time doing something funny to each other, and then we have to go over there and pull their chestnuts out of the fire!'

Before I could frame any more questions, she threw down the dishcloth with a splat and stalked out of the kitchen singing 'Over There' at the top of her lungs.

The awkward age lasted through my first year in high school, but in the second year my fat fell away and I became pleasing to passing strangers again. Soldiers downtown kept asking me for directions to the White House.

I did not date in high school. I was not forbidden to; like the books I read, it was my choice and I chose not to. My reasons were mixed. The simplest one had to do with the custom of neighborhood schools prevalent at this time. Many of the boys in high school had been my classmates ever since kindergarten; we had thrown up together, farted together, wet our pants together, picked our noses together for so many years that we looked on each other with the dull eyes of the long-married.

The rezoning that grew out of the Powell and Central transfers had thrown a lot of new boys into my life, but pride kept me from dating them. They had seen me in the first year of high school when I was still in the awkward age, and it gave them an advantage I did not want them to have.

My biggest reason for not dating was the old one of peer problems. I had physical desires and enormous curiosity about sex; I wanted to neck and pet but I did not want to play knock-knock jokes at marshmallow roasts or sing endless choruses of 'Goodnight Irene' on hayrides. I wanted to dispense with the social aspect of dating and get down to brass tacks, but it was impossible. You couldn't meet a boy one moment and get your tongue sucked the next; you had to go out with him. Not just once either, but several times. I did not see why I had to sit through movies I could just as well see alone and then adjourn to the Hot Shoppes when I could just as well feed myself, all in order to get what I wanted, which was the same thing the boys wanted. But there was no way out of this conundrum if one wanted to remain a nice girl, and at this point I still did.

I would not have minded being a bad girl in my own mind, and I certainly had no fear of going to Hell; I shared Herb's belief in reincarnation and couldn't wait to see who I was going to be next. What I did mind was the idea of not being treated right by boys. A girl who Went Too Far was considered 'fair game.' Once the boys found out about her, they became what Ann Hopkins called 'fierce.' Fierce boys wrote a dirty girl's name and phone number on the bathroom wall. She got a lot of phone calls but no specific invitations, just, 'You wanna go out with me?' This euphemism was always accompanied by sounds of snickering in the background as the caller's friends gathered round the phone and listened in.

Granny's songs had accustomed me to the idea of righteous wrath. Her lyrical heroines were a touchy lot ever ready to snap 'Take back your gold!' or 'My mother was a lady!' These ostensibly pathetic Nells and Marys wrote the book on assertiveness. They thought nothing of standing outside saloons and singing about empty larders and consumptive babies until Father gave up and came home, and they never hesitated to interrupt a wedding in progress to lay a fatherless child in the arms of a mortified bridegroom. They caused uproars wherever they went; trains, hansom cabs, and sweatshops were constantly subjected to indignant cries of 'Have you a sister, sir?' Even mansions of aching hearts knew no peace. How Gay Nineties whores ever made any money was a mystery. As soon as the customers arrived, the madam started giving them hell for being the cause of it all, until they broke down and started sobbing about Indiana.

Having been nourished on this musical diet, the idea of being treated as anything less than a queen made me furious, so my sex life took place exclusively in my mind. I fantasized about a room where I could go with a fallen boy. It would contain a couch where we would do the things I wanted to do, and when I was finished, I would turn his picture to the wall and forget about him until the next time. Being easily shamed like all fallen boys, he would permit himself to be forgotten. He would not give me knowing leers when he passed me in the hall, or tell the other fallen boys that I had taken liberties with him. He would be exactly like a genii in a bottle. I would rub the bottle to make him appear, and then he would rub me.

I became known as 'the girl who doesn't date.' Ironically, it won me my first real popularity.

'God, you must have strict parents,' Ann Hopkins said in heartfelt tones. The other girls at the lunchroom table nodded and breathed, 'Yeah . . . God.' Everyone was gazing at me with deep sympathy and understanding, obviously thinking that I wasn't so bad after all. They reminded me of Greer Garson in *Blossoms in the Dust*, ready to stand up and cry, 'There are no peer-problem children, just peer-problem parents.'

It would have been so easy to keep my mouth shut and let them think what they already thought, but somehow I could not do it.

'No,' I blurted, 'my parents aren't a bit strict. They'd let me date if I wanted to, but I don't want to.'

The sympathy and understanding vanished.

Under ordinary conditions they would have persecuted me in that subtle way of females; a few of them tried, but it never amounted to more than a giggle behind a hand when I passed. They were intimidated by the cachet I now had. At long last I belonged to a select in-group, democracy's version of sixteen quarterings and a unicorn *gules*. I was college-bound.

The term had different meanings depending upon one's sex. College-bound boys associated freely with their non-academic confrères and looked up to them as avatars of bad-ass masculinity. Cars, sports, and gang showers created a male society that was by and large classless, but no such equality existed among the girls. For us, academic status bestowed an almost unbridgeable social status as well. Some girls were more equal than others, and I was a some. It was the same kind of unavoidable elitism that had plagued the suffragettes and would plague the feminists of the seventies. There is no such thing as a fallen woman; when she steps out of her place, she always steps up.

Our group was called 'the Brains.' It consisted of all the Jewish girls, all the Chinese girls, all the Diplomatic Corps girls, some of the Greek girls, and a tiny minority of straight-A Southern Wasps. Our motivations were as different as we were.

The Jewish girls had a tradition that exalted booklearning; the diplomatic girls were the daughters of a foreign intelligentsia who took 'taking a degree' for granted (Ranni Das Gupta was a brahmin); and the ethnic girls came from families who cherished the American Dream.

Southern Wasps stood outside this charmed circle. Our families looked down on the American Dream, muttered about old maids and bluestockings, and were only slightly closer to the intelligentsia than the Jukes and the Kallikaks. Our compensatory advantages were that quality of personality that comes to fullest flower in a Protestant whose mind is made up – 'Here I stand, I can do no other' – and one sane relative who supported us against the rest. Mary Jane Magruder (that's an old Maryland name) had a Brooklyn-born aunt who silenced the impassioned wails of 'You think you're better'n us!' with 'Shaddup, ya hicks!' I had Herb.

If any of us had heard the word 'feminist' we would have thought it meant a girl who wore too much makeup, but we were, without knowing it, feminists ourselves, bound together by the freemasonry that exists among intelligent women who know they are intelligent. It is the only kind of female bonding that works, which is why most men do not like intelligent women. They don't mind one female brain if they can enjoy it privately; it's the idea of two or more on the loose that upsets them. The girls in the college-bound group might not have been friends in every case – Sharon Cohen and I gave each other the willies – but our instincts told us that we had the same enemies.

The non-academic girls, a much larger and more homogeneous group, did not have a name. This struck me as odd, so I told Herb about them and asked him to think of something to call them. He came up with 'malkin,' a Shakespearean word meaning a woman of the lower orders.

I felt it was too strong. A few of the girls in this group were trashy and some were common (never mind the difference, it would take another whole book to explain it), but the rest were neither. I had lost Peg to this group but I knew she wasn't trashy or common; nor, I had to admit, was Ann Hopkins. Certainly they were not all stupid; quite a few of them had been tracked to 7A3 with me, so we must have had about the same IQ. Therefore, it was something else that made a girl a . . . Oh, hell, a malkin.

Ann was their undisputed leader, so I used her to construct a profile. First, there was the purple ink. Next, the circled *i* dot. Third, whenever someone asked a malkin what she was going to be, she always answered with her steady boyfriend's name: 'Mrs John J. Smith.' She spent her study hall scrawling *Mrs John J. Smith* over and over in her notebook.

Malkins did the most dating but they were also the most puritanical, seeming compelled to explain their dates with 'I just like to have a good time,' as if denying all interest in necking and petting. Yet they were obsessed with going steady, and if a boy did not suggest it after a certain number of dates, they accused him of 'wasting a girl's time.'

Malkins cared more for appearance than appearances, arriving at school with their hair in pincurls under kerchiefs and going immediately to the restroom to comb it out. They all seemed to have a Rapunzel complex; not only was their hair much longer than ours, but presumably much cleaner, because they were always saying 'I've got to wash my hair.' They continued their grooming operations in homeroom, picking and pulling at themselves and each other like baboons. Ann used her eyelash curler while all heads were bowed for the Lord's Prayer and thrust her hand inside her blouse to dab perfume on her breasts during the pledge to the flag.

Malkins were always having intense feuds, and leaned heavily on the verb 'to cuss out' when they related details of their confrontations. 'I really cussed her out,' they would say, yet their cussing never exceeded 'damn' and they invariably mouthed 'shit' or said 'shh . . .' substituting raised eyebrows for the second syllable. It paled beside Mama's muleskinner glories.

It occurred to me that Mama, academically anyhow, would have assayed out to malkin in her schooldays, yet I knew she wasn't one. What *was* it, then, that made the difference? I consulted Herb again.

'Malkins leave nothing to chance, but your mother leaves no stone unturned.'

When I frowned in confusion he began one of his Socratic dialogues.

'Would a malkin have stolen Charlie's lamb?'

'No,' I said promptly.

'Why not?'

'They'd be afraid of getting in trouble or being talked about.' I paused, reviewing everything I knew about Ann Hopkins. 'They'd be afraid of not being like everybody else.'

'So the key word is?'

'Afraid.'

He nodded.

'That's why your mother is a gentlewoman.'

I took three more years of French in high school. In third year we read that unsurpassed satire on machismo, *Tartarin de Tarascon* by Alphonse Daudet. Next came *Le Livre de Mon Ami* by Anatole France, which brought me up against the realities of translation. We had to do the 'O ma génie et ma fée' passage from the chapter *Marcelle aux Yeux d'Or* in a literary rather than a literal rendering – i.e., we could not say, 'Oh, my genius and my fairy.' The narrator is an adult man recalling his boyhood crush on his mother's beautiful friend, so I settled on 'graceful sylph.'

Fourth year was taken up with a line-by-line study of *Cyrano*. I found the story ridiculous but the speeches rang like deep resonant bells and the title role seemed made for Mama. It would have been just like her to call somebody a jackass and get into a swordfight.

Fifth year was the happiest interlude of my life. I might have been attending an expensive private academy instead of a public school; there were only eight of us in the class – the minimum for forming a class – and all of us were girls. We began each class with a pep rally. '*Mesdemoiselles, levez-vous!*' the teacher would say, and we would rise and sing '*La Marseillaise*'. It gave me a delicious frisson; even francophobic Mama liked it ('I'll say one thing for 'em, they've got a good "Star-Spangled Banner"').

As we sang, we raised our eyes to the steel engraving of bare-breasted Marianne hoisting the tricolor and walking over dead bodies as she urged her male comrades to the fray. We made a strange sight, eight little honor students all in a row, singing lustily of bloody standards and cutthroats. We did not know it, and there was no name for it in 1953, but we were into consciousness-raising.

In fifth year we read the verse plays of Jean Racine. For once I was studying something that stirred Granny's interest. When I told her about Phèdre's tirades, she perked up and asked, 'Is she having the Change?'

My favorite Racine play was *Bérénice*, based on a true story, whose plot turns on a situation that was dear to Herb's heart. When I translated Titus's refusal to abdicate and become

Un indigne empéreur, sans empire, sans cour
Vil spectacle aux humains des faiblesses d'amour

into 'A disgraced emperor, without an empire, without a court, a vile example of love's weakness in the eyes of all mankind,' he said, 'Sounds like that bloody Duke of Windsor.'

The messy passions of *Phèdre* reminded me of humid summer, but *Bérénice* was crisp autumn, full of the clean cool air of passion renounced and dignity preserved. I loved autumn because it symbolized school, but I did not love passion, I merely had it. I did not even like it because I did not really like boys, I merely needed them. Once exposed to the neo-classical restraints of *Bérénice*, I began to resent males for their power to distract me from the life of the mind I craved.

Bérénice replaced Dominique Francon as my ideal role model. Henry Adams's theory was now my yardstick for measuring all women, but when I tried to fit Bérénice into it she eluded definition as either Virgin or Venus. The Virgin was not yet generally known or revered in A.D. 70 when the events of the play took place, but Venus was everywhere in the Roman-dominated world Bérénice inhabited. She should have drawn her strong sense of identity from the goddess of love, but it was obvious she did not. She was a surprisingly masculine woman who put duty before love. Queen of Palestine in her own right, she was able to understand the political reasons why Titus, being Emperor of Rome, could not marry her. Instead of collapsing and having to be carried to the infirmary like Ann Hopkins when her boyfriend asked for his ring back, Bérénice walked off stage with dry eyes and full honors.

I was thrilled by her exit lines.

> *Je vivrai, je suivrai vos ordres absolus*
> *Adieu, Seigneur, régnez; je ne vous verrai plus*

'What's that mean?' asked Mama.

'"I will follow your wishes to the letter, but I will survive. Farewell, my lord, keep your crown; I will never see you again."'

'Good for her! She should've shot the sonofabitch!'

'Oh, Louise! I think it would make a nice sad movie with Barbara Stanwyck. She goes away real good.'

Herb put his head in his hands.

*

My French teacher recommended that I become a translator.

'You'd work for a book publisher, or several of them,' she explained. 'When they bought the American rights to a French book, they'd pay you to translate it. You could work at home, at your own pace.'

The idea appealed to me and I made it my ambition. I would be like the lady named Constance Garnett whose name appeared on all the Russian novels. Herb was full of enthusiasm for my plans. Once, when I kept fiddling with a sentence because 'It just doesn't sound right,' his eyes lit with empathy.

'You have an ear for music gone awry,' he said, smiling.

Now that I had a clear picture of my future, my tepid interest in marriage faded. I would be a career woman and have affairs, like George Sand. This decision brought me up against a double-barreled problem. I wanted no babies growing out of these future affairs and I was tired of losing valuable study time because of menstrual cramps. Since both problems could be solved with a sweep of the surgeon's knife, I decided I wanted a hysterectomy.

Knowing better than to broach the subject to our family expert, I looked around for a woman of detached scientific bent to consult. The school nurse was a Yankee so I assumed she was free of womb-lust. I was wrong.

'You want to have an *operation*?' she gasped, eyes popping. 'Oh, but – but – that's against the law! A young girl like you . . . no doctor would ever . . . Where did you get such an idea?'

My heart sank, as it always would whenever I put my faith in a woman and she turned out to be a malkin. But it was too late now; I was already up Mama's favorite creek without a paddle and there was no turning back. I plunged on with as much calm assurance as I could muster.

'I want to be a career woman. My periods interfere with my work.'

'But you wouldn't even be *you* without your . . . er . . . the part you want removed. That's the part that makes you a *woman*.' Her hand fluttered to her breast, a gesture I knew well. 'Without your . . . er . . . that part of yourself, you'd be nothing but an *empty shell*!' She put a suitably hollow ring in her voice.

'Why?'

'Because an *operation* would mean that you could never have children!'

'I don't want any.'

She looked as if she'd been stabbed. She did some lip-licking, then pulled herself together and gave me that confident puckish smile people use when they are getting ready to utter a cliché.

'You'll change your mind when you have some,' she said softly. 'When you hold your first baby in your arms, you'll *know*.'

Suddenly she tilted her head to one side like an inquisitive terrier and winked.

'Now don't let me hear any more of this silly talk. Remember,' she added, sobering suddenly, 'when a woman has an *operation*, hair grows on her chin. You don't want a beard, do you?'

'No, ma'am. Those who study Greek must take pains with their dress.'

She frowned. 'I thought you were the one who was so good at French?'

As good as my school was academically, its guidance counseling was almost nonexistent. Most counselors at this time were teachers who had caved in; unable to cope with the rigors of classroom life, they sat out their pensions in the guidance office. Actually, there was very little for them to do. Most of the students in the school were the first members of our families to go to college. We and our parents believed that a college was a college; one was as good as the other, and a degree was a degree. As long as we went to *some* college, we felt we would have a passport to what was then called the 'Good Life,' and would earn, as Mr Koustopolous said to Helen, 'a million dollars a year.'

Everyone was so firmly convinced of this that we had no need of guidance counselors, nor would we have listened if a good counselor had told us otherwise. Familiar with these lower-middle-class attitudes, the counselors, such as they were, made life easy for themselves and let us think what we wished. It was a conspiracy between battle fatigue and ignorance.

I knew about Ivy League schools, but I thought their superiority lay in social rather than academic areas. I didn't care about going to the 'right' school, I just wanted to go on studying French. Thus, when I won a four-year scholarship to a Washington college, it seemed to be a perfect solution to my academic aspirations and my family's limited finances. I could live at home, and there would be nothing to pay for except my textbooks.

It sounded so good that I did not even bother to apply for any other scholarships, but took the first one I was offered.

9

On a hot September day I sat in the college's auditorium with the sweating, exhausted Class of '57. It was Orientation Day and the president was giving us a welcoming address.

'Now some people ask, why bother to send a girl to college? A woman's place is in the home, they'll tell you. Educate a woman and you'll ruin a good wife and mother. Well, I have an answer for people who say that – an educated woman makes a *better* wife and mother!'

He flashed a smile and went on with energetic enthusiasm. The newspapers called him a 'dynamic, progressive educator.'

'A wife has to entertain her husband's business associates,' he went on. 'How is she going to do that if she isn't well educated? She's got to be able to talk to her husband intelligently, to meet him on his own level. She can't do that without a college education. So you girls here, don't you let anybody say to you, "What good is it to send a girl to college?" Tell them that as a future wife you've got to help your husband get ahead. You girls get your degrees so that your marriages will be equal partnerships!'

He grinned and winked.

'Now don't misunderstand me. I'm not saying that I don't like a woman to be a real woman.'

A titter of approval went over the audience. He looked immensely pleased.

'Don't you agree with that, fellas?' he boomed.

A dull roar of enthusiasm rumbled through the muggy room. The sound had the loutish quality of still-young male voices.

'I'm not saying that I want you girls to go out and become hard, aggressive career women, because no man likes women who *compete* with him. You know the old saying: "A smart woman is one who's smart enough to know when to be dumb!"'

The loutish sound rose again but this time it was matched by the fluttery giggles of the girls.

'But suppose a woman doesn't marry?' the president demanded. He held up his hand like a policeman directing traffic. 'Now I know that's a horrible thought to you ladies and I don't mean to imply that anybody here is going to be an old maid – not as pretty as you girls are. But suppose that you don't marry . . .' He dropped his voice to an ominous pitch. '. . . Ever.'

Several girls groaned and the boys guffawed.

'There's where your college education will come in handy, because for a woman, a degree is something to fall back on. But don't you worry,' he went on, all Edmund Gwenn again, 'the ratio here is four to one! Now how about that, girls? You can get your M-R-S degree here, can't you?'

He left the subject of marriage and started talking about the sororities and fraternities on campus.

'I'm glad we have Greeks here. It makes for a good campus social life. Each of our frats has a sister sorority. That means that the boys in that frat date the girls in that sorority. Of course, you don't *have* to,' he said with a grin, 'it's just a custom. I recommend the Greek life to all of you. It's the best way to meet people and have lots of dates, and I know all of you – especially you girls – want lots of dates. Maybe that's why some of you ladies came here, eh? Ha-ha-ha.'

He took off his glasses, polished them on his tie, and waved them merrily.

'I want to say that I've never seen a prettier collection of females in all my days. You've got a fine supply of heifers for the barbecue tomorrow, fellas. Ha-ha-ha. Now I don't want to hear about anybody missing the barbecue,' he added with mock truculence. 'We need all the girls there that we can get, thanks to our four-to-one ratio.'

The speech over, I went to my advisor's office to register for classes. The name plate on the door said: J. WILEY RUDD, ASSOCIATE PROFESSOR OF SOCIOLOGY. I knocked and a hearty voice yelled, 'Come in!'

I opened the door. A man of about forty-five spun around in his swivel chair and grinned. He had a moon-round face, dimples, a skullcap of curly black hair, and twinkling blue eyes. It was the most open, friendly face I had ever seen.

'How do you do, sir. My name is—'

'What, what, *what*? No formality allowed around here, honey. And you don't have to knock, either. Just march right in, I'm happy to see you anytime.'

He seemed to be shouting through a megaphone. I handed him my registration card. As he read it, something in his face changed and his beaming smile receded a little.

'So you won a scholarship, huh? Very nice, sweetie, very nice. Well! We gotta plan your schedule, don't we?'

'Yes, sir,' I replied automatically.

'Ruddy,' he corrected. 'All the kids call me Ruddy.'

I said nothing. He waited, his teeth set in a smile. The way the top and bottom rows met made him look as if a dentist had just said, 'Do this.' As our eyes held, his gaze hardened in a way that made me remember Miss Tanner. He was a huggybear. I didn't know they had them in college.

Suddenly he clapped his palms on his knees.

'Well, Flo! What we usually do in freshman year is get

those nasty required subjects out of the way. First, English Comp.'

'I waived it,' I said, handing him an exam slip.

He looked at it a long time.

'You know,' he said at last, rubbing his chin, 'it's a good idea to go ahead and take it anyhow. A good brush-up never hurt anybody.'

'The test was easy. I don't think I need it.'

'All right,' he said tersely. 'Now, freshman history.'

'I waived that, too,' I said, handing him another exam slip. This time he did not argue.

'Science,' he said, going down the list. 'You have to have six credits in either physics, chemistry, or biology.'

'Biology,' I said quickly.

His good nature returned.

'I thought you'd pick that.' He smiled. 'Everybody does because it's the easiest. Now, let's get you some electives. Most kids take a little of everything in the first two years. You don't know what the heck you're going to be majoring in at this point so—'

'French.'

His lips twitched.

'French?'

'Yes, sir. I've had five years. I want to start sixth year now.'

'Whoa, whoa, *whoa!*' He reached out and patted my hand. 'Flo, take it from me, I've seen a lot of freshmen. I'll bet you dollars to doughnuts you don't know what your major is going to be yet. Why, most kids change their majors two or three times before they graduate.' He grinned. 'Especially girls. You know how it is. You get interested in a guy who's majoring in Soc, so you switch to that so you'll have lots of classes with him.'

'I don't care what boys major in. I want to major in French.'

Two bright pinpoints appeared in his eyes.

'A pretty girl like you doesn't care what boys do?' he said softly. 'Oh, come on, I just don't believe that.'

It was like a dream in which a simple destination kept eluding me. He hated me for winning a scholarship, for knowing what I wanted. He was trying to thwart me. Suddenly I was terrified.

'I have to take French.' My voice shook and his mouth curved into a smirk as he heard it. I forced a shrug and spoke as matter-of-factly as I could. 'You can't let a language drop, you know.'

The 'you know' came out with Herb's clip. J. Wiley Rudd did not like that, either.

'Veddy British, aren't we?'

'My father is!' I snapped. Now I had sassed a teacher . . .

He shrugged. 'Everybody waits till their junior year to start their major. That gives you plenty of time to get all the credits you need. You only need thirty.'

'I don't want to take credits, I want to take French.'

He lifted his hands and let them drop with an air of despair and resignation.

'Okay, okay, okay, you can take French. Anything to please a lady. I'll put you down for intermediate grammar and comp. Now are you happy?'

'We finished grammar in third year.'

This time his face twisted with raw loathing.

'Lit courses are junior and senior level! Freshmen can't take them. Intermediate is for freshmen who've had French in high school.' He made it sound like a disease.

'I've had *five* years. We started literature in fourth year. In fifth year we read Racine.'

He made a knock-knock joke.

'Racine with the moon,' he sang in adenoidal imitation of Vaughan Monroe.

'They gave waiver exams in freshman English and history,' I argued. 'Why can't they give me one in French?'

'You'll have to see the French lady about that.'

'Who?'

'Paula Hale. She teaches those lit courses.' He handed me my schedule card. 'You two gals have a parlay-voo and get her to initial this.'

I went in search of the French professor. I found her office but there was a note on the door saying she would be back in an hour. My knees were trembling. There were some benches down at the end of the hall but I didn't dare leave that door. I leaned against it and waited.

At last I heard light footsteps on the stairs and a woman appeared. She was small and pretty with neat gray hair and an air of tired sweetness. She reminded me of Fay Bainter. She smiled pleasantly when she saw me.

'Professor Hale?'

'Mrs,' she corrected. 'What can I do for you, dear?'

We went into her office. There was a verb chart leaning up against her desk.

j'ai
tu as
il (elle) a
nous avons
vous avez
ils (elles) ont

I stammered out my story. She nodded and made sympathetic sounds.

'Five years of French? Oh my, you must be a very good pupil. I see no reason why you can't take the literature survey course.'

There was something wrong that I couldn't put my finger on. She seemed abstracted, like someone trying to be polite to a door-to-door salesman. She made no effort to test me by speaking French, and she gave off an air that made me reluctant to change languages. I had a feeling that if we had been speaking French and someone had come in and caught us at it, she would have been embarrassed. Her kindness was making me almost as uncomfortable as Rudd's hostility.

It hit me all of a sudden that she lacked a quality I had cut my teeth on: grandeur. I thought of Granny's bustling imperiousness, Mama's swagger, Jensy's metaphysical certainties. The three women in my life all held facts instead of opinions, but now I was telling my troubles to a woman who was whispering in her own office. She was a malkin. A well-bred one, a well-educated one, but a malkin just the same.

'I'm afraid we don't have a French major here, dear. I can't imagine why your advisor didn't tell you. The courses we offer add up to only eighteen credits, and some of them are in English. Language people go to Georgetown as a rule. The Foreign Service School, you know. But Georgetown is a man's school. There – is something wrong, dear?'

'No, ma'am.'

'Perhaps in your junior year you can transfer to another school. Wellesley, perhaps. They have an excellent French Department.'

'I can't transfer anywhere. I won a scholarship here. If I don't go here, I can't go to college at all.'

'Oh, I see, I see . . . Dear, you look so pale. Are you sure you're feeling well?'

'Yes, ma'am. It's just that it's so hot.'

'Isn't it?' she said brightly. 'It's been a frightful summer, hasn't it?'

Now that we were discussing the weather, she relaxed for the first time. I thanked her and left.

While I was crying in the ladies room, a senior girl came in. Her breasts looked like a pair of collie muzzles; grazing on the left one like two roaches on a piece of sugar were a sorority pin and a fraternity pin with chains crossed like the cavalry sabers on my great-grandfather's uniform hat. She put her arm around me.

'Are you sick?'

I shook my head.

'Did somebody die?'

I shook it again.

'Did you break up with your boyfriend?'

'No.'

Her catalogue of tragedies exhausted, she went into a stall and peed. When she came out, she washed her hands carefully and thoroughly the way women always do when someone else is in the ladies room, so I would know that she had been raised to wash her hands after she peed.

As she left, she put a clean hand on my shoulder.

'You'll find somebody someday,' she assured me.

I took the French literature survey to spite Rudd and to supply a French grade to show Herb to keep him from wondering why I had suddenly dropped the subject I loved. I could not tell him what had happened, not yet anyway. It was better to let him go on thinking that a college was a college; it was his sole area of ignorance and I had to use it. Otherwise, he might blame himself for being unable to send me to a better school and perhaps go back to work in order to do so. I did not want him to go back to work; I wanted him there when I got home.

There was no point in asking Granny for the money to go to a better school. Even if she had not disapproved of higher education for women, there was still her Lady Bountiful complex to contend with. To get her for a patron, you had to be a physically sick stranger about to be evicted, deserted by your ungrateful kin, and constipated. Her philanthropy never rose above the waist, and my needs were above the brow. Hers was both a personal and a group tic. An ethnic woman enjoys telling people she scrubbed floors to put children through college, but a Wasp Lady Bountiful would rather be famed as an angel of mercy who got there just in time with the soup and the blankets. She sees herself as a Seventh Cavalry who arrives quietly; paying college tuition simply doesn't turn her on because it would inspire no one to say, 'They would have died if she hadn't come.'

It's a miracle I managed to get myself home that day without getting run over. I was covered with cold clammy sweat and my legs felt like rubber hoses. I ached everywhere, phantom pains of a body refusing to accept the indignity of amputation. I was in a state of ambulatory shock, as much a member of the walking wounded as Evelyn Cunningham. I had lost my femininity; my *elle*, my *ette*, and my *euse* had gone splat and I had no sense of myself as a female. The Henry Adams problem that I had held in abeyance during the French years closed in on me with an either/or finality. Of its two behests, only one was part of my nature, so I heeded a quintessentially American inner voice that said, 'Be your own Venus.'

10

Sex is the only American invention that does not save time and trouble. I still wanted to go to my fantasy debauching room with a faceless fallen boy, but there was simply no way out of the dating game.

My first project was to get kissed. The mores of the fifties held kissing on the first date to be a device of the Evil One. There being no way to reach the second date without going through the first one, I accepted an invitation to a fraternity party proffered by my biology lab partner as we bent over the formaldehyde vat to fish out our pig.

His name was Larry. As I sat beside him on the sprung sofa in the frat house drinking beer and wax flakes from a paper cup, I wondered if any of the other girls were putting up with the party in order to get sex? Somehow I doubted it; they just seemed to want to have a good time.

Suddenly my vision blurred. It was Larry waving his hand in front of my face.

'Hey, come back!' He laughed nervously.

I forced a gay smile. It would have made an excellent death mask. Larry looked worried, as well he might. Evelyn Cunningham needed a deserted backyard or a dark road to wander off, but I could do it without leaving the room. I did not want to wander off; I wanted Larry to like me so he would ask me for that all-important second date, otherwise I would have to start the whole hideous business all over again with somebody else. I saw myself condemned to an endless string of first dates, never getting kissed, a celibate Sisyphus pushing my rock up Fraternity Hill. Boy after boy would ask me out once and spend the evening saying, 'Hey, come back!' until I became known as the sleepwalker of Sigma Chi.

I had to say something peppy, fast. It was like being back in elementary school and having to race around the playground in a state of bogus joy, pretending to release restless high spirits I did not have so the huggybears let me alone. 'Harbor Lights' came on the phonograph.

'Let's dance!' I cried.

We walked out on the floor. The state that bad novelists call 'as if I were standing outside of myself, watching myself as if in a dream' is a boon to dancing. Spirit-light and unresisting, I followed with spectral grace wherever Larry led.

'Gee, you're a terrific dancer,' he said.

When he took me home, he bade me a kissless goodnight and invited me to the movies the following week. I accepted.

Movie night came and he held my hand during the show. No one had done that since I learned to cross streets by myself. Afterwards he took me to the Hot Shoppe, where I ordered a hamburger and coffee. His face fell.

'Don't you want a shake?'

'I'd rather have coffee.'

'You can have a shake if you want, it's okay.'

'I like coffee.'

'You don't have to get coffee, I can afford a shake.'

It sounded like a situation in a traveler's phrase book. I did not want my first kiss ruined by a beating nose bridge so I had to say something peppy, fast.

'I just *love* coffee!' It sounded like a stranger. I just don't talk that way.

I got the coffee, and later on I got the kiss. It was, of course, a dry one. The first one had to be; it could last indefinitely but the tongue could not enter into it. Since it is impossible to dry-kiss indefinitely, ours lasted about ten seconds. When it was over, Larry asked me to a semi-formal (cocktail dress) dance on the following Saturday and I accepted. I looked forward eagerly to the dance because the second kiss on the third date could be wet. Like the tortoise, I was getting there.

My first wet kiss was immensely pleasurable. It took place in Larry's car and lasted several minutes, but officially it was only one kiss because we did not break. Stopping for breath or to rearrange noses marked the beginning of the second kiss, which could lead to a third, which was necking, which was forbidden until the fourth date.

He asked me for a fourth date and I accepted. We went to another frat party and at some point in the evening we decided to park in the grove near Fraternity Row. Leaving a party to go neck in a car was permissible on the fourth date, but if matters got out of hand it was called 'the girl's fault.' Matters got completely out of hand and it was my fault.

I failed to 'draw the line,' i.e., I let him touch me 'up top.' Covered tit was for the fifth date and bare tit was for the sixth date, so when I let him unhook my bra, I was two tits too early. Nor did I stop him when he reached under my skirt and lowered the seventh veil – a terrible mistake because diddling was for couples who were going steady.

Suddenly the door flew open and I fell out of the car.

'What's going on here?' a gravelly voice barked.

It was Matthew X. Kearny, the campus beadle, who deserved to have *in loco parentis* carved on his tombstone. A retired cop who looked like a Celtic Agrippa, it was his job to see that things did not go too far. He roamed the grove with a flashlight looking for cars that appeared to be empty. If he saw two heads more or less side by side he did not interfere, but one head, or none, brought him out of the bushes like a wild boar.

He shone the flashlight on me as I lay sprawled at his feet. Seeing my déshabille he quickly turned his back.

'Cover yourself, girlie.'

When I had repaired my dignity, he beckoned me grimly over to the road for a lecture. He was famous for his lectures; having had five daughters of his own, he considered himself the father of us all.

'Ever a bridesmaid but never a bride,' he sighed, shaking his huge gray head. 'That's what's gonna happen to you if you don't straighten up and fly right. How you gonna get a fella to marry you if you let him make free with you like that? Don't you know that fellas *test* a girl to see how far she'll go? If she goes too far, it's curtains!' Here he drew his finger across his throat. 'You're headed for trouble if you don't mend your ways, girlie. It's like the song says, "Fallen and forgotten, without a good man's name . . ." Well, I forget the rest, but—'

'"She dreams of Indiana while she walks the streets of shame,"' I supplied.

Kearny dismissed me and I got back into the car. Larry looked unaccountably miserable. He said very little on the way home and did not kiss me goodnight or ask for another date. The following Monday when we fished our pig out of the formaldehyde vat, he looked worse than the pig. I never saw such a tormented face; it would have been perfect for a Gogol dust jacket.

'Look,' he said in a voice from the lower depths, 'I don't think we should see each other again.'

'What?'

'You're a nice girl. That's why I don't think we should see each other again. I don't want . . . to hurt you.'

'Hurt me?'

'I think you're getting too serious about me.'

'What do you mean?'

As he struggled to articulate his thoughts, his fingers nervously twisted one of the pig's ears. It came off.

'You're a nice girl,' he said again, 'so I know you must be in love with me because a nice girl doesn't let a guy do . . . that . . . what you let me do, I mean, unless she's in love with him.' He took a deep breath and gagged as the formaldehyde fumes went up his nose. 'I'm not ready to fall in love,' he choked.

His coughing fit gave me time to think, otherwise I would have blurted out what I wanted to say, which was, 'I'm not in love with you.' It was the most self-defeating statement a girl could make in those days. He had handed me what he considered a golden rationale for my behavior. If I rejected it, *he would scorn me with words fierce and bitter, and laugh at my shame and downfall, and tell all the boys at the frat house that I was the cause of it all* . . .

He was forcing me to choose between pity and censure. I wanted to hit him with the pig but I couldn't do that, either; it would have demolished our already hash-like dissection and made us both flunk lab. My only recourse was dignified passivity.

'All right,' I said. 'We won't see each other again.'

Relief flickered over his face when he realized that I was not going to go to pieces. He was so relieved that he had to add something.

'I want you to know that I still respect you, though.'

That did it.

'I respect you, too, Larry. If any other girl lets you do those things to her, you tell me, and I'll beat her up for you.'

'Huh?'

I felt I had won one for Mama the Gipper.

I don't know whether Larry told the boys about me or not. Probably he did, but they did not get 'fierce' with me. Though

I did some pretty heavy stuff with a number of different dates, my reputation remained more or less intact and I was regarded as an official Nice Girl. There were three reasons for this.

In the first place, sexual respect was the only kind of respect available to women in the fifties, so men bent over backwards to bestow it to keep us from developing a yen for the important kinds. Because they sensed that sexual aggressiveness is the first step to general uppityness, 'Keep her respected' replaced 'Keep her barefoot and pregnant' as the best way to put women down and neutralize all of our aggressions, sexual and otherwise. It was a maddening attitude but it was also convenient: I could do anything I wanted short of actual fucking and still come out of it as an official Nice Girl.

Second, I looked like a Nice Girl. There was nothing outwardly sexy about me. I had the fresh-faced daisy-in-the-dell look that the fifties cherished while it drooled over Marilyn Monroe and Jayne Mansfield. Having a big bust was all it took to make people think the worst, but I wore a 32B so I was a Nice Girl. It was a Wasp decade, the way the sixties were black and the seventies ethnic. Being dark, or short and stocky, or having sensual lips or any other exotic feature could change entirely the way girls were perceived; but I was five feet six, small-boned, fair-haired, blue-eyed, and had the kind of lips Thomas Hardy described as 'meeting like the two sides of a muffin,' so I was a Nice Girl.

I tugged heartstrings all over town. When I ate dinner in a crowded downtown cafeteria on my way to my part-time job, old ladies invariably headed for my table like hounds on the scent.

'When I saw you sitting here I said to myself, I said, "I'm going to sit with that nice girl."'

By the time the meal was over, I had been told I was the hope of the future.

'When I think of all the terrible things going on today, what with girls running around in cars with boys and all, it does my heart good to meet a girl like you. Why, anybody could just look at you and know you're a lady to your fingertips.'

I collected St. Georges wherever I went. One evening as I ate a hamburger in a Little Tavern, some men started arguing and emitting damns and hells. The tattooed counter man turned to them in fury and shouted, 'Hey, knock it off! There's a lady in here!'

He gave me a stricken look and apologized. 'I know a girl like you ain't used to hearing that kinda talk.'

I managed to keep a straight face. He kept wiping my area of the counter as though there were something on it that would bring a blush to a maiden's cheek, and when I left he told me to 'stay as sweet as you are.'

Servicemen on F Street tried to pick me up but they were always tentative: 'I guess you wouldn't want to go to the show?' I found several of them attractive and fleetingly considered going to a hotel with them; sleeping with someone I would never see again would have been an ideal solution to the reputation problem, but I was afraid of getting pregnant or murdered – in that order.

My third cachet was grades. To the adolescent male mind, anyone capable of mental concentration must be free of distracting sexual desire. This is what boys meant when they said, 'Girls get good grades.' Interest, ability, ambition had nothing to do with it; an A was proof of what the Book of Common Prayer calls 'the gift of continence.' The gift I actually had was the female's cyclical lust. Sometimes when I tried to study, my mind wandered and I got so horny I had to change my pants, but the rest of the month I was a calm little honor student. Thus, when the first semester grades were posted in February, I could have run naked past Fraternity Row and all the boys would have said, 'There goes that nice girl.'

Sorority Row also took note of my grades when the groups

looked around at unpledged freshmen for someone who could help them win the scholarship cup. I was invited to a tea and given a bid. I accepted it because fraternity boys were reluctant to date an Independent girl, and most of the boys on campus belonged to fraternities.

Over my protests, my sisters began calling me Flo. No name was too short or too formal for a nickname; our sorority ritual was full of references to sisterhood but nobody knew what it meant, so we settled for diminution. Ellen was El, Charlene was Char, and Fay was Faysie.

Each of the sororities had an alumna advisor, suburban housewives in their late thirties or early forties who could have substituted for Pat Nixon without Dick's being any the wiser. We were Nice Girls and the advisors were Nice Women. Ours gave us advice on premarital sex ('If you love him, you *won't*') and described, with eyes closed and speech measured for dramatic effect, what it was like to give birth. 'Having . . . a . . . baby . . . is . . . the . . . most . . . wonderful . . . experience . . . on . . . earth.'

Whenever she left or whenever her name came up, we were supposed to turn to each other and say, 'Isn't she *terrific?*'

She was fond of claiming that nothing had ever shocked her except the time she found a bidet in her hotel room on her first trip to Europe. She said she had not at first known what it was for, and related with merry self-deprecation all the uses she had put it to before finding out what it was. She washed her undies in it, soaked her feet in it, chopped ice in it, and tried to develop film in it.

'What *is* it for?' asked El.

'People who don't have nice bathrooms sit across it and wash . . .' She pointed to her lap.

As I pictured in my mind the trail of ruined bidets she must have left in her wake, with enamel hacked away or decomposed by developing fluid, all I could think of was a line from

Coriolanus: 'You would be another Penelope, yet they say all the yarn she spun in Ulysses' absence did but fill Ithaca full of moths.'

Being in a sorority gave me a place to spend the night after on-campus dates, no mean consideration for one who lived all the way across the city. Three of the Virginia commuters had the same problem, so the four of us fell into the habit of sharing a guest room fitted out with two double-decker bunk beds.

We discussed the vital topics of the day, like finger-fucking, a widespread substitute for coitus practiced by pinned couples and me whose *glick-blick-sloosh* sound effects enabled even El to answer correctly that standard lit exam question: 'Define onomatopoeia.' My roommates and I differed in that I finger-fucked with every boy I dated, while they did it only with the boys they loved. According to sorority consensus, it was something you did not for yourself but 'for him,' though how any girl could believe this was a mystery to me. Finger-fucking was hard work. Once the boys had satisfied their curiosity about what the inside of a vagina felt like they did not especially want to do it, but they did it anyway to strengthen their case that a hand job was the proper quid pro quo. The 'I did it for you' argument always worked, whether a girl was motivated by Southern do-rightism, English fair play, or free-floating female guilt.

What was to stand as the sorority's most memorable crisis started the night Faysie burst through the door of the guest room with semen all over her skirt.

'It got on me! It got on me! I'm P.G., I know it!'

She spread the voluminous folds of her ten-gore taffeta cock-tail dress and showed us the wet spots.

'Look! If it gets *on* you, anywhere *near* you, you can get P.G., it *has* happened. Did you read in *Coronet* about the girl in the swimming pool?'

She sank down in a chair and sobbed. Reaching into her

coat pocket for a Kleenex, she pulled out her pants instead. As she was about to dry her eyes on them, she realized what they were and dropped them with a moan. She opened her bag and pulled out something white but it was her bra.

'Oh, God!'

Char gave her a Kleenex. She snuffled into it for a moment and then continued her story.

'He asked me to . . . you know, play with it. I didn't want to do it but I *love* him! I mean we're pinned! It's all right to do it when you're pinned! Everybody does it when they're pinned! It's *okay*!'

'We know that, honey,' Char soothed.

'If one, just *one*, hits you in the leg, it can get into your bloodstream and travel all through your system until it reaches you-know-where!'

Something of Mama's easily stirred irritation came over me. 'For God's sake, they're not buckshot.'

'But if it gets *on* you, anywhere *near* you, you can get P.G., it *has* happened! Did you read in *Pageant* about that girl in New York who used her brother's bathwater during the water shortage?'

'Oh, no,' said Char, closing her eyes and putting her hand over her mouth.

Faysie spent the next two weeks counting on her fingers and asking frantic questions like 'What day was it that your mother bought you the green sack dress that you hated and traded to Ginny for the black suede heels? For God's sake, you've *got* to remember!' Her terror was so convincing that we began to wonder if we might be pregnant, too. We were all virgins, but then so were the unfortunates in *Coronet* and *Pageant*. The drumbeat of '*on* you, *near* you, *in* you' throbbed in our brains. I had recently enjoyed a dry screw on a dark dancefloor; maybe it wasn't as dry as I thought; maybe one, just *one*, came through his pants and swam through my skirt and then swam through my pants and then . . .

The counting and babbling continued.

'I was in my middle the night it happened even though it was three days before my usual middle because last month was February and that always messes up the count because it's so short. Wait! Is this Ground Hog Year? That adds another day, doesn't it? Oh, I'm P.G., I know it!'

By the time she got the curse, the rest of us were destroyed. She, of course, was the first to recover.

'I wasn't really worried.' She smiled.

A good sex manual would have helped, but the fifties offered nothing but marriage manuals. Their chief object was to deny the importance, and if possible the existence, of clitoral orgasms. Consequently, when Char had a clitoral orgasm during a diddling session, she had hysterics as well.

The source of her woe was an author whose theory of the subcontracted orgasm read like a directive from the Interstate Commerce Commission. He said that while the clitoris was not licensed to operate independently, it was a spur line of female pleasure that helped carry the delirious consignment to its final destination. It did this by transferring its sensations to the vagina; the vagina then signed for them, and had the orgasm for the clitoris.

Char reasoned that since her clitoris had made an orgasm run all by itself, she must be a nymphomaniac.

Another manual discussed the morning erection in a way that made the penis sound like a bird's cloaca. In a passage hauntingly reminiscent of 'Your grandfather was a perfect gentleman,' the author cautioned husbands against waking a hardworking wife and mother to get rid of a morning erection. Morning erections should *never* lead to intercourse because they had nothing to do with sexual desire, he said, and proved it with a golden example of *post hoc ergo propter hoc*: 'Empty the bladder and the need is met.'

Our most tangled web grew out of El's treatise on the oversized penis.

'I don't expect the man I marry to be a virgin, but I don't want somebody who's done it with hundreds of girls.'

'Did he tell you he had?' asked Faysie.

'No, but he's got such a big you-know-what that he must have. The men in those Charles Atlas magazines get those big arm muscles from lifting bar bells, so it stands to reason.'

After marriage manuals, the favorite sorority reading matter was magazines. El read them aloud to us.

'Listen! Oh, this is so true. "For the sex act to be fully satisfactory to a woman she must, in the depths of her mind, desire deeply and utterly to be a mother."'

'Who said that?' I demanded.

'It's an excerpt from a book called *Modern Woman: The Lost Sex.*'

'It's a bunch of bull.'

Her eyes widened in horror.

'Have you . . . gone all the way?' she croaked.

'No, and neither have you, so you don't know whether it's "so true" or not. But we've all enjoyed everything else we've done with boys, and God knows none of us wants to be a mother.'

'Not *yet*,' she corrected. 'But someday . . . someday . . .' She smiled moistly and began rocking back and forth like the extras in *The Snake Pit*. It was Ann Hopkins all over again.

'The only reason I'd have a baby is to cure my cramps, and then I'd give the little nerd away.'

'Oh, Flo! How can you say that? I have cramps just as bad as you do, but I *love* my period and my cramps, too, because they *prove* that I'm a woman.'

'Why do you need blood and pain to prove that you're a woman? Why do you need anything to prove it? You *are* a woman, that's that.'

'Ye-e-e-s-s, but it makes me feel feminine.'

'Why do you need blood and pain to make you feel feminine?

Do you feel masculine the rest of the month?'

'Oh, no! I mean, God . . .'

'Then if you don't ever feel masculine, why do you need proof that you're feminine?'

'Well, God, Flo, I don't know, it's just natural.'

'Henry Adams said it's impossible for an American woman to be feminine.'

'What frat is he in?' she asked indignantly.

'Oh, never mind.'

11

In my second year of college, all the boys started chasing freshman girls and the 'sophomore slump' dominated sorority conversations. My sisters were terrified that they would never 'find somebody.'

In 1954, 'finding somebody' was a euphemism for what Granny called 'catching a man.' Her field & stream idiom vanished from the female vocabulary when *McCall's* invented Togetherness. Merely being safely married was no longer enough. Girls dreamed of eternal bliss in suburban snuggeries, love and marriage turned into a horse and carriage, and there was horseshit everywhere.

My career was gone, but I still did not want to find somebody. The only thing about marriage that appealed to me was sex without scandal: husbands could be counted on not to ask, 'How come you let me go all the way?' Everything else about marriage appalled me, with children leading the list, but I was an exception.

The campus resembled a swamp wafting deadly vapors of marriage fever. Even the women faculty members were infected. A few had Ph.D.'s but none wished to be called Doctor. 'Mrs,' they corrected with sweet smiles, like Paula Hale of the token French Department. One of them was famous for making her preference known first crack out of the box to each new class.

'If you call me Doctor, I won't answer,' she cried gaily. 'I'm Mrs Thornton.'

'Isn't she terrific?' El asked after class.

'No. I'm sick of terrific women. I prefer women like Angélique Paulet.'

'Who's she?'

'She was the mistress of Henry the Fourth of France. She never married because her fiancés kept getting killed in duels with her lovers.'

'I think that's sad.'

El's favorite course was Preparation for Marriage, which proved so popular that they had to split it up into three sections and hold them in the ROTC armory. I was the only member of our sorority who did not take it, but I might as well have; El read her notes aloud in the suite.

'Use bathroom together. He shave, you tub, make closeness.

'That sounds like Hemingway. Long ago good, now not good.'

'Oh, Flo, why don't you take it, too? Everybody else is,' she added reproachfully.

Soon it was impossible to find a free washing machine in the dorm because all the girls in Marriage Prep were washing their boyfriends' socks.

'Grad. intro. wife duties,' El explained.

'What he do hus. intro.?' I asked.

'Wash my car, except I don't have one.'

My favorite course that year was Medieval Portraits: Literature as History, taught by the campus heartthrob, Dr Newton. The library's copy of *The Directory of the American Historical Society* fell open to his page because so many girls had looked up his biog that the spine had broken. He was in his late thirties, muscular, with a sandy crewcut that looked like a newly mown lawn. Though he was known as a hard grader who never fraternized with students, girls like El took his classes anyway because he was so 'cute.' It was the presence of so many malkins in Medieval Portraits that led to the fight over Patient Griselda.

'Patient Griselda was the Melanie Wilkes of medieval literature,' Dr Newton lectured, 'except that Melanie was married to a gentleman and Griselda was not. Griselda's husband demanded proof of her devotion, and so he beat her and set fire to her wimple and put her through various tests to see if he could make her lose her temper and criticize him. But she never did. She simply went on making cloth for the manor, hence the famous line, "Patient Griselda, always spinning."'

'Awwww . . .' sighed the malkins.

'Shit-eater,' said a boy behind me.

'Griselda crops up quite often in medieval literature,' Dr Newton went on. 'Chaucer and Boccaccio used her, and so did many minor folklorists and ballad-makers. For this reason many scholars consider her to be the representative woman of the era.'

I raised my hand.

'Miss King?'

'How could a woman that meek be representative of the Middle Ages? She lived at a time when the Virgin Mary was the leading symbol of power. Men were in awe of the Virgin then, so it wouldn't have taken much to put them in awe of all women. I think Chaucer and Boccaccio were poking fun at Griselda for being too dense to realize what she had going for her. Their works about her are actually satires.'

El was waving her hand frantically. Dr Newton called on her.

'But the Virgin Mary was meek, too, just like Griselda,' she said eagerly.

'No, she was good,' I countered. 'There's a difference.'

'Yeah,' said the boy behind me.

Dr Newton heard him. 'Mr Panelli, do you have a comment?'

'The Blessed Mother had a lot of sorrows and she suffered a lot, but she didn't let anybody shove her around. Griselda was a doormat. She was probably one of those dames that if you slug 'em, they worry about whether you hurt your hand. That makes a guy want to slug 'em again.'

Gasps of shock punctuated the malkin corner. 'What frat is he in?' El whispered indignantly. 'He isn't,' somebody replied, 'he's a Korean vet, that's why he's *older*.'

I raised my hand again. Dr Newton nodded to me.

'Henry Adams said that women in the Middle Ages were supreme in a way that American women could never be, because the power of the Virgin rubbed off on them. It's American women who are powerless; Griselda had clout if she had wanted to use it.'

'Oh, Flo!' El wailed.

'Do you wish to comment on Miss King's statement, Miss Parker?'

El clasped her hands and pressed them to her heart. 'I just want to say that it's not things like power and clout, it's *love*. Griselda was right to be so patient and loyal because that's the way women are supposed to be. I don't say her husband was right to beat her or to set fire to her . . . her . . . to her thing, but if he needed proof of her love that much, she must have done *something* to make him think she didn't love him. They should have sat down and talked it over. I mean, marriage is a *partnership*.'

'Patient Griselda, always spin-drying,' I said.

That summer I worked for a State Department annex called the Human Relations Area Files, where I filed information sheets on the sort of countries Granny lumped under the collective name of 'Timbuctu,' inhabited by the sort of people she called '*foreign* foreigners.' The files were open to State Department personnel, which is how I met Lloyd, who ate me, proposed to me, and taught me how to drive. Of these three proofs of love, the last shall always be the first.

He was five years my senior and lived with his well-fixed widowed mother in a Maryland suburb. She was away much of the time tending her late husband's business interests, so Lloyd and I used his bedroom for my ultimate venture into Everything But. I had heard about oral sex – known in the fifties by the sweeping name of '69' – and that summer I got hooked on it. I did not go down on him, nor did he ask me to. Nor did he ask me to fuck. He seemed content with a humble hand job. I have never figured out whether he was what was then called 'weird' and what is now called 'kinky,' or whether he actually did love me in the old-fashioned honorable way which was not entirely old-fashioned at the time. As I say, he taught me to drive on his brand-new 1955 Buick, so you figure it out.

I was not, to put it mildly, very lovable. Lloyd belonged to that breed of hesitating men who keep clearing their throats. His passivity brought out the most unattractive aspects of my personality and I treated him the way Mama treated Preston. The very name Lloyd irritated me beyond all reason; his habits pushed me to the brink. The way he dunked his shrimp into the little paper cup of tartar sauce enraged me so much that I longed to wreck the restaurant. I lay awake nights contemplating his pointed earlobes until my stomach was a mass of trembling knots. In short, I behaved like Mildred in *Of Human Bondage*.

I reduced him to a mouth and a rapidly circling tongue. When he invited me out during my period, I sneered 'What's the point?' One day when I was feeling especially horny, I insisted we leave a movie he was enjoying and go home and muff. Occasionally I suffered guilt pangs and tried to be kind to him, but the slightest decency on my part invariably encouraged his smarmy, masochistic gratitude, which made me mad again.

'What did I do?'

'Oh, shut up!'

'I love you.'

'Oh, damn you!'

Granny, of course, was crazy about him. I didn't dare tell her he proposed, but *he* told her, and so she helped him press his case. 'You'll die on the vine if you don't marry Lloyd' went on all summer, and I kept finding women's magazine inspirational verse tucked into my current book. They were the kind of 'pomes' whose lines all ended with a repetition of the title: *Who is the rock in the stormy sea? My Husband!*

'Anybody want to hear "Casey at the Bat"?'

'Oh, Louise!'

Ironically, I liked Lloyd's mother as much as he liked Granny. She told me all about her real estate deals and took me with her one day when she made her rounds: threatening contractors, bullying bricklayers, and eyeing virginal stands of Maryland timber in a way that would chill an environmentalist's blood. Afterwards, she took me to lunch.

'Lloyd will never be anything but a bureaucrat,' she said contemptuously. 'But you'll amount to something – you're like me. The idea of leaving my business to Lloyd when I die gives me the willies, but if I knew that a sharp gal was around to keep an eye on things, I could rest easy, you know what I mean?'

She looked up from her martini and gave me a wink. I was positive she and Granny had gotten together.

Soon it was time for me to return to college for my junior year. I did not know what to do about Lloyd. He was driving me insane with his lovesick gazes and perfect patience, but I wanted to keep him around so I could go on enjoying what he did so well. I wished there had been some way to keep only his head and carry it around with me under my arm like St. Denis coming down from the Mont des Martyrs. Having spent the better part of the summer with a tongue in my twat, I could not now conceive of a life without cunnilingus. On the other hand, I could not conceive of a life with Lloyd.

Meanwhile, classes started and I had to choose a major. I chose history and promptly tumbled into bittersweet memories of French like the heroine of one of Granny's fallen women songs remembering her first beau. My sex drive vanished and I constructed a pristine fantasy, imagining myself on the faculty of a girls' boarding school, dressed in a tweed suit and walking shoes and having tea with intellectual spinsters similarly attired. There were no students in my imaginary grove of academe, just a school and a female faculty who took walks together arm in arm along paths strewn with crackly red and yellow leaves.

It was easy enough to analyze. Fall was coming, school was starting, and I wanted to be back in that select, all-girl, fifth-year French class where I had known perfect happiness. The spinster teachers were my classmates grown to womanhood and the school without students represented a world without males. *Adieu, Seigneur, régnez; je ne vous verrai plus.*

I broke up with Lloyd and all hell broke loose at home. Granny sighed and surged, wept and wailed, spoke in choked tones of great-grandchildren, and made a Sarah Bernhardt production out of calling for her digitalis.

'You killin' yo' big momma!'

'It's all that education! A whistling woman and a crowing hen always come to a tragic end!'

'Lor' blimey . . .'

'Everybody shut up! *The Pride of the Yankees* is coming on!'

Granny continued talking about whistling women and crowing hens, and I continued having my fantasy. The image of myself in a severe tweed suit filled me with a strange, private happiness at whose core lay an even stranger sensation of sly mischief, as if I had a secret that I was keeping even from myself. I was caught up in a mood of sexless sensuality that revolved around attractively unattractive clothes.

I had no trouble finding an excuse for what I wanted to do. Everyone goes shopping when school starts, so I did, too. The frilly fifties were no time to outfit the new spinsterish me, however; the kind of tweed suit I wanted – herringbone with a single-breasted man-tailored jacket and a straight skirt – simply did not exist. The closest approximation would be today's dress-for-success suits, but nobody was dressing for success in 1955. All the suits I saw had flared skirts, and jackets with Peter Pan velvet collars and gathered panels, something like a cross between a valance and a mudguard, to emphasize the waist and hips.

Even more discouraging, I looked great in a 1955 suit. I had a tiny waist – three motherly salesladies tried to span it with their hands – a long neck, and a statistically average bust that fit exactly into the spaces made by all the darts and tucks and gathers that graced the jacket. It was like putting hands in mittens.

Next I tried to put something together from separates, but that was impossible in the fifties, too. The only jackets around were blazers in red, navy, or green, and every co-ed in America had one. Without the suit I wanted there was no point in shopping for walking shoes, and in any case there weren't any. In 1955, people thought nothing of driving two blocks to the drugstore. There were styles called 'sporty' shoes ('cute 'n' comfortable classics!') but they looked like ballet slippers. In an era that would have needed very little encouragement to design spike-heeled sneakers, the kind of ground-grippers I craved were found only in orthopedic stores.

I bought a new pair of loafers exactly like my old pair and strolled down F Street in a resentful mood. Coming to a tailor shop, I stopped and gazed hungrily into the window at the sumptuous English tweeds spilling artfully from arranged bolts. For a moment I thought of having a suit made, then dismissed the idea as impossibly expensive. Still, I continued to think about it, enjoying my thoughts with the same sensations of happy sadness that memories of French days gave me.

My tailored suit would have an inside breast pocket made of thick satin. I would not be able to carry anything in it because it would give me a lopsided bust, but that was unimportant. It was not a question of using the pocket but of having it; just knowing it was there would be enough.

My enchantment with inside breast pockets seemed to be a new idiosyncrasy growing out of my fantasy, but it was not new at all. I had merely forgotten about it for a long time. Now, looking into the tailor shop window, I remembered how I used to try on Herb's tuxedo jackets when I was little. I was fascinated by the smooth satin lapels because they felt like 'a lady's clothes,' yet they were part of a man's suit. I liked to stroke them, and one day while I was stroking them I reached inside and found the strange, hidden pocket. It was satin like the lapels and felt huge as I buried my small hand in it. I asked Granny what it was and she explained. 'I want one in my coat,' I said eagerly.

'Ladies' coats don't have them, they're for men.'

'But it's satin,' I argued.

'Be that as it may.'

Suddenly a simple solution came to me. Why couldn't I buy a man's ready-made sports jacket in a small size, or a boy's? I crossed the street and headed for a haberdashery, working on an excuse to give the salesman as I walked. I could claim a puny brother with a birthday coming up, or I could tell the truth and say the jacket was for myself. But what reason could I give for wanting a man's jacket? (It never occurred to me that I was not obligated to give a reason, but remember this was 1955.)

'For horseback riding,' I said. 'Something very tailored that'll go with my breeches.'

The salesman nodded without surprise and showed me a rack of small sizes. The smallest jacket would not button across the chest, and the one that did was far too long in the sleeves and too big in the shoulders. I was attracting attention and starting to blush, so I gave it up as a bad job. The salesman recommended a riding apparel store. I knew that no woman's jacket was constructed with an inside pocket, but I went to the equestrian store anyway and promptly collided with that us-against-the-world psychology of the horsey set.

My first mistake was asking for a riding jacket. It's called a riding *coat*. My second mistake was buttoning the third button. The third button is *never* buttoned; they will throw you off the field if you button your third button. My third mistake was complaining about the long length and odd flare that all the riding coats shared. This was the *traditional* cut, the style that *hunt matrons* had *always* worn, but now there were *some* people who wanted to *change* it!

It was like talking to the Daughters. I left.

It was while I was in the dimestore buying school supplies that I finally found something that took my eye, but it was not wearing apparel. It was a blue willow cup and saucer. The sight of it sent a shimmering yearning through me. It made no sense; I had spent the day longing for mannish tweed suits and inside breast pockets, but now I was responding to the 'nice things' instinct that women are supposed to feel when they look at china and silver. The cup was not china, and at ninety-eight cents it was not at all nice, yet I had to have it.

My desire for the cup was actually the other side of the suit coin, but I did not realize it, nor the precise significance of blue willow, until that night at dinner when Mama inadvertently analyzed it for me. She had been having a grand time all summer tormenting Granny about Lloyd. Now, seeing the cup, she picked it up, thrust it under Granny's nose, and said, 'See, Mother? She's buying old maid dishes now.'

It was only to be expected that El would get engaged while I was experimenting with celibacy. She came back to school that

September with a frat pin over her heart and a gift album of Ravel's *Bolero*, which she called 'passionate.' It was 'their' song. She played it over and over again on the sorority phonograph and went around humming 'DOOP-doopy-doop-doop da-da DOOP doopy-doop-doop' until a curious springiness marked her walk.

In recognition of the greater intimacy of betrothal over going steady, she now washed his underwear as well as his socks. She also washed, starched, and ironed his shirts, folding them into perfect rectangles over cardboard and sticking pins in various locations to hold her coolie creations neatly in place.

Every time I saw him he was handing her a bundle of dirty laundry. She explained that they were saving money for their marriage and showed me a spiral notebook marked *Marriage Fund* to prove how big a portion of his former laundry bills was now going into their joint savings account. She said she had learned how to keep such records in Preparation for Marriage. It was a remarkably neat notebook with none of the chaotic scrawls and scribbles that marred her academic notes and the pride she took in it touched me in spite of myself.

I made an oblique contribution to the Marriage Fund when she asked me to lend her fiancé my two-volume text for Survey of English Literature. They cost six dollars each, a fabulous sum for books in those days, and being a business major, he was trying to avoid buying books he did not need to keep. Because I felt sorry for her, and also because I felt superior to her, I gave her the lit books and she passed them on to the beloved.

Her own reading matter that year was the 1955 bestseller, *Making the Most of Your Marriage* by Paul H. Landis.

'Listen!' she said. 'Oh, this is so true. "Except for the sick, the badly crippled, the deformed, the emotionally warped and mentally defective, almost everyone has an opportunity to marry."'

Suddenly her smile vanished and she looked up from the page with stricken eyes.

'What do you suppose he means by "almost"?'

'Don't worry, you're home safe. He means me.'

'Oh, Flo! That's not true. You'll find somebody.'

'I don't want to.'

Her eyes bugged out. 'You don't want to get *married*?'

'No. I want to be an Almost.'

I meant I wanted to be an independent woman, but there was no name for it. It's a chilling tribute to the thoroughness of fifties propaganda that I, with my vast reading, had never seen the word 'feminist' in print, much less heard it spoken. There were two or three lines in a history text about Susan B. Anthony and the 19th Amendment, but the word used was 'suffragette.' Basically, what I was going through proved the truth of the Yiddish proverb, 'What the daughter does, the mother did,' though in this case mother and daughter had such different styles that the core resemblance eluded most people. One of us used a sledgehammer and the other a stiletto, but both of us had declared war on femininity and now my fight was beginning in earnest.

As long as my sex drive was quiescent there was no reason to date, so I stopped. My absence from Greek social functions caused consternation on Sorority Row; peer pressure mounted, everyone took me aside for talks, and once again I found myself playing my old familiar role of Horatius at the bridge.

It was worth it. The benefits of having no social life were immediate and startling. I already knew I hated dating on general principles, but now I compiled a dossier of specific resentments that I had never articulated before. I saw how dating chipped away tiny pieces of a woman's self-confidence; piece by piece, date by date, she was diminished by some form of unnatural behavior forced on her by social usage. The most hateful custom was sitting serenely in the front seat of the car while the boy ran around to open the door. It made me feel like a cripple. Staring into space with an air of utter detachment while he paid the check made me feel like a schizophrenic deadbeat. Crossing a street and having a boy make a quick run behind my back to get on the outside again reminded me of the switcheroo tricks Charles Boyer played on Ingrid Bergman in *Gaslight*, and when a boy gripped my arm just above the elbow as we walked, it felt like a citizen's arrest.

Not the least of my reasons for hating to date was the diminishment that social usage forced on Mama when boys called for me at home. Herb was naturally polished, and Granny and Jensy were naturally charming and gregarious, so all they had to do was be themselves; but Mama had to step totally out of character to get through the amenities. Seeing her on her good behavior and hearing her speak in a normal tone of voice destroyed my security and sent me forth into the night in a state of nervous collapse. Ten minutes without a single reference to assholes, sonsofbitches, and Our Lord Jesus Christ made me feel like a motherless child.

Keep dating and you will become so sick, so badly crippled, so deformed, so emotionally warped and mentally defective that you will marry anybody.

El's fiancé did not return my lit books after spring finals, so I asked him for them.

'What books?' he said innocently.

'The books that El asked me to lend you. I gave them to her to give to you. She said she did.'

'She didn't give me any books from you, Flo.'

'You know damn well she did. Where are they?'

'Flo,' he said with infuriating emphasis, 'I didn't borrow any books from you.' His mouth twisted into a confident smirk. 'Ask El if you don't believe me.'

I found El and told her what he had said. She wrinkled her brow melodramatically.

'Gee, Flo, I kind of remember something about books but . . .'

'You asked me for them and I gave them to you. I saw him carrying them plenty of times. Now he won't give them back to me.'

She gave her forehead a little self-deprecatory slap.

'It's been such a long time. You know me.' She laughed. 'I just *can't* remember.'

'He sold my books! What are you going to do about it?'

'Me?'

'Yes, you! He's your boyfriend. If he won't do right, you have to. I want those books or I want twelve dollars.'

'Now wait a minute, Flo. If he said he didn't borrow them, then he didn't borrow them. I'd help you if I could, but I just can't remember!'

'You're afraid of losing that frat pin, aren't you? If you took my side against him, he might ask for his pin back and then you wouldn't have a man to make you feel like a woman!'

'Flo, so help me God, I *swear* I don't remember!'

I looked into the labored innocence of her wide eyes. This was her version of femininity. Carried to its logical extreme, it was the psychology of the gun moll, the perjured witness, the accomplice. So far I had heard femininity defined as nervous breakdowns, insanity, spontaneous hysterectomy, and illiteracy. Now to that glorious list I could add defect of character.

'Malkin!'

I slammed out of the room. That was the day I joined the Marines.

It was Career Week. The campus was full of folding tables piled with brochures and presided over by smiling men in gray flannel suits who had come to tell twenty-year-olds about pension plans. This was the boys' version of 'finding somebody.'

Total security appealed to Roosevelt babies; the girls wanted to marry a man who would solve everything and the boys wanted to work for a man who would solve everything.

There were hardly any tables for girls, but there was one in the lobby of the dorm. At it sat a woman in a magnificent blue uniform with captain's bars on her redpiped shoulder tabs. The sight of it sent a thrill up my spine. I approached and spoke to her. She told me she was a procurement officer for the Woman Officer Candidate School at Quantico. She explained that as a rising senior, I could take the twelve-week course that summer and be commissioned a second lieutenant when I graduated from college a year hence.

It sounded like the answer to my problems. While hardly the idyllic grove of academe of my spinster fantasy, the Marine Corps was an elite closed society with limited appeal for most women and none whatsoever for malkins. Second, it would be a job. I had no postgraduate plans, and I had chosen a major that, even more than English, left one with no choice but to teach. A career in the Marine Corps would save me from a fate worse than death. Third and best of all, I would get to wear that uniform.

Most people with a lust for uniforms also have certain other characteristics that go with uniforms. These include team spirit, conformity, reverence for authority, a capacity for blind obedience, a bureaucratic turn of mind, and a serious outlook on life. All I had was a lust for uniforms; even my different drummer heard a different drummer. I was too *engagée* to give this minor point any thought, though, so I signed the papers.

Mama: 'If I were younger I'd go with you!'

Herb: 'Life is a vale of tears, its wonders to perform.'

Granny: 'They're all morphodites!'

Jensy: 'Yo' big momma be right!'

Granny continued to talk about morphodites up to my departure for camp. It was her all-purpose word for sexual abnormality, serving her for everything from homosexuals to carnival freaks, both of whom she swore she had never laid eyes on. I don't know whether she was trying to say 'hermaphrodite' and missed, or whether 'morphodite' was the going word in her youth, along with 'waist' for blouse and 'stout' for fat. Herb and I looked it up and found it was spelled with an *i* instead of an *o*. The definition of *morphidite* said: 'A pair of compasses or calipers with one straight pointed leg and the other leg bent inwards at the end; – called also *moffs*, *oddlegs*, and *jenny*.'

A few days after the school year ended, I took the train the short distance to Quantico. Several girls got on at Alexandria, presumably after having debarked from a plane at National Airport. It was obvious that we were all going to the base, so we talked about what made us decide on a Marine Corps career.

'They take care of you,' said one. 'Medical, dental, food, housing, pension.'

'You get stationed in neat places like Hawaii where you can work on your surfboarding,' said another.

'You meet a lot of guys,' said a third.

I kept quiet about Henry Adams.

Our train was met by a hearty sergeant with a beautiful permanent wave. Every Woman Marine, officer and non-com alike, had one; carefully coiffed and curled hair seemed to be the order of the day. It was, in fact, an obsession. Discovering that many of the O.C.s had butch cuts, the captain chewed them out for not having a 'softer' hairdo.

They gave us a lecture on hair. What they wanted was a medium bob or short pageboy – clubwoman hair, First Lady hair – short enough not to touch the collar (a regulation) but long enough to look like a woman from behind. The captain did not put it quite that way, however.

'It looks more feminine,' she said carefully.

My vacation from femininity also included a lecture on

lipstick and nail polish. All of the Women Marines wore bright red lipstick regardless of their complexions because regulations demanded that lipstick match the red piping on the dress blue uniform and the red-bordered chevrons on the green one. This being the case, nail polish had to match both. Many of the Women Marines wore nail polish, which I found surprising. Officially it was 'optional,' but there was so much talk about matching it to lipstick that I smelled peer pressure. Remembering Granny's uproarious talk of morphodites, I realized that the Marine Corps was worried about the Lesbian image that had plagued the women's services since their inception. Those who study Greek must take pains with their nail polish.

They were also worried about the tramp image.

'A Woman Marine never smokes on the street.'

As soon as we got our uniforms, the Public Information Office requested an O.C. to photograph for publicity shots to show America what a Woman Marine looked like. Guess who they picked?

'King!'

They woke us up at 5:55 A.M. by blowing a police whistle. Mama would have been up and at 'em before the last roll of the ball; but I had Herb's metabolism. We had to have the bed made regulation-style by six and ourselves ready to march to breakfast by six-thirty. After breakfast they marched us to the drill field for inspection. My O.C. pins were upside down. After inspection they turned us over to male drill instructors who had been picked for their unblemished service records and solid domestic histories.

After drill we had sports. They gave us a choice of softball, sailing, and horseback riding. I picked riding because it gave me a chance to sit down. We had to groom our mounts ourselves and mine stepped on my foot. When I took off my shoe and sock, my toes looked like a tit after archery. They sent for an ambulance and took me to the base hospital where a medic almost broke my leg trying to get my foot in the right position for the X-ray machine. I had to fill out an Accident Report Form in quintuplicate. When the captain read it and found that I had referred to the medic as Attila the Honey, she tore it up and made me fill out a new one.

'No humor in official reports!' she barked, and marked me down in Attitude.

A good attitude was known as 'gung-ho.' It meant having a singleminded love for the Marine Corps and exhibiting hearty good cheer under stress and pain, the kind of response that might have come from Patient Griselda if somebody had told her to keep her pecker up. It also meant singing 'The Marine Hymn' and 'Lady Leathernecks' while we laundered and starched our green fatigues and spit-shined our shoes.

A Marine is neat. Spots on uniforms were removed by carbon tetrachloride. I left my bottle on a sunny windowsill and it blew up. I was marked down in Safety. A Marine is clean. I neglected to dust my bunk springs and got marked down in Area. I stored my toothbrush in my helmet and got marked down in Hygiene. They took us to a weapons demonstration and I fell asleep while shells exploded all around me. I flunked Alertness.

My sole area of excellence was military etiquette. Forbidden to address officers in the second person, we had to say, 'Does the captain wish anything else?' It was so much like Granny's grace notes that I never forgot the form.

By the middle of the course I knew the Marines were not for me, but I hung on because of the money. It was the best summer job I ever had; we got corporal's pay the first six weeks and sergeant's the second, plus room and board. (The food was delicious.)

Knowing that I was going to flunk, I salvaged my pride by

quitting a week before the end. After filling out the termination forms, I had a final interview with the colonel.

'I'm sorry to see you go,' she said. 'If you want to return next summer and try again, I'll give you a recommendation myself. I think you'd be a credit to the Marine Corps.'

She leaned back in her swivel chair and surveyed me with a fond smile.

'You're a lady to your fingertips.'

12

Coming back from Quantico, I could not decide whether the clicking train wheels were saying *feminine – feminine, lipstick – nail polish*, or *softer hairdo – softer hairdo*. I was sure of one thing, though: at last I had the concise one-sentence definition of 'malkin' I had been seeking since high school.

A malkin is a woman who worries about her femininity.

That absolved Granny, who worried about everybody else's, but it cast a comprehensive net over all the other women who had ever driven me nuts, from Miss Tanner and Ann Hopkins to burly lady leathernecks red in tooth and claw.

I arrived home at three in the afternoon and went directly to bed. For the next six days until classes started, I caught up on my sleep and exorcized the turgid prose of the *Marine Corps Manual* with Nancy Hale's *The Prodigal Women*. Exorcizing the wishful thinking of Granny and Aunt Nana was harder. Neither wanted to believe that the horse had merely stepped on my foot; one pressed me for a kick in the stomach and the other for a kick in the head. Evelyn Cunningham had calmed down considerably in the last couple of years and they needed a new doppelganger.

More wishful thinking awaited me on campus. When I walked into the sorority room, everyone jumped up and saluted, then dissolved in giggles. I stiffened warily, detecting some-thing new in the air, and I was not mistaken. After the general questions were asked and answered, they raised the specific one that was on their minds. El kicked off in a stage whisper.

'Did any fairies bother you?'

'Are you kidding? They ran us so ragged we were too tired to lift a finger.'

I swear to you, nobody caught that. They sat there staring at me with intensely curious, eager eyes full of the hard bright shine of cattiness waiting to pounce. By joining the Marines I had given them a perfect chance to round on me. At last they could get their druthers for all the poisoned darts I had sent their way, and supply themselves with a neat explanation of why I was 'different.'

'Did you have to take showers together?' Faysie asked.

'There was one shower room but it had separate stalls – just like ours.'

'Did they get in any free feels during inspection?'

'I didn't feel a thing.'

'Did anybody stare at you real hard?'

'Only during inspection.'

Five pairs of lips twitched with skepticism. El, the squad leader of the assault, heaved a deep sigh and gave the signal for a round of patronizing comments.

'I feel sorry for women like that.'

'They have to turn to each other because they're so unat-tractive that no man will look at them.'

'I don't understand what two women can *do*.'

'I'd die if a woman touched me.'

'I'd feel robbed of my femininity.'

'If one makes a pass at you, it means you don't have any femininity. They can always tell.'

Listening to their lugubrious, cliché-ridden talk, I wondered why on earth I had ever joined – yes, *joined* – a sorority. But of course I knew why. To get dates, which I hated, so I could play Everything But with fraternity boys, whom I despised. Suddenly I thought of my class-mates in high school French. Where were those girls now, I wondered. I wished I had them back. A wave of loneliness washed over me, surprising me with its intensity. I had never admitted it before; or even realized it, but I was lonely. I had never had a woman friend, but now, even though I despised women, I wanted one. I did not know how both things could be true, but they were.

'I still don't understand what two women *do*.'

'They kiss each other you-know-where.'

'Oh, you're kidding! They do *that*?'

'I'd vomit.'

'I could do it to Susan Hayward,' I said.

Silence. Five pairs of eyes widening in horror, five mouths dropping open in a death-in-life rictus, five audible swallows like rusty clicks. I rose and picked up my books.

'If y'all are against Lesbianism, it can't be too bad.'

I was thrown out of the sorority, except they didn't call it that. Just as there are former Marines and dead Marines but no ex-Marines, there are no ex-sorority girls. Being privy to the secret password, handshake and knock, I was in the position of a defrocked priest whom nothing short of a lobotomy can divest of heard confessions. They called it 'going inactive.' As for the charge, they came up with my old theme song, 'anti-social attitudes.' Ayn Rand would have loved it. I was allowed to keep my pin, which I hocked. I also saved six dollars a month in dues and a small fortune in contributions to bridal and baby showers.

If my summer with the lady leathernecks had brought on a bad attack of malkinitis, starting senior year brought on an even worse one. With graduation looming, I was destined to be tarred with the malkin brush whether I worried about my femininity or not. Come June I would have to get a job, but there were no good jobs for women. I would end up in a malkin pool, no different from the women I saw on the streetcar during rush hour, 'government girls' in Washington, secretaries and typists elsewhere, anonymous everywhere.

Being a college graduate would not raise me above the mass, except perhaps to give me a grandiose title. From my various part-time and summer jobs I had learned that a file clerk with a college degree was called a 'depository administrator' but she went right on filing. The classified ads lured educated women with come-ons like 'Career-Minded Miss!' but whatever autonomous glories they promised, most of them ended with 'Relieve PBX.'

I wasn't used to being anonymous; the thought of joining a faceless, powerless regiment of women revolted me. Ever since high school I had been one of the special girls because of my grades; A's were the source of my power, but A's came from school and school would soon end. When it did, I would go from 'God, she's a brain,' to 'Hey, she's a secretary,' except I did not know shorthand.

My mounting panic was exacerbated by the silent nagging I endured at home. Mama and Herb, like so many unsophisticated parents, still assumed that I would walk off the commencement stage and into a walnut-paneled executive suite where I would earn the proverbial million dollars a year for 'running' some organization or other. There was no way to dislodge them from their blind spot; Herb was locked up in his ivory tower and Mama was immersed in the female-dominated telephone company where she had been promoted once again and was now a trainer of new operators. Having several dozen thoroughly cowed young women under her aegis ('When I say shit, they squat!') had made her blissfully unaware of sex discrimination, so there was no point in trying to get through to her.

My communication problem was complicated by the fact

that to the Southern mind, 'discrimination' meant only one thing. Using the word in reference to myself would have brought down the house, with Jensy hooting the loudest. There would have been jokes about having a touch of the tar brush, mock-reverential observations along the lines of 'She sho come up light, dint she, Miss Lura?' and reminders to get my hair straightened before I went job-hunting. As for Miss Lura, she would have said what she had been saying ever since I could remember: 'A woman can get anything she wants, an-nee-thing.'

I was too much a product of my time and place to think of my problem as discrimination. A passion for social change was not part of my rebelliousness; I was content to let the world stay exactly the way it was, provided I could have special privileges. I wanted to be a token. I saw the situation in individual terms, and I was the individual who mattered. All I knew was, I couldn't get a decent job because malkins had given women a bad name. 'Women quit to get married,' employers said, and they were absolutely right. Not satisfied with gumming up the classrooms of America, malkins gummed up the working world as well. 'I want to work for a couple of years to save money for my wedding,' they said prettily, flashing their quarter-carat diamonds. Those who were not already engaged went to work solely for the purpose of finding a husband, quitting as soon as they discovered that their offices did not contain any eligible men.

They were my pawnbrokers, my badass razor-toters, my Mafia with garlic breath; I was Gustavus Adolphus and they were Onkel Axel. I understood perfectly how Jensy felt, so much so that I adopted her standard philippic for my own purposes. '*You rents to one malkin, she bring in all her friends, an' 'fore long you looks up an' you sees dem sleepin' wid dey feets hangin' out de winda!*'

I always thought I would be an exception because the three

women who raised me all behaved like freewheeling, slightly mad Popes. All I had to do, I reasoned, was copy them and let the malkins hang themselves. But it was not that simple; there were too many of them. They had purple-inked the entire female sex into a corner.

The solution to my job problem came to me in Renaissance England, taught by Dr Newton, who had refereed the Patient Griselda fight. Thanks to Granny, I had become his pet. Impressed by my ability to read a genealogical chart and keep all the kings and queens straight, he always called on me to untangle royal relationships. On this particular day, we came to one of history's finest scrimmages, Lady Jane Grey's claim to the throne.

Dr Newton began his lecture.

'Edward the Sixth died childless in 1553. The three claimants to the throne were his half-sister Mary Tudor, daughter of Henry the Eighth and Catherine of Aragon; his half-sister Elizabeth Tudor, daughter of Henry the Eighth and Ann Boleyn; and, as usual, Mary Queen of Scots. However, both of the half-sisters had been declared illegitimate and Mary Stuart was Catholic. They had to find somebody who was both legitimate and Protestant, so they picked Lady Jane Grey.'

He looked up with a smile. 'Why did they pick her, Miss King? Tell us about it.'

It was nothing compared to the descents I had heard Granny trace. She had corkscrewed and serpentined herself all the way back to Richard the Lionheart, so Lady Jane Grey was a piece of cake.

'She was the great-granddaughter of Henry the Seventh,' I began. 'Henry the Seventh's youngest daughter Mary married Charles Brandon, Duke of Suffolk, and had three daughters. The eldest was Lady Frances Brandon, who married Lord Henry Grey, Marquess of Dorset, and also had three daughters, the eldest of whom was Lady Jane Grey.'

My Daughterly presentation was greeted with 'Whew!' by my classmates. A boy who had finger-fucked me turned around and gave me a look to which I had grown accustomed: part resentful, part puzzled, and part grudging admiration. It was a look that took me seriously, a look that *saw* me. I needed the hostility it contained. I did not like to tease men – that hurt me as much as it did them – but I did like to disturb them, even if it made enemies of them, because I loved to bring forth that all-shook-up look. It was solely for this purpose that I had made myself an expert on that tangled web, the annexation of Schleswig-Holstein. Now, scholarship and 'the look' were one and the same in my mind; once I left school and joined the ranks of so-called career women, I would stop getting it. I must never stop getting it; therefore, I had to stay in school.

After class I stopped by the podium and spoke to Dr Newton.

'I want to go to graduate school. I need to find out about fellowships. May I have an appointment with you to talk about it?'

He snapped his fingers. 'We must be telepathic. I made a note on my calendar to call you in about that. You want a fellowship here? I'll fix it up.'

'Not here,' I said quickly. 'I was born and raised in the District. I'd like to see another part of the country.'

'That's always a good idea. What part did you have in mind?'

'The Deep South,' I replied, remembering Herb's theory about Virginia's dearth of belles. 'I'd like to see how women there compare to Upper South women.'

'Well, how about the University of Mississippi? You can't get any deeper than that.'

'All right.'

It was much simpler than I expected. He wrote a letter, I supplied a transcript, and a few weeks later I had a fellowship to Ole Miss: free tuition plus a stipend of one hundred dollars a month. Dr Newton gave me a money-saving tip.

'Write to the Dean of Women and ask for a dorm proctorship. You get a free room in exchange for tucking the little girls in. They like graduate students for that – more mature, settled down, good example for the co-eds.' His glance flickered over my face. 'Enclose a picture of yourself,' he added.

It worked. The dean replied saying that she was assigning me to a freshman dorm. *I am sure you will help us maintain the highest standards of Southern womanhood*, she wrote.

Winning the fellowship filled me with triumph and confidence. Now that I had it, my final semester's grades didn't matter, so for the first time in my scholastic career I goofed off. I settled for a lady's B and looked around for other forms of fun and relaxation.

The one I wanted most was normal genital intercourse. I was tired of finger-fucking; now that I was twenty-one it seemed perverse. I was ready for the real McCoy. But winning the fellowship made me more afraid than ever of getting pregnant – a baby would keep me from going to Ole Miss.

It dawned on me all of a sudden that it was not concern for my reputation that had kept me virginal thus far. I could have handled 'fierce' boys, or found an older and more sophisticated lover who was unconnected with the gossipy fraternities. The campus was swarming with marvelously oversexed foreign students who had sent a delegation to the Dean of Men to ask him where Washington's whorehouses were; the dean had reputedly answered, 'If you find out, let me know.' Being, outwardly at least, the personification of all-American girlhood had made me the target of smoldering stares from hooded eyes; I could have had a sheik or a gaucho or a maharaja, as long as Jensy didn't find out about it. There would have been no reputation problem because the foreign students were a little afraid of American women, and men who wear turbans do not fret over why you let them go all the way.

No, I had refrained from fucking because of that ceaseless,

gnawing, paranoid terror of getting pregnant. Yet it was not the baby or the ruin that terrified me; babies could be given away, and Mama could be counted on to shout Granny and Jensy down. I was terrified of getting pregnant because 'She had to leave school' was a metaphor for malkin. I had not dared combine coitus with matriculation; for four years my subconscious motto had been: 'Graduate first.'

Now I was forced to consider a charming conundrum. If I carried out my burgeoning plan to become a fellowship bum and stay in school as long as possible, I would not be able to fuck until I was thirty.

There was only one solution – a diaphragm. I knew all about them thanks to Evelyn Cunningham, who had shown us hers one day out at the house. Incapable of editing herself, she had delivered a treatise on the care, use, and efficiency of diaphragms, speaking so volubly and steadily that Granny did not get a chance to say, 'Mr Ruding was a perfect gentleman,' until it was all over. Proof that diaphragms worked was the fact that Evelyn, to whom unplanned things were always happening, had only two planned-for children (both of them boringly normal).

The problem was how to get one. You couldn't buy them without a doctor's prescription and nearly all doctors refused to fit unmarried women. Somehow I had to find one of the renegade few who were said to fit engaged women. How? Whom to ask? Remembering my high school infirmary nurse, I was reluctant to ask anybody. Not that I had much choice; since leaving the sorority I had gone from near-friendless to friendless in a trice, so that I did not even know any malkins now.

I ended up asking a woman I hardly knew. She was one of the bohemians in Contemporary Appreciation, a fine arts course I had signed up for in the usual final-semester smorgasbord way, chiefly because it dovetailed with my bus schedule.

Her name was Patsy but should have been Tanya. She wore black leotards with pink ballet slippers, dirndl skirts, peasant blouses, and paisley shawls fastened with old Stevenson buttons. She was married but childless, she said, because she refused to bring a child into This World. (I had figured her for an apocalypso dancer.) She also said she wanted to stamp out ignorance, so I asked her to stamp out mine.

'A diaphragm?' she repeated loudly, giddy with uplift. 'There's a dedicated woman doctor in one of those residence hotels down by Union Station. She *knew* Margaret Sanger. Just tell her you're getting married – that way, she's covered.'

'Suppose she asks me why I don't have an engagement ring?'

'Tell her he's saving his money to go to graduate school. She won't ask, though.'

I made an appointment and took the streetcar downtown.

The doctor's waiting room contained a nurse-secretary at a scarred desk, and two plastic couches with chrome legs. As I sat down, the inner office door opened and a young woman emerged carrying a small package. She paid her fee in cash and gave me a tiny conspiratorial smile as she left. Evidently it was a diaphragm mill.

My turn came. The doctor was extremely short and plump, with grizzled hair and glasses that kept slipping down her nose. I told her what I wanted and named a June wedding date. She nodded and told me to undress and get in the stirrups. A rubber glove snapped and she bobbed up between my knees like a buoy with a set of fitting rings around her finger.

'Have you ever had a baby?'

'No, ma'am.'

'Have you ever had intercourse?'

'No, ma'am.'

'Well, you probably take a sixty.'

I didn't take a sixty, or a seventy, or a seventy-five.

'Eighty,' she pronounced, peering up at me from her burrow. 'Are you sure you've never had a baby?'

'Yes, ma'am.'

'Let's put it this way. Have you ever been pregnant?'

'No, ma'am.'

'You can tell me, I don't care. I'm just curious, that's all.'

'I'm telling the truth, ma'am.'

'Hmmp,' she grunted, shaking her head.

'Is there anything wrong with me?'

'No, you've got a healthy-looking pelvis. But eighty is a married woman's size as a rule.'

So I had terminal *ultima thule*. It was all those fingers, I thought dismally. Had I ruined myself for fucking? What would I say when I got laid? Would I ever have a satisfying sex life? Men might marry women with big twats but they didn't run around with them.

I was afraid to ask any more questions for fear she would ask some more. When she reached for a number eighty diaphragm from among the boxes on her shelf, I turned my head away, certain it would look like a dinner plate. I kept my eyes closed while she smeared it with jelly and stuffed it in me. Satisfied that it fit, she took it out and made me insert it.

It wasn't nearly so big as I expected; in fact, it was only about three inches in diameter, but that still seemed big. I was shaking so badly that when I pinched it into the requisite figure-eight to insert it, it flew out of my fingers and rose up like a pop fly. The doctor caught it and handed it back to me. I finally got it in.

'What's the biggest size?' I asked obliquely.

'A hundred-five. Generally you find that in women who've had lots of children.'

Her *generally* was as ominous as her *as a rule*. If I was an eighty now, what would I be after fucking? I felt like Pinocchio.

'Now remember,' she said, summing up her instructions. 'You

must smear vaginal jelly *all over* the diaphragm before you put it in. Using a diaphragm without a spermicide is almost as bad as using nothing. And you *must* douche with plain warm water before you take it out, then douche again after you take it out. Whatever you do, don't take it out until six hours after intercourse. *Six!*' she repeated, thrusting her head out at me. Her glasses slid down her nose.

She gave me a tube of vaginal jelly and I stopped by the drugstore to buy a douche bag. Now my mission was complete; I was ready to fuck.

Whom? My preferred candidate was Dr Newton, for three reasons. I did not require love, but I did want compatibility, and we certainly had that. Second, I found him physically attractive. Third, he was married, which meant that I would not have to date him. Married men can't take you anywhere except to bed. I couldn't tell whether he was attracted to me or not, but I kept thinking about his allusion to our telepathy and wondered if it had reminded him of the telepathy scene between Jane Eyre and Mr Rochester. It was the most famous instance of telepathy in literature, so it must have crossed his mind. If so, he had entertained at least one non-professional thought about me. It was a start.

My fucking equipment was proving hard to carry, so I went to Woodward & Lothrop and bought the biggest shoulder strap bag I could find and dumped everything into it then and there while the saleslady cut off the tags and put my old pocketbook in a paper bag.

A horrible thought struck me as I left the store. If Dr Newton took me to a motel, how could I douche six hours later except at home? And how could I douche at home without Granny finding out about it? What would I say when she asked me why I was douching? Where would I keep the douche bag, the jelly, the diaphragm? Granny and I had separate bureaus but we still shared a room – I had to masturbate in the bathtub – so how could I open a drawer and pull out a douche bag?

There was nothing to do but keep all the fuckiana in my new handbag and sneak the douche bag into the bathroom when I needed it. Presumably that would be late at night when Granny was asleep. If by some chance she happened to see it, I would claim a minor gynecological ailment – something virginal, like an itch – and say the school nurse had recommended douching.

I could blame the itch on the chlorine in the college pool. Granny could never remember the difference between chlorine and fluoride, and all the Daughters were against fluoridation.

Needing a summer job as well as proximity to Dr Newton, I killed two birds with one stone and got a job as the History Department's typist. I started three weeks before graduation, right after the seniors' early exams. I was the only female in the office.

History Departments are macho in the best sense of the word. The English Department across the hall ran to shrill types with that air of timid ruffianism that comes from carrying a razor blade to cut the pages of European paperbacks, but the historians came on like erudite lumberjacks in a smoke-filled, book-lined back room. The jokes were bawdy but they always depended upon a solid grounding in the field: the War of Jenkins' *What?* and the Woodrow Wilson Misprint ('The President was observed entering Mrs Galt, who appeared to enjoy his sally') were typical daily fare, blending food for thought and sexual awareness in perfect proportion.

In this atmosphere there was no ice to break with Dr Newton. The turning point came much sooner than I expected and with very little effort on my part. It happened around four-thirty on the Friday of the second week; everyone else had left early and we were alone in the office. I had been wearing scoop-neck blouses and bending over a lot. Now, I took his letters in

to him, dropped an envelope, picked it up, and looked at him.
I caught him in the act; his eyes shifted quickly to my face.

'Well,' he said, leaning back in his swivel chair and folding
his hands behind his head. 'Graduation's a week off. What are
you going to do with yourself this summer? Besides putting up
with us, I mean.'

'Oh, nothing much.'

'No beach? Weekend trips? Parties?'

'Not that I know of.'

'What's the matter with the guys around here?' he demanded
gruffly.

I laughed. 'A lot.'

His pupils distended a little. 'Callow youth, huh?'

'Very.'

'Maybe Ole Miss will have something better to offer.'

'Maybe.'

'One of those Beauregards will sweep you off your feet.'

'That sounds interesting. I've never been swept off my feet.'

'No?'

'It's not a specialty of callow youth.'

I held his glance for the barest second and then lowered my
eyes with a flutter of lashes. Southern flirting is fun when you
have a specific lascivious purpose in mind. Besides, it works.

He looked at his watch. 'Say, how about some chow? There's
a place down on the avenue. It's just a beer joint – but they
have good hamburgers.'

My ruin was coming along nicely considering I had never
even set foot in Indiana. One of these days I was going to have
to go out West and take a look at that state. I left the office with
Dr Newton feeling like a soiled dove about to soar.

As we drove crosstown past the heavy north-south com-
muter traffic inching toward the Key Bridge, he sighed happily
and beat a little tattoo on the wheel.

'Look at those poor bastards. I won't have to do that again

till September. When I pulled the National Archives Summer Institute, Curtis in Poli Sci sublet me his apartment in town.'

'Oh? Where is it?'

'Just off Wisconsin and Porter.'

'That's convenient.'

'No point in dragging out to Falls Church with the family away. We've got a cottage at Rehoboth Beach.' He paused. 'My wife and kids are there now. They left last week.'

'Are they going to spend the whole summer there?'

'Yes.'

'How nice for them.'

'I figured they might as well enjoy the beach even if I can't. I'll grab a weekend now and then, if I can get away.'

His arrow of self-sacrifice went far wide of the mark. He was as bad an actor as I was an actress. Suddenly I wondered if he had been planning a summer bachelorhood all along, numbering me among his possibilities just as I had numbered him among mine.

The conversation continued in the same loaded vein when we got to the beer joint. He led me to a tall wooden booth well in the back and suggested that we have a drink.

'What the hell, you're twenty-one,' he said cavalierly.

I wondered if he meant to verify my age for purposes of his own. If he was worried about my majority, he might also be worried about my virginity. I had already told him that I had never been swept off my feet; suppose he was the type who refused to 'lay a finger' on a virgin? Granny had a song about that. A roué finds his long-lost daughter's picture in another roué's pocket and reforms on the spot.

'What are your children?' I blurted.

'Huh?'

'Boys or girls?'

'Oh. Two boys.'

Never inject the subject of domesticity at a time like this. It took us a while to get the conversation back to its former tumescence. By the time we did our glasses were empty, so he ordered two more highballs. As we drank and talked, we manifested those classic signs of sexual undercurrent: playing with the cardboad coasters and compulsively fitting our glasses into the wet circles on the table that the coasters were meant to prevent.

We talked about 'life' and finally it came:

'Are you a virgin?'

'Not the way you mean.'

'How do you know the way I mean?'

'Telepathy. You said we had it.'

'So I did. You mean you've lost your cherry and your innocence, but you haven't gone all the way, is that it?'

I nodded.

'That's what I thought. We *are* telepathic.'

As our eyes met, the denouement became a foregone conclusion. Reader, I fucked him.

I slipped into the phone booth to call home. Mama answered.

'I'm working late tonight. One of the professors needs a long article typed. It might take quite a while but he's going to drive me home afterwards.'

'Okay,' said Mama. 'See you later, alligator.'

I wanted to rent her to Marjorie Morningstar.

Dr Newton – by now Ralph – drove us to our house of assignation with such extreme caution that I felt like a DMV examiner as I sat beside him. We did not speak, but when he braked to a glass-smooth stop at a red light he reached over and gave my knee a squeeze.

The apartment was an efficiency with a convertible sofa that had not been made up. The sheets were the plain white ones that nice people still preferred in 1957 ('Those color sheets are trashy!'). Ralph pulled me down on them and we messed them up some more with a long rolling embrace.

'You don't have to worry,' he murmured. 'I've got safes.'

'I've got a diaphragm.'

'You do?'

'It's not . . . I have to go into the bathroom for a minute.'

He let me up and started unknotting his tie. Feeling like Harriet Mudd, I picked up my loaded-for-bear haversack and beat a retreat. Why did I have to blurt out the news of the diaphragm that way? Now he knew I had planned it all. I couldn't decide whether I was honest or just dumb.

The diaphragm went in like greased lightning. I breathed a sigh of relief. Though I had practiced insertion with excellent results, I had been dreading this first real moment, visualizing mishaps involving air shafts and open bathroom windows with Catholic priests standing in range. I put my pants in my purse, washed my hands, and left the bathroom, fully dressed except for pants and carrying my handbag.

Ralph was in bed naked, the sheet pulled up to his waist. His chest was roped with muscles and covered with a mat of hair much darker than his sandy-blond crewcut.

'May I watch you undress?' he asked softly.

I nodded and unzipped my skirt. This was a performance I had orchestrated mentally many times, guided by a cold assessment of my assets and liabilities. Deciding to leave the best for last, I promptly removed my bra. I hated my breasts because they did not look like funnels or collie muzzles. They had when they were still sprouting, but around age fourteen they rounded out and developed a convex line on the undersides that prevented me from passing the pencil test. Years later I would realize that there was nothing much wrong with them, but in the fifties, tits weren't up to snuff unless they could be used to put out Gloucester's eyes in *King Lear*. I was convinced that I looked like a Bolivian wet nurse.

Next to go was my halfslip. My pants were already off so the first thing he would see was my crotch. Having no basis for comparison, I did not know if I came up to Napoleon's estimate of Josephine – 'She had the most beautiful cunt in the world but she lied too much' – but in my own way I was the soul of honor.

In any case, when I stepped out of the circle of my halfslip my hour had come, because nothing beats garter belt, stockings, and high heels for showing off legs.

As I reached down to unfasten the garters, his voice cut through the turgid silence.

'Leave that on.'

He pulled me down on the bed. The shoes came off but the whorish prop remained to cast its unique spell over the occasion. It turned into a glorious melee with no real caresses but a lot of leg-wrapping and rolling around on top of each other. His cock was short but very thick with a tip the size of a tangerine; it was like being hit in the twat with a fist. When it was all the way in I felt very full and not at all big.

'Remember,' he said as I got out of the car, 'tomorrow morning at ten. We'll spend the whole day together.'

It was like asking me to remember my own name. Tomorrow was Saturday, his Rehoboth Beach day, but he was not going.

It was nine when I got home so I could not douche until two A.M. I was too excited to sleep so I had no fear of missing it. I wanted to lie in bed and think about what had happened, but I was destined to be thwarted. Granny wasn't sleepy, either.

'What *was* that woman's name?'

'What woman?'

'*You know*,' she accused. 'The one that had the son with the ears.'

'Granny, everybody's got ears.'

'Not like that. Oh, you know who I'm talking about! They lived next door to that friend of Aunt Nana's who lost her mind.'

'Which one?'

'She used to bake cakes and take them out to the cemetery and put them on her husband's tombstone. The gravediggers ate them, but when she found the empty plate on the tombstone, she thought her husband did. Oh, *what* was his name?'

It went on for over an hour. Every time she remembered a name, it reminded her of some other name that had slipped her mind. My reverie was destroyed. I wanted to think about big fat cocks, but by the time she fell into a querulous, snorting sleep, my mind was crammed with ears, shock treatments, and people who had choked to death on fish bones.

Two o'clock came at last. I slipped silently out of bed, picked up my carnal valise, and tiptoed into the bathroom. I debated whether or not to lock the door and finally decided against it. None of us ever did, so it would only arouse suspicion, especially at two in the morning.

My douche bag was the hanging kind. I filled it with water and then looked around for a place to hang it, but of course there wasn't one. My heart sank. Like the master criminal who forgets one small detail, I had forgotten to put up a nail.

There was a clothes hook on the back of the bathroom door but it was sagging out of the wood from the weight of all the robes and nightgowns that Mama and Granny put on it. To their way of thinking, it was easier to sling a garment on the hook than to take the trouble of putting it away properly. A sizable part of both their wardrobes resided on the hook at any given time, so there was neither room nor fortitude for a douche bag.

I would have to remember to put a nail in the wall for future douches. Meanwhile, there was nothing to do but hold the bag over my head with my left hand while I performed the ablutions with my right. I sat down on the toilet.

'Give me your tard, your poah . . .'

It worked fine until the bag was half-empty and it was time to remove the diaphragm. Pressing the clamp to shut off the water, I held the nozzle in my teeth while I probed for the diaphragm. I pulled it out, sat it on the edge of the basin, and stuck the nozzle back in my twat.

Just then I heard a scuffling sound in the hall. Before I could move, the door flew open, the hook gave up the ghost, all the clothes fell in the bathtub, and I lost my balance and dropped the douche bag.

'Oh, Law!' Granny screamed.

The nozzle was still in me. I plucked it out and hauled in the rubber tubing; the douche bag came flapping into my lap like a fish. The gooey diaphragm had fallen into the basin and lay there just out of my reach. Granny had not seen it and probably couldn't without her glasses but she would if I stood up and tried to rescue it. I stayed put and hoped for the best.

Just then a familiar voice rang out.

'Goddamnit! What the hell's going on?'

The Gipper joined us. Granny pointed a Zola-esque finger at me as I sat huddled on the john.

'The child was taking a douche!'

Mama looked at the floor. 'She missed.'

'Oh, Louise! I heard a splashing sound and thought she was sick, and when I came in, there she was just as big as life, taking a douche!'

Mama's eyes flickered over to the basin and rested for a second on the diaphragm. She turned back to Granny.

'Well, let her take it. For God's sake, Mother, do you have to run everything? Go back to bed.'

'But why was the child taking a douche?'

'The nurse at the infirmary recommended it,' I said. 'I had an itch.'

Granny's suspicious expression faded and she perked up.

'An itch? What kind of itch?'

'A real bad one,' I said in my best Evelyn voice. 'There was a discharge with it.'

'Really? Was it white or yellow?'

'White.'

'White. Did it have—'

'It's the Upton crud, Mother, now go back to bed.'

'—little nodules in it like cottage cheese?'

'No, just mucusy. The nurse said it came from using the swimming pool. A lot of girls had the same thing.'

'Chlorine!' Granny cried, her curlers quivering with righteous wrath. 'They're putting it in everything! It's a Communist plot to poison us all! Mrs Baldwin read a paper on it at our last meeting.'

'Jesus Christ on rollerskates! To hell with the Russians! Go back to bed!'

Mama took Granny's arm and steered her firmly into the bedroom. Just then Herb called up from the foot of the stairs.

'What are you people up to?'

'Nothing that concerns you. Just keep on reading John Quincy Shitass.'

She stalked back to her room and slammed the door. When I had stopped trembling, I mopped the floor, hung the clothes on the shower rack, washed the diaphragm, dried the douche bag, and staggered back to bed with my pocketbook. Now I was sleepy but the night wasn't over yet.

'Those Communists will do anything. Look what they did to that poor little girl. Took her down the cellar and blew her brains out! But they say she's still alive somewhere. They're holding her money for her in a Swiss bank. The poor, poor little soul . . . Oh, *what* was her name?'

'Anastasia,' I groaned.

Already unique in the annals of motherhood, Mama now went herself one better. She never said a word about the diaphragm or the douche, or questioned me about my private life. She gave Ralph a shrewd look when she met him at graduation, but she never mentioned him to me.

It was a charmed summer in every way. I even had the foresight to get the curse on the weekend that his wife abruptly demanded his presence at the beach. By the following Saturday I was in flat-bellied fucking trim.

Our assignations were deliciously salacious and occasionally perverse. There were no whips or bondage games but we did everything that he called 'the things I've always thought about.' (There were as yet no official fantasies, and the word, when it did appear in print, was spelled with *ph*.) We took a lot of showers, for the practices that require absolute cleanliness, for the ones that require thick slippery soapsuds, and for the one that requires a drain.

As things turned out, we did have one date after all. The week before I left for Ole Miss, he took me out to dinner. He was in the process of drinking coffee when I glanced out the window and stiffened.

'Look at that woman. She's smoking on the street.'

There was a wheezing sound of bubbles in distress; then a fine spray of coffee rained down on the table and me.

I never saw him again. Our goodbye that night was like the whole affair – friendly rather than tender. Later on I realized that except for first names and fucking, that summer was no different from the student-teacher friendship that began in my sophomore year when I took my first class with him. We had some good conversations and some good laughs but there was no talk of love and no terms of endearment, even in our most frenzied moments. It was always an affair, never a 'relationship,' and that's what I liked about it and him.

I knew I was going to miss him sexually, but it did not stop me from feeling a certain relief when I embarked for Memphis a few days later. I still liked 'overness' and there was still a part of me that wanted to wave at the railroad men when the train went through.

13

My South was a region of narrow red brick Federalist houses and vast rolling acres of cobblestones. I had never seen naked children playing with a dead snake nor a four-year-old standing up to nurse at the breast of a mother seated on a porch, but these riveting sights were mine from the window of the Memphis–Oxford bus.

Oxford itself was a pretty town with a courthouse on the square and a Confederate statue in front of it. It was almost dark when the bus pulled into the depot. As I got off, a taxi driver spotted me for a student and jumped forward, tipping his cap.

'Carry you up to campus, l'il lady?'

His idiom for 'drive' was another first; for a moment I visualized myself arriving in a swoon in his skinny arms. He loaded my luggage and I gave him the name of the dorm the dean had assigned me to.

'That's Miz Arvella's dorm,' he said, referring to the house-mother the dean had mentioned. 'A fine woman.'

Proctors had to arrive two days earlier than the other students, so the campus was empty and unlighted when he pulled up before a dimly outlined rectangular house set in a copse of dark overhanging trees. In the tradition of Gothic paperback covers, one light burned in the house. The driver shone his headlights on the walk so I could see and I mounted the porch and rang the bell. I heard footsteps and then the door opened.

'Hey, Miz Arvella!' the driver cried happily.

'Hey, Mistuh Reece! How you doin'? How you been? You have a good summuh?' She turned to me. 'You must be Flarnz. Are you Flarnz? Are you the proctuh named Flarnz? They said you wuh comin' tonight. The Dean said to me this mornin', she said, "Flarnz is comin' tonight." Did you get heah awright? How you doin'?'

Everybody started talking at once; the driver answering his questions, I answering mine, and Miz Arvella asking more. It made walking through the door difficult; other people enter houses but Southerners surge in on wings of speech. Miz Arvella was the same age and shape as every other old lady I had ever known, but there was nonetheless something un-Daughterly about her. The word 'askew' came to mind. I was used to rigidly glued gray fingerwaves and personalities to match, but Miz Arvella looked as if she had been cut out of her own speech pattern.

I reminded myself that I was getting a free private room out of this. Miz Arvella took me upstairs and showed it to me as the driver followed behind with my bags. It was huge and attractively furnished and sans Granny – my first room-of-one's-own. I paid the driver and he left me alone with the fine woman.

'Come on down aftuh you wash up. We'll have us some coffee and Ah'll explain your duties,' she said, and waddled out.

I washed up and looked out the window but could see nothing except an amber patch made by my own light; beyond it lay the wet black velvet of a Southern night. It was as still as death, yet there was something pervasively alive about it, a sense of things unseen moving among the trees on soundless wings. No wonder so many of the early settlers had gone mad. ('One Nathaniel Upton was floggèd for shewing himself in publick unclothèd.')

I went downstairs to join Miz Arvella. She led me to a little room with a wall board that contained buzzers and corresponding room numbers. Next to the board was the proctor's desk and a table containing the sign-out book. According to the dean's letter, I was to alternate odd and even nights with Miz Arvella, each of us having every other weekend off. There was very little to do and I could study at the desk once the girls were out on their dates. I had to check them in, keep track of late records and grace periods, chase any boys out of the lounge when the witching hour struck, and lock the doors.

As a woman of legal age, I had no curfew. I could go out after I locked the magnolia blossoms in, and stay out all night if I wished. My job entitled me to a key to the dorm, which Miz Arvella issued me now.

Next she explained the buzzer system. This is what she said:

'When a guhl has a phone call, you know what Ah mean, when the telephone rings, when somebody is callin' huh up. When a guhl has a phone call, you press huh bell once. When she has a calluh, when a boy comes in to get huh, you know what Ah'm tryin' to say, when they've got a date that night and he picks huh up, when he comes in and asks for huh in puhson 'stead of callin' on the phone, you unnerstand what Ah mean? When she has a calluh, then you press huh bell twice. That way she knows whethuh she's got a phone call or a calluh. 'Cause see, if she has a calluh and you press huh bell once 'stead of twice, she'll think it's a call 'stead of a calluh. She'd come downstairs in huh dressin' gown with huh hair up in cullahs, and there stands huh calluh just standin' there right in front of huh just as big as life. She'd just die of embarrassment, you know what Ah mean, she'd just fall down dead is what Ah'm sayin', she'd just perish!'

She invited me to dinner in her apartment but I pleaded travel fatigue and escaped to my room. I poured myself a drink from Herb's Prohibition flask, which he had filled with Scotch and given me for a going-away present. I heard the phone ring in Miz Arvella's bedroom. A call, not a calluh. I put my hair up in cullahs, had another drink – you know what I mean, I poured some more whiskey out of the flask and drank it is what I'm saying – and fell into bed.

I slept twelve hours and awoke to the kind of morning that can turn night people into morning people. The warm sunny air was so fresh and sweet that I actually stuck my head out the window and inhaled. Ole Miss had a bona fide campusy look that my city college had striven for and missed. It was enough to make a graduate student feel like a co-ed at last, instead of the strangely haunted, secret-drinking proctor of Miz Arvella.

No sooner did this thought pass through my mind than I heard a tap at my door.

'Flarnz? You there, Flarnz? Come on down and have breakfast. Miz Zaviola's heah. She's one of the othuh housemothuhs and she's just dyin' to meet you.'

I was starving to death, so with two of us in extremis there was no reason to try and get out of it. I dressed and went downstairs, sniffing appreciatively at the aroma of Miz Arvella's home-baked biscuits.

The other housemother looked more like my kind of old lady but she sounded exactly like Miz Arvella. This is what she said over breakfast:

'When Ah heard they wuh lettin' the freshmen guhls stay out till midnight on Saddy, Ah saw the handwritin' on the wall. Ah said to myself Ah said Ah can just see the handwritin' on the wall if they let those guhls stay out till midnight on Saddy. Ah said the same thing to one of the mothuhs that called me. She asked me what did Ah think about them lettin' the freshmen guhls stay out till midnight on Saddy and Ah said to huh Ah said Ah can just see the handwritin' on the wall.'

My stomach was shaking. I was sorry because I had always

enjoyed old ladies and I wanted to enjoy these, but I had to escape the echo chamber. As soon as I could politely do so, I excused myself and went for a walk around the campus. It was nearly deserted without the students but I had an imaginary companion. As we strolled through the grove in front of the white-columned Lyceum, Somerset Maugham whispered in my ear: '*It requires the feminine temperament to repeat the same thing three times with equal zest.*'

Maybe. Probably. But there was something a little too sweeping about Willie's theory. The most feminine temperament I had ever encountered belonged to Evelyn Cunningham, but though she was a chatterbox, she was not a repeating rifle. No matter how much she talked she always moved forward, usually too fast; her needle never got stuck. Compared to Miz Arvella and Miz Zaviola, Evelyn was taciturn.

I stayed out as long as I could, but with the campus closed and no car to take me into town I was thrown back on the dorm. That meant having my meals with Miz Arvella because – I want to emphasize this – she was what the South calls 'a good soul.' She would give you half of anything she had to eat and three of everything she had to say.

As long as I had to endure her echolalia, I decided to analyze it. Perhaps she had been the youngest in a large family and had trouble getting people to listen to her. When she told me she was the oldest of seven and had raised her siblings after their mother's untimely death, I decided that her thrice-told tales sprang from saying 'No, no, no' to children while she herself was still a child. When both housemothers told me their late husbands had been farmers, I blamed isolation in the country with laconic men. This did not explain the absence of echolalia in farmwives in other parts of America, especially New England, but by then I was in no condition to pick a fight with myself.

All of my theories collapsed on the first day of school when the dorm was invaded by girls and mothers from every part of

Mississippi, representing every social background and sibling rank, who all said everything at least three times.

'Well, lemme tell you, Ah've been on the horns of a dilemma evva since we got up this mornin' to drive Tulaplee up heah from Jaspah City. Ah've nevva seen a fuhst day like this one. Ah tole Jimmy Lee while we wuh drivin' up heah, Ah said Jimmy Lee Ah said, Ah'm on the horns of a dilemma, that's what Ah tole him. When we got to Clarksdale, Tulaplee remembuhed that she forgot huh opal necklace and we had to tuhn right around and go back home and get it. By the time we got stahted again, Ah was on the horns of a dilemma the likes of which you have nevva seen.'

'Mary Lou's upstairs just cryin' huh eyes out 'cause it's the fuhst time she's evva been away from home. But Ah tole huh, Ah said Mary Lou Ah said, there's no point cryin' your eyes out 'cause there comes a time when the Mama bird pushes the babies out of the nest. You know what Ah mean, Ah said Mary Lou Ah said, Nature tells Mama bird to push the babies out of the nest, so you hadn't ought to cry your eyes out like that, 'cause the time has come for you to leave the nest, that's what Ah tole huh. But she kept cryin' huh eyes out, so I went and got huh Daddy and Ah tole him Ah said T.J. Ah said, you make that chile unnerstand that she's just got to leave the nest. So T.J. talked to huh a long time, a right good while, and finally she dried huh eyes and she said to me, Mama, she said, you're right. Ah've just got to fly.'

The front door burst open, crashed against the wall, and shuddered on its hinges as an embattled mother and daughter surged through the foyer and stormed upstairs. This time it was the daughter doing the talking.

'Ah got sick and tard of listenin' to all that ole hoorah so Ah tole him Ah said Purvis Lee Thornton Ah said, Ah don't want to heah another word out of you, so you just hush your mouth right this minute, that's what Ah tole him. And he said to me he said Jackie Sue he said, Ah know good 'n' well you been datin' Lamar Creighton on the sly, and Ah said now listen heah Ah said, that's the biggest bunch of hoorah Ah evva heard! Ah said you just take that up the road and dump it, Ah said, 'cause you're just as full of hoorah as you can be, that's what Ah tole him.'

Thus vanished my slim hope of blaming it on the menopause. I took four aspirin, helped Miz Arvella get everybody squared away, and then escaped to the all-male world of the History Department to sign up for my classes. I took Ancient Greece, Ancient Rome, the Age of Reason, Historiography and Historical Research, and Thesis I. After I registered, I had an interview with my thesis advisor.

'I see from your transcripts that you've had six years of French,' he said. 'I assume you're planning a topic from French history, since you can do the research in the original. How about Syndicalism?'

Ralph had warned me about professor-generated topics. ('You can bet he's writing a book on it and wants a free research assistant.')

'Labor movements don't interest me,' I replied, 'and besides, it's too recent. I like the distant past.'

Having blurted these sentiments to the only liberal at Ole Miss, I was smoothly but quickly transferred to another advisor, but he too pounced on the French, albeit with much more chronological empathy.

'How about Pippin the Short?'

'I'll think about it,' I lied.

I wanted to write on the historical Bérénice, but I hesitated to say so for two reasons. First, very little was known about her and I was afraid there would not be enough to make a whole thesis. Second, I did not want to suggest a female topic after two men had suggested meaty male topics. I knew what History Departments thought of 'hen scholars poring over *Godey's*

Lady's Book.' I decided to see if I could solve both of these problems by fleshing out Bérénice with Titus and her father and grandfather, Herod Agrippa and Herod the Great. The latter's policy on watery moles was bound to be an inspiration.

Next I went to the library to get my carrel assignment. The study nooks for graduate students, smaller versions of Herb's first alcove at Park Road, were on the top floor of the library. The room was blessedly quiet and deserted. My carrel was next to a half-moon partitioned window that faced east and got the cool morning light. The desk was a Formica slab bolted to the wall, which made me think of the stationary desks bolted to the floor in high school. I gazed around the partitioned little space and smiled. It seemed more like my first private room than the one I had in the dorm. I ran my hand along the bookshelf above the desk. I was going to like studying here.

I heard a chair scrape and turned around. A woman stood in one of the cubicles in the back of the room with her arm draped over the top of her partition. The sleeve of her white shirtwaist was rolled up to the elbow in a businesslike way but the arm was languidly, almost bonelessly Southern. Just then she moved, seeming to push herself off the partition with a conscious effort, and started up the aisle toward me. She looked slender even though she wore a gathered skirt, so the body under it must have been thin. Her hair was dark and wavy and twisted carelessly up on the crown of her head in a chignon from which a few strands escaped and straggled down. She was taller than I, and as she came closer I saw that she was older. She looked about twenty-seven.

It seemed to take her forever to get from her carrel to mine. Southerner she undoubtedly was but a repeating rifle, never. Her smile was slow and lazy, too, but her undernourished air did not extend to her teeth. They were strong, perfectly aligned, and as white as her cotton blouse.

'Hey,' she said.

It meant 'Hi.' Her eyes were dark grayish-green with golden flecks. I wondered what she put down when she filled out an application. She wore no makeup at all.

'Saw you get in a cab last night. I was going to carry you up to campus but you got away.'

I was still not used to 'carry' for 'drive' but her voice was as soft as velvet. I introduced myself and she responded with something that sounded like 'breast.'

'Beg pardon?'

She gave a resigned smile as though she had been through this many times before.

'B-R-E-S. Rhymes with dress. My mother's maiden name was Le Brés. Huguenot. We're from the Gulf.'

'Are you a graduate student?' I asked

'Graduate assistant. Classics. I got my master's last year. I'm doing independent reading this year.'

'You mean Latin and Greek?'

She nodded. 'But Latin's my specialty.'

It explained her oddly un-Southern, elliptical way of speaking. The military precision of Latin would necessarily eliminate the Mississippi daisy chain. I was terrifically impressed. As I tried to think of something ungulpy to say, she looked at her watch.

'Want to go get some coffee?'

The jukebox was playing 'Tom Dooley' when we entered the snack bar. It would continue to play all that year and become the song I afterwards associated with her, incongruous as it and she were. Several people gave her a quick glance and then looked speculatively at me. She continued on through the main part of the shop and led me to a smaller annex around a corner. I put my books down beside hers on the table she chose and we went to get our coffee.

'That's our section,' she said, jerking her head back toward the annex. 'It's known as the Poet's Corner. The campus cuties

and the meatheads always sit in the main section. It's called segregation,' she added with light irony.

I decided to test her. 'I call campus cuties malkins.'

She knew what it meant. 'Yes, they are that, but campus
cutie is a proper noun around here. Capitalized. An official
title. An award.'

'You're kidding.'

'No. The student newspaper picks a Campus Cutie of the
Week. Black.'

'What?'

'No, I mean the coffee.'

We returned to the table and I told her about my idea for a
thesis on Bérénice. Once again she picked up the intellectual
ball and ran with it – much farther than I could.

'Hmm. Not much to go on. Tacitus mainly. "*Titus reginam
Berenicem, cui etiam nuptias pollicitus ferebatur, statim ab Urbe
dimisit invitus invitam,*"' she quoted rapidly. Something that was
pure joy went through me. 'There's a little more in Dio Cassius,'
she continued. 'And the New Testament. Saint Paul met her.
Bet that was an interesting occasion.'

Two co-eds at a table at the end of the main section were
peering around the bend and staring at us. When I looked at
them, one smirked and jabbed the other with her elbow. They
whispered together and giggled. That's when I caught on.

'Do you live in a dorm, too?' I asked.

'No. Faculty Shacks. Apartments. Full-fledged faculty have
houses. Oh, here comes the Grope.'

She gave a slow-motion, flat-handed Jackie Gleason wave to
an assortment of people coming in the side door of the shop.
They were the other denizens of the Poet's Corner – Ole Miss's
handful of bohemians who had baptized themselves the Grope
for 'the Group.' Though I was to like all of them, at that
moment I would have gladly zapped them into dust. I wanted
Bres to myself.

Southern bohemians never quite make it. An embroidery hoop containing a half-finished sampler fell out of the Army B-4 that Sorella used for a book bag. Augustus carried in his chinos an heirloom pocketwatch with an inscribed lid. Lucius kept his place in *Tropic of Capricorn* with a strip of leather containing the tenet, 'I Know That My Redeemer Liveth.' The most startling evidence of conservative raffishness was provided by a girl my age named Vanny who launched into a complicated story about an experimental theater performance that was interrupted by a loud fart, which she archly called 'a fanfaronade of flatulence.' The surliness that marks artistic types striving for existentialism was totally absent as they acknowledged Bres's introduction; I was drowned in a sea of 'How do's.'

All of the Grope members were connected somehow to the English or Fine Arts departments; an instructor, a graduate assistant, and two fellows like me. There were three or four others who kept a foot in both worlds and sometimes sat in the mainstream section of the coffee-shop, but the hardcore Grope was before me now.

Bres was obviously their leader, and a few minutes' conversation revealed her as the only bona fide intellectual among them. They readily acknowledged it, deferring to her in almost obsequious ways that betrayed the depths of their cultural roots. The Old South had revered the civilizations of the ancient Mediterranean; it was why Southern mansions had Doric columns, why Ole Miss and several other Southern schools still offered a classics major, and why two young men in 1957 bore names like Augustus and Lucius. As a classical scholar, Bres was more truly Southern than the girls who called themselves belles, and the Grope knew it even if the campus cuties and meatheads did not.

Poet's Corner or not, the talk quickly turned to the subject that dominated Mississippi conversations at this time. The state was completely dry, so alcohol and where to get it obsessed everyone. For my benefit several legendary 'hooch run' stories were retold. The time Sorella hit a cow on her way back from the bootlegger's. The time Lucius made gin in the chemistry lab and 'evvrabody got dyreer.' The time a professor returned from Memphis 'with so much hooch in the trunk that the back bumper started draggin' and struck sparks and the gas tank blew up.' The time a federal employee at a Labor Department regional office used a government car to drive to the boot-legger's. 'Being a Yankee, he didn't know what seeing a government *anything* does to bootleggers, so 'fore he knew what happened, they shot out all four tires and had his pants down and were threatening to castrate him, and he was so scared he shit all over evvrabody.'

'Bres, tell about the time you found a jug of shine in Sardis Lake,' Vanny urged.

'Saw a rope, pulled it in, and there it was.' It sounded like *veni, vidi, vici*.

I learned about the unabashed 'Blackmarket Tax' that was actually on the Mississippi statute books so the state could make money off of the bootleggers it had officially outlawed. I was told that behind the WELCOME TO MISSISSIPPI signs one could expect to find lurking state troopers looking for cars with low trunks. I heard about the bootlegger who ran 'Johnny's Grocery' who became so undone by hypocrisy that he eventually came to believe he really was a grocer and started attending meetings of the Retail Food Merchants Association.

The strangest story they told me was about the local option situation over in the next county. Anyone with a powerful thirst could drive thirty miles to Batesville where there was a tavern that sold perfectly legal malt liquor. Not beer, malt liquor.

'Why malt liquor?' I asked.

Nobody knew. 'That's just the way it is,' Lucius said with a shrug.

It was an example of those recumbent QED's that so infuriate Northern liberals. Another is: 'It's always been that way.'

Suddenly I found myself dying for a drink. I was not much of a drinker at this time, and it was only mid-afternoon, but going to live in Mississippi was like being transported back to the 1920s: I wanted it because it was against the law to have it. The others evidently felt the same way; all had a parched, panting look. I was about to suggest a drive to Batesville when Augustus spoke up.

'Hey, I've got a jug of Thunderbird wine in my room. How about if we take it down to Bres's apartment and drink it?'

I had never drunk Thunderbird but like all city people, I was familiar with the vintage, having seen empty bottles bearing the label scattered in alleys. Bres agreed to the suggestion and we left the coffeeshop.

First, we had to stop by Augustus's dorm and stand watch while he brought out the jug in his laundrybag, surrounded, for authenticity's sake, by a bundle of his underwear. I expected to hear sirens closing in on us. It was a heartrending example of the sanctity of states' rights.

The six of us walked down to the well-named Faculty Shacks, tiny frame houses like beach cottages whose peeling exteriors evoked the old saying, 'Too poor to paint, too proud to whitewash.' Each little house was a separate apartment with its own driveway; Bres's contained a 1954 Ford with Pearl River County tags. She opened the door of the house and we trooped in.

The uncarpeted living room was like an oven. While she was in the kitchen getting ice, I looked around. The furniture consisted of two mattress-on-a-door couches facing each other and separated by a cable spool coffee table; the lamps had been made out of green wine jugs weighted with pebbles, and the bookcases from planks of lumber and cinder blocks. All in all, bohemian done to a turn.

She was fairly neat but not shockingly so; her slut's wool was coming along nicely and her window ledges contained that undisturbed layer of aristocracy to which I was accustomed. There were books everywhere, in and out of the bookcases, and an enormous collection of grant literature: prospecti and brochures on Fulbright-this and Guggenheim-that. Lucius noted my interest in them.

'If you want to know how to live on grants forever, ask ole Bres. Freighters to Europe, too. She's got the schedules memorized.'

It was exactly what I did want to know. I imagined the two of us living in Paris, studying at the Sorbonne and sharing a Left Bank garret. It was an easy dream to realize in the fifties; grant money fell like rain and Arthur Frommer was the Vagabond King.

Bres brought in the ice and we started drinking the awful wine. I could barely swallow it but everyone else lapped it up. Still thinking about the Southernness of classical studies, I ventured my opinion and asked the others what they thought.

Bres shook her head. 'That was true once but today's Misissippians wouldn't buy it. One way or another, Latin makes them mad.'

'Why?' I asked.

'Three reasons.' She shot a long index finger out of the relaxed curve of her fist. '*Primo*, it's Catholic, so the Baptists hate it. *Secundo*, it's *the* symbol of scholarship, so the anti-intellectuals hate it. *Tertio*, the campus cuties hate it because it has a reputation for being hard to learn, and that makes it unfeminine.'

She turned to me with the barest inquisitive glance. I had difficulty swallowing, but this time it had nothing to do with the wine.

'Actually, they're right for once,' she went on. 'It is unfeminine. It's ideal for writing military reports, which is what

Caesar's *Gallic War* is. The *g*'s and *c*'s are hard – the Church has ruined the real Roman pronunciation, you know? – and then there's that marvelous brevity. Southern women like to put things in, but Latin takes things out. Like "Where is the mirror?" *Ubi speculum est?* You don't need "the."'

Once again she looked at me. Her glance was wry at first, but as I held it her eyes widened with unmistakable meaning. Suddenly she put down her wineglass and raised graceful arms to her hair and began to reorder it in that half-abstracted, half-automatic way of women who wear their hair up, swiping at the nape of her neck to catch loose strands and tucking them into the chignon at the crown. As I continued to watch her, she removed a bobby pin and opened it with her teeth. There is no gesture more womanly, yet it has all the carelessness of a little girl who loses her sweaters and breaks her Thermos jars. Something melted inside of me, a hard tight ball in whose center lay a tenderness I had never acknowledged or expressed. I wanted to hug her, to pull her into my lap and rock her. When she smiled shyly up at me from under the bow of her bent arms, it was all I could do not to cry.

The ghastly wine was nearly gone. I had drunk only one glass but my tongue tasted like a Croatian army sock. I shuddered as the others drained their glasses in one gulp and smacked their lips appreciatively; evidently Mississippians would drink anything. Sorella suggested that we turn our afternoon into a night of serious drinking, and the Grope started discussing a gas station near Water Valley where, it was rumored, you could buy a pint of applejack. Not whiskey, applejack; not gin, applejack. It being impossible to telephone ahead and ask point blank if the gas station sold illegal hooch, they were willing to drive all the way down to Water Valley on the strength of this uncertain gossip.

Reluctantly, I looked at my watch. 'I'm on the desk tonight.'

'We'll make a hooch run when Florence can go with us,' Bres ruled, and the argument subsided at once.

We all went to the cafeteria instead. I should have been hungry but I could barely finish a hamburger. I had fallen in love at last.

14

A hooch run to Memphis was planned for the following Saturday. Meanwhile, all of us were busy with a new school year, so I did not see Bres alone for the rest of that week. I think she was letting it build up, and in a way I was glad. I had never known real yearning before and I had to admit there was nothing quite like it. It was completely different from the brutal anticipation I had felt with men. That was directly carnal but this was carnality once removed, lust's distant cousin whose genealogy keeps getting lost in the dense foliage of a tree chart. I daydreamed about her long fingers rising out of her fist *primo, secundo, tertio*; my mind took imaginary darts in her baggy shirtwaists like a little French dressmaker enjoying the occasional accidental pass. Not that I did not imagine her naked breasts and myself kissing them – that picture was constantly in my mind – but because we were both women, my thoughts kept returning to darts and tucks and loving exasperation: why in the *hell* did she buy blouses that were too big for her?

I did my best to concentrate on other things. Working as a dorm proctor gave me an ideal chance to study the classic Southern belle. My education began the night Tulaplee told me she wanted to be an actress and I asked her what role she would most like to play.

'Mildred Pierce's daughter. Ah think it's right for me.'

Her name was actually Tulip Lee, a fact I discovered when I saw the picture she drew in the sign-out book. It looked like a yellow twat with a green Tampax string hanging out of it. She liked to make her mark rather than write her name and had a four-color, twenty-four-carat gold mechanical pencil for this purpose – a gift from her daddy, she told me, who had taught her to sign herself this way back when she wasn't hardly old enough to hold a crayon.

Most of the space in the storage room was taken up by her trunks, and Daddy had paid for a triple room so she would have enough closet space. She had what looked like a Dickensian strongbox that turned out to be a portable file containing records of all her clothes on five-by-seven pastel index cards – when they were sent to the cleaners, when and where she had worn them last, comments received, and so forth. She used blue cards for dresses, green for skirts, yellow for coats, lavender for sweaters, and pink for evening gowns. The dress file, rather than homework, took up most of her study time. Seeing her at this massive labor was like coming upon Erasmus in drag.

Handling her calluhs made me feel like a maternity ward nurse saddled with expectant fathers. A boy would come in, ask me to 'please ma'am ring Tulaplee,' and the countdown would begin. The pendulum of the grandfather clock in the visitors' lounge ticked off ten minutes but no Tulaplee appeared. I gave her another ring. Ten more minutes passed but still no sign of her. Boy starts to sweat. The crunch of a breath mint. Tick-tock, tick-tock, tick-tock. Adam's apple bobs in small spasm. Wristwatch synchronized with grandfather clock. Diffident attempt to thumb through a magazine does not come off; magazine is upside down. Bony knee begins to jerk. Another breath mint. Boy accidentally crunches down on inside of cheek. Tick-tock, tick-tock, tick-tock.

At last, as the moon crept over the yardarm, there came

Tulaplee, flicking the lead buttons on her pencil. She was half an hour late right on the nose but her calluh had to wait still longer while she created her signature. Choking on silent screams of torment, he took surreptitious peeks at his watch while he listened for the click of her pencil that meant she had changed colors and started on the stem.

I had to hand it to her. The malkins I had known all lacked the courage to treat males so brutally. They were too afraid of being stood up or losing a boy's love, but Tulaplee had none of their insecurities. The idea of not being loved clearly had never occurred to her.

One night she came in ten minutes early and agreed to sit in the lounge with her date. It meant that she had agreed to neck, but as the boy lowered himself onto the sofa beside her she gave a cry of despair.

'Oh! Ah left my scarf in the car! Would you be a sugar-plum and run out and get it for me right quick?'

The boy hurried out the door. When he was gone, Tulaplee stuck her head around the office wall and gave me a conspiratorial wink.

'Ah didn't really forget it. Ah stuffed it down unda the seat on purpose. Ah wonda how long it'll take him to find it?' Suddenly she blew out her cheeks and made a squirty sound of repressed laughter through her stretched lips. 'Ah just love to send 'em on air-runds, don't you?'

It took me a second to realize she meant 'errands.' Her magnificent chocolate brown eyes glittered with sadistic joy. She looked so maniacal that I decided it was the better part of wisdom to agree with her.

'Keep 'em on the run,' I said.

She circled thumb and index finger and winked again. The boy returned too late to neck.

By the end of my first week at Ole Miss I could state with certainty that Tulaplee was not a malkin in any way, shape, or form. She was a cuddly barracuda; mad, bad, and dangerous to know, but she commanded respect. It's not often one meets a woman who is honest enough to compare herself to Veda Pierce.

I called home late Friday night. The three ladies of the house were getting ready for bed but Herb was entering his owl stage so I told him about the echolalia.

'Hmm. Compulsive repetition, eh? Most interesting.'

'What do you think causes it?'

In the background I heard Mama bellow, '*I don't own the phone company, I just work there!*'

'My ancestry is about to be defined in no uncertain terms,' he said quickly. 'We mustn't dally any longer. Besides, it's better if you piece these things out for yourself. I'll give you two hints. Do you remember the clipping Mrs Ruding gave you about how God made the Southern woman?'

'Who could forget it?'

'Righto. Now the second hint: do you remember the time I took you over to the Franciscan monastery and we heard the monks chanting?'

'. . . Yes, sort of. That was a long time ago. What do monks and monasteries have to do with Baptist women?'

'Just think about it. Cheerio.'

I tried to figure it out as I lay in bed but I could not concentrate. All I could think of was the whiskey run planned for the next day. The Grope was going, too, of course, but I knew Bres could get rid of them later if she wanted to, and I was sure she wanted to. So sure that I told Miz Arvella I might be away 'visitin" for the whole weekend. She beamed with extroverted Southern joy and told me – three times – that she was glad I had made friends so quickly.

We left at eleven in the morning, the four girls in Bres's car and Augustus and Lucius following behind. Most of the campus population must have decided to go to Memphis that day, too; the first familiar face I saw was Tulaplee's when she passed us on the road in her brand-new white T-Bird doing about seventy-five.

'She's goin' shoppin',' Sorella said. 'Dudden have a thang to wear.'

'You know who she is, don't you?' Bres asked me. 'Her daddy owns half the Delta. They say he still owns slaves.'

When we got to Memphis, Bres headed straight for the city's biggest liquor store. It was a drive-in but the parking lot was full, so we had to leave the cars several blocks away. In the store I saw the chairman of the History Department, the coach, a couple of clerks from the bursar's office, the public relations director, and the taxi driver who had carried me up to the dorm. The air was thick with familiar greetings and unabashed ecstatic smiles.

It was obvious that most of the Mississippi customers either knew nothing about liquor or, what was more likely, did not care what they bought as long as it had alcohol in it. As a bartender's daughter I knew, for example, that Dewar's Scotch, while not the most expensive, has the truest Highland flavor – i.e., smoky. I bought two fifths and tried to convince the Grope, but they would not listen. The idea was to get as much hooch as possible for the least amount of money; if it was light brown and under four dollars they would buy it even if the label said *Auld Eagle Piss*. The conversations I overheard were beyond belief. 'Ah lak to mix me some Morgan Davis wine in a l'il Sebben-Up . . .' 'My wife is a churchgoah so Ah put sloe gin in strawberry Kool-Aid and she don't know the difference . . .' 'You evva taste thet 'air cream dee coco? Sure beats vanilla extract.'

We left the store laden with brown bags. The worry set in at once. 'If we drop it, I'll just die,' Sorella moaned. 'Imagine what you'd feel like if you dropped it. Oh, I can't stand to think about it!' Other exiting customers were evidently in the throes of the same dread, clutching their bags like Roman mothers protecting their babes from Alaric's Goths and walking with their eyes on their feet. It was the Mississippi version of 'Step on a crack, break your mother's back.'

We put all of the purchases in Bres's car because it was well known that the state troopers waiting behind the border signs rarely stopped women. Next we wadded old blankets around the bags to keep them from breaking in the trunk. When that was done, Sorella began worrying that somebody would break into the parked car and steal the cache while we were eating lunch. Lest you are wondering, as I was, why we did not wait and go to the liquor store at the end of our Memphis excursion instead of at the beginning, the answer is simple: my new friends were afraid that Something Would Happen to keep us from getting to the store before it closed. As Vanny put it: 'Suppose we got run ovah and had to go to the hospital!'

Sorella's fear of hooch thieves infected Bres, so we unparked both cars and drove around town looking for a restaurant with big picture windows and parking spaces out front so we could watch the car while we ate. Passing Lowenstein's department store, we saw Tulaplee coming out the door with her arms full of dress boxes. When we stopped for a light, the occupants of the car beside us emitted a football cheer: 'Hotty-totty, gosh awmighty, who the hell are we? Ram! Bam! Grand! Slam! OLE MISS BY DAMN!' A cab driver leaned out his window and yelled, 'Bust 'Bama!' and the students responded with a chorus of 'Dixie.'

We finally found a restaurant that met our security requirements. After lunch we walked up to Confederate Park on the bluff and looked across the Mississippi River to Arkansas. I would have liked to stay longer and enjoy this breathtaking view, but they were all worried about the hooch, so we hurried back to the cars and set off on the seventy-five-mile drive back to Oxford.

As we approached the WELCOME TO MISSISSIPPI sign, conversation ceased and the atmosphere in the car grew tense. Bres, who was inclined to speed, slowed down, and Sorella began chewing on her thumbnail. Vanny alone showed true courage. Leaning forward over the back of the front seat, she offered us a piece of advice which proved that the gentle breast of Southern womanhood is the repository not only of hope, but of eternally springing resourcefulness.

'I heard about this girl who was stopped. They say she sucked his peckah, so he let her go without confiscatin' her hooch.'

'Ah oughta be a state troopah,' Bres murmured in an exaggerated drawl.

She got rid of the Grope. As we pulled into Faculty Shacks, she turned to the back seat and said, 'Florence and I have to discuss her thesis on Titus.' *Finis.* It proved that Kant gave us excellent advice when he said, 'Never complain, never explain.' Sorella and Vanny fairly leaped out of the car and signaled the boys behind us. Bres opened the trunk, the hooch was unswaddled and distributed, and the girls climbed in with Augustus and Lucius. The latter lived in a garage apartment on the edge of town so they decided to do their drinking there. As they drove off, I wondered how much they knew. One thing was certain: bohemian honor required them to be blasé about everything and Bres took full advantage of it.

We entered her house and went at once to the kitchen with the bags. This, I discovered, was standard Mississippi practice regardless of weather: after the hooch was comfortably settled, she went back and closed the front door. She had bought a plenteous if miscellaneous supply of potables, so we discussed what we would have. I offered my Dewar's.

She shook her head. 'You're in my house.'

I knew she would say it; I would have said it, too. A polite
Northerner would have made the same refusal, but not with
'You're in my house.' The idiom forged a pleasant Southern
bond, and lowered the sexual tension that had throbbed
between us in the car. We were hostess and guest now, tem-
porarily caught up in the minuet of hospitality to the exclusion
of all else. I had to admit it was convenient; ritual behavior
soothes the nerves.

'How about martinis?' she suggested.

'Fine.' I paused, remembering the overheard conversations in
the liquor store. 'Would you like me to mix them?' I asked casually.

'No, you just go on in and sit down.'

That was Southern, too, but it forged no bond, just triggered
visions of Kool-Aid, leftover coffee, and Vicks cough syrup. I
went into the living room and sat down on one of the mattress-
and-door couches. In a moment Bres came in with the ice
bucket – a steel scrub bucket that was saved from being the one
she used to scrub the floor only because she never scrubbed
the floor – and a sloshing plastic picnic jug full of martinis.
There was a little spigot on the jug like an appointment on a
miniature sink. The two glasses she held pinched between
thumb and forefinger were what were then called lowballs and
are known now as on-the-rocks. They were big enough for
triple Old Fashioneds, and still showed traces of peeling mar-
malade labels. In Mississippi the important thing is hooch, not
bar equipment.

She shoveled her hand in the ice bucket and scooped out
some cubes, dumped them in the glasses, and held each glass
under the spigot until it was full to the rim. There were no
olives, lemon peel, or pearl onions. She handed me my drink
and we clicked glasses and drank.

'How is it?'

Not like Father used to make. 'Perfect.'

Soon, very soon, my lie became the truth. Martinis are like that, especially when shared with someone whose name you have whispered to yourself just for the magic of its sound. We had executed the requisite hospitality step and now the tension rose again. Her slate green eyes were the strangest color and, I was certain, twice as big as mine; optically speaking, I was an A cup and she was a C.

'How do you like living in a freshman dorm?'

'It sounds like Mr Rochester's attic.'

She grinned and I was pathetically grateful. It was wonderful to make a casual literary reference and know that she would pick up on it. My life with my own sex had been an endless parade of puzzled, frowning faces saying, 'Huh? What do you mean?'

Suddenly I thought of the arcane clues Herb had scattered over the echolalia mystery. Bres would be an ideal detective to assign to the case. I described the thrice-told tales. She hooted with laughter and delivered a perfect imitation of Miz Arvella that was nonetheless uniquely Bres.

'Ah said to Cataline, Ah said Cataline Ah said, you got to stop messin' with our mores, 'deed you have, that's what Ah tole him.' She took a big swig of martini and shook her head. 'They all do it. My mother does it, too. Ashley Montagu said it was hysteria caused by racial tension, but there must be a few things down here that are caused by something else. What does your father think?'

I repeated Herb's clues. Her eyes sharpened when I mentioned Granny's clipping.

'Is that the piece that goes ". . . all heaven veiled its face, for lo, He had wrought the Southern girl"?'

'Yes! Do you know it?'

'Know it? Honey, it was one of our boys that wrote it. Some stump politician back when I was in high school. He put it in a speech he made and it caused a sensation. Everybody wanted a copy, so he had batches printed up and gave 'em out all over the state. Lord, every picture framer in Jackson was going crazy! All the girls in my school got one for Christmas – my mother hung mine over my bed just like a crucifix. Then the wallet-sized copies turned up and all the fathers started carrying them around next to their hearts. I'm not surprised that it ended up in the Daughters' magazine, it was reprinted everywhere. It even got in *The Mississippi Hog Farmer*.'

Our glasses were empty. She threw some more ice in them and held them under the spigot.

'How does it tie in with the monks?' I asked.

She smiled, and swayed gently back and forth, sing-songing in a rich contralto: 'Mystical rose . . . *Ora pro nobis* . . . Mother of Hope . . . *Ora pro nobis* . . . Star of the Sea . . . *Ora pro nobis*.' She looked at me questioningly.

My memory stirred. 'That's what the monks were chanting!'

'It's the Litany of the Virgin. You could replace any one of those lauds with a description of the Southern woman from the clipping and it wouldn't sound any different. Try it,' she challenged.

'Rose's ruby heart . . .'

'*Ora pro nobis* . . .'

'Lily's petal . . .'

'*Ora pro nobis* . . .'

'Star-strewn vicissitudes . . .'

'*Ora pro nobis* . . .'

I had to be drunk if I was singing, but I hardly felt the gin, so intoxicating was the intellectual puzzle that was falling into place.

'Repetitive speech comforts people,' I began, 'but the Baptist Church has no litanies. Henry Adams was right. The American woman does have to invent her own feminine ideal, and the problem gets worse the further south you go. The Maryland woman *is* Catholic, so she's already got the Virgin. The Virginia woman is Episcopalian, which helps some because the Episcopal Church is soft-shell Catholic. But Deep South women don't have any Virgin at all, so they keep saying everything over and over – it's a way of saying rosaries to themselves.'

I felt so triumphant that I drained my glass in one gulp. Bres poured us yet another and we toasted Henry Adams.

'There's one thing I can't figure out,' I went on. 'Where does Bérénice fit in? A Jewish woman would have to reject both Virgin and Venus because they represent alien religious and political enemies, yet Berenice had no female identity problems. Do you suppose Jewish women have some kind of secret?'

'I don't know about that, but I can tell you about Bérénice. She was the third V. She was a virago.'

I stopped my glass at my lips. 'Oh, come on, she wasn't a bitch.'

'Virago has come to mean bitch because people prefer to forget what it really means,' Bres said softly. 'The first definition the dictionary gives is the right one: "a woman of great stature, strength and courage who is not feminine in the conventional ways." It comes from the Latin *vir* meaning male.'

I wondered how eyes already so huge could grow still bigger, then I understood. It was because they were coming closer. I tasted gin – mine, hers, ours, in a kiss of warm lips and cold tongues. My first thought was how soft her mouth was compared to a man's. I did not have a second thought. The best description of what happened next can be found in the Book of Revelation, in the verse that describes the end of the world and predicts that 'the sky shall roll up like a scroll.' I have always believed that St John the Divine could not have written this apt line unless, at some point in his career, he had drunk too many martinis, because that is exactly what it feels like when they hit.

My blouse was unbuttoned and Bres's fingers were loosening my bra strap. My breast came free and she cupped her hand around it. I put my head on the back of the bolster and waited for the dizziness to pass, telling myself that it would surely pass, that it was just momentary. If only I kept perfectly still, everything would be all right.

My stomach issued its final warning just as she took my nipple into her mouth. Lurching to my feet, I zigzagged into the bathroom not a moment too soon. The last thing I remembered was the pain that coursed through my knees when they hit the hard tile floor in front of the toilet.

I came to on the bathroom floor with my head on a dusty shower rug. After a moment or two I remembered what had happened and cringed in mortification. Getting stiffly to my feet, I stuffed my breast back into my bra, rinsed my mouth, and went out to the living room to apologize to a scornful, disgusted Bres.

But she was beyond scorn or disgust, passed out on the couch with her long graceful arm dangling on the floor in that same bonelessly Southern way I remembered from our first meeting. I aimed for the other couch, landed on it, and passed out for the second time. The lights were still on. When I awoke some indeterminate time later they were off and there was a light cotton blanket over me. My mouth was as dry as flannel. Staggering up, I felt my way over to the coffee table and drank the melted ice out of the bucket, then crashed back down on the couch.

The third time I awoke it was early morning and Bres was standing beside me with a bubbling, fizzing Alka-Seltzer. I took it in two shaking hands and chugalugged it.

'Child, child,' she murmured, stroking my hair back from my forehead. She wore a long chenille robe and smelled warm and soapy.

I handed her the empty glass and looked at her ruefully.

'I'm sorry,' I mumbled.

She shrugged. 'Everybody throws up.'

'You're just saying that to make me feel better.'

'There's no reason to try and make you feel better. Why, you're practically a Yankee when it comes to getting sick. All you did was throw up. You should have seen Vanny the time she mixed the wintergreen alcohol in the fermenting peach juice and—'

'Please don't tell any of those stories.'

'—had fits. I'll get you some tomato juice.'

She returned with the juice and I chugalugged again.

'I slept in my clothes,' I said disgustedly, flapping my arms. 'I feel all sticky.'

'I'll run you a bath. I just had one.'

She seemed so matter-of-fact that I suspected her of not remembering last night. Was it possible? No, I decided. She was a Mississippian; she could stick a straw in a gas tank and drain it dry without turning a hair. If she did remember, was she planning to pick up where we left off?

'There's a terrycloth robe on the back of the door,' she called over the rushing water, 'and some Ivory Flakes so you can wash out your things.'

The girlish euphemism for underwear sounded bizarre tripping off a tongue that had licked my nipple. I picked up my handbag – I had optimistically packed my toothbrush in anticipation of an overnight stay – and went into the bathroom. I brushed my teeth, washed out my underwear and stockings, and got into the tub. In a few moments the steam joined forces with the Alka-Seltzer and tomato juice to make me feel almost human.

When I was stretched out in sybaritic glory, the door opened and Bres came in with a sweating mug of beer.

'Ice cold. Best thing for a hangover.'

Sitting on the edge of the tub, she held the mug to my lips. As I drank, I looked at the place where her robe had gaped open and saw something that made me remember the famous line from *Auntie Mame*: 'Agnes, you *do* have a bust! Where on earth have you been keeping it?'

When I finished the beer, she put the mug on the toilet seat lid and proceeded to take up where we had left off.

In the South, Sunday morning sex is accompanied by church bells. Ole Miss had a carillon; we were serenaded with 'In the Garden,' 'Shall We Gather at the River?' and, later in the afternoon, a terrestrial medley that included the old temperance song, 'Lips That Touch Liquor Shall Never Touch Mine.'

There were other regionalisms to cope with. Bres confessed that she had received several anonymous phone calls the previous year and two more already this year. She explained that the White Citizens Council had reputedly recruited student operatives to spy on people and report any political irregularities. According to the tenets of Mississippi logic, what we had just done automatically made us 'niggah-lovin' Jew Communists.'

She took my hand. 'We'd better not spend any more nights together. Daytime is better, they never call then. They seem to think that nobody would make love except at night.'

She leaned over me and blew on the line of sweat that had formed between my breasts, and I returned the favor. We lay apart in the afternoon heat, trying to cool off.

'How did you know about me?' I asked.

'Oh, something about the way you were looking at your carrel, caressing the desk and all.' A chuckle crept into her voice. 'You were making love to that tight little space. Then later on in the coffeeshop, something came over you when you talked about Bérénice, a kind of glow. I figured if you fell in love with a woman who's been dead for two thousand years, the odds were in my favor.'

We stayed in bed until it began to grow dark. Bres drove me back to the dorm and thereafter we met in the daytime. I suffered no coming-out trauma; Bres, who had come out at sixteen, said she hadn't either. Our reactions were not unusual. Southern women tend to go completely to pieces after a homosexual experience and have to be 'put away,' or else we take it eerily in stride. The middle ground, as in so many other Southern reactions, simply does not exist. In both extremes the joker in the deck is the South's worship of femininity. Viewed through this lens, Lesbianism can emerge as conventional behavior. I doubt if there is any other place in the world where eating pussy makes a woman feel like just plain folks.

In short, I was happy, but of course that didn't stop me from trying to analyze my happiness. I wanted to know why I had turned to Lesbianism, but when I tried to engage Bres in group therapy, she wouldn't play.

'My mother wanted a boy,' I threw out.

'All mothers want boys, unless they already have two or three. Then they say, "It would be nice to have a girl."'

'I have a passive father and an aggressive mother.'

She shrugged lazily. 'Who doesn't?'

It was *finis* time. For all her intellectualism, she took a dim view of hypotheses. Analytical meandering irritated her; the classical rigor of her Latin-trained mind rejected the loose construction of speculative thinking in much the same way as the legal mind scorns imagination. She had analyzed Herb's echolalia clues only because they had to do with Latin; otherwise, she was one of the period-paragraph people. She balked at looking into herself. She was a Lesbian because she was a Lesbian. *Finis*.

Actually, she was right; her 'Who doesn't?' was an accurate two-word social history of every advanced civilization. America was full of passive fathers and aggressive mothers, but whatever was happening to their sons, their daughters continued overwhelmingly to turn out heterosexual. Therefore, my Lesbianism had some other cause. Once I dispensed with Freudian clichés, I began to understand what it was.

Lesbianism is a mirror-image, and most women do not wish to contemplate themselves in anything but a looking glass. When malkins said, 'I'd die if a woman touched me,' they were telling the truth. The enhanced self was their nemesis, but it was the staff of life for Bres and me. Neither of us could accept diminishment. The ego of the female is rarer than the male's but much deadlier, and we both had one. We needed the I-ness of Lesbianism, the unbroken circle of self in which she was me, I was her, and we were us.

Though I entered into our affair knowing perfectly well what two women 'do,' I was unprepared for the intense physical passion we had. Thanks to the silence surrounding the subject of Lesbianism in Lesbian novels, I had imbibed the quaint but very common assumption that Lesbians skipped eroticism per se and took off for fastidious realms of ethereality where grunts and groans were never heard and lubrication turned into some sort of Grecian nectar.

Bres became an entirely different woman in bed, exchanging her mannered complexity for a rural directness and turning country-girl hot in a way that is uniquely Southern. In fact, she turned just plain lewd and it was wonderful because it implied no threat. There are no trashy women in Lesbianism and hence no ladies either. The nagging worries that go with the heterosexual territory (Does he try *that* with other women? What will he think if I ask him to stick his finger up my ass?) never came between us. We could let ourselves go.

We tried Sixty-Nine a few times but neither of us liked it. Since no two people ever come simultaneously, I felt it had all the disadvantages of intercourse: a tendency to concentrate selfishly on one's own pleasure, a loss of enthusiasm by the one who finishes first, and a fear of taking too long. When I said this to Bres she agreed and confessed to another objection as well.

'It reminds me of Uncle Antoine.'

'You mean he . . . molested you that way?'

'Oh, no,' she said airily. 'But he does parlor tricks. He's always demonstrating how he can write with both hands at once, and pat his head and rub his stomach at the same time.'

Taking turns making love to each other satisfied our need to experience total aggression and total passivity with no fear of settling permanently into either condition. It's something heterosexual lovers would like to do but can't. I always felt silly whenever I got on top of Ralph, but when Bres's thighs were locked in the vise of my elbows, I really was in charge; yet when we changed places and she did the doing, I could let down my guard and wallow in submission without worrying that she would get 'the wrong idea.'

I had to admit I missed being fucked. Bres, who had slept with a man out of curiosity, said she liked it, too. We did our best with what we had but finger-fucking is inadequate even when you do it with someone you love. There is another problem for two women unless both of you are nail-biters, and neither of us was. Bres enjoyed it more than I did because she did not associate it with dates and fraternity boys, but every time she went inside me I could hear Faysie babbling, 'I mean, it's *okay* because we're pinned!'

We had a few wistful discussions about getting a dildo but they were not sold openly then. Undoubtedly they were covertly available if you knew where to look, but we didn't, and in any case, no Mississippi resident would have had the strength to embark on such a search. Considering what we had to go through to buy hooch, God only knows what buying a dildo would have involved.

As for other foreign objects, we never used them.

> *Candles melt*
> *Carrots are tough*
> *Bottles can hurt you*
> *You might as well muff.*

On a more mundane level, I decided that Lesbianism saved time, energy, and money. Had Bres been a man, I would have gone shopping at once for some new 'things,' mostly black lace things. I had done it at the beginning of the summer when I decided to go after Ralph; every woman does it when she starts an affair with a new man, but now I did not have to. The hassle of romance, the harried, exhausting, distracting, dashing-down-town, color-coordinating, sets-of-three *shit* of romance (what malkins call 'the fun part') vanished from my life. Women do not vamp each other, and in any case, Bres's underwear looked as if it should have been stamped LAMBETH WORKHOUSE, so I did not have to worry about mine.

The major drawback was, of course, coping with two men-strual periods. The good news is that my cramps went away; the bad news is that we never managed to fall off the roof at the same time.

One such day, Bres, who did not like tampons, came into the bedroom wearing plain white cotton underpants with san-itary belt and pad underneath. She always felt especially sexy during her period, so when she finished making love to me, I pulled her across me and played with her nipples while she rubbed herself against my knee. She came quickly and sprawled, panting, across the bed, her hair tumbled and her cheeks flaming.

She looked the picture of Woman incarnate, as gloriously feline and sensual as a long, dangerous cat, yet suddenly I had an overwhelming urge to protect and shield her. It was the white cotton pants with the menstrual harness showing through; they made her look so inexpressibly dear and vulner-able that I thought my heart would break. In that moment she was my little girl, and the fierce tenderness welling up inside me was the maternal instinct I thought I had been born with-out.

'It's getting dark,' she said. 'The phone calls . . .'

At the tremor in her voice, fear wove through me, a special Mississippi fear I had never expected to have. Fear of cars slowing down, stopping, doors slamming – the fear of night. Until now, night had been Herb time, book time, best time, but now it was fear time because Bres and I were nigger-loving Jew Communists.

15

Having found my Bérénice in the flesh, I applied myself to my thesis with lover-like concentration and soon had almost as many note cards as Tulaplee had dress cards. An interesting commonality, because sometime near the end of October the biographer of the world's foremost Jewish princess entered into a conspiracy with Ole Miss's foremost Southern belle.

One night while I was on the proctor's desk, I heard Tulaplee screeching. Hardly an unusual occurrence, but this time she was screeching about an academic matter.

'They let me in conditionally 'cause Ah flunked French in high school, and now Ah'm gonna flunk it again and get expelled and Ah won't get to be a Campus Cutie or join a sorority and Ah'll die, Ah'll just die, Ah'll just fall down dead!'

She was taking what amounted to Remedial French, except that it had a more tactful name. Her classmates were other freshman girls like herself, their freshman male equivalents, and a few members of the football team. The text was a paperback with a title like *French Without Tears*.

'We got to put these ole things in French!' she shrieked, waving a mimeographed sheet. 'She's gonna give us one a week and that's gonna be the grade! She said we could use the dictionary, but what good is that when Ah don't know how to do those funny things that keep changin'?'

I presumed she meant verbs. Catching her eye, I signaled her over to the desk and asked to see the exercise. It was slightly above the *plume de ma tante* level. Taking out a sheet of notebook paper, I began writing rapidly while Tulaplee leaned over my shoulder in openmouthed awe.

'Ah don't believe it . . . Ah'm dreamin' . . . you are not of this world . . . Ah can't believe ma eyes!'

I handed her the finished translation. 'Now listen,' I said, 'I've done this exactly right but don't *you* do it exactly right – make a few deliberate mistakes.'

She circled thumb and forefinger in her now-familiar gesture and gave me her conspiratorial wink.

'Bring me the others as you get them and I'll do them for you.'

'Lawd . . . Oh, Lawd, Ah just don't know how to thank you!'

'Quietly,' I suggested. She nodded vigorously, winked again, and scurried upstairs.

On her next shopping trip to Memphis she brought me back a bottle of Guerlain's Mitsouko. Not a phial, a bottle. She proffered it literally under the counter as I sat at the proctor's desk, but this time her Medici wink did not quite come off. There was a note of shyness in her manner and it was ingratiating.

'Ah'm partial to White Shoulders myself, but Ah gave it a good deal of thought and Ah decided that this is more you. Ah hope you like it.'

I was touched. My first sniff renewed my faith in Mississippi tastes: they knew a lot more about perfume than they did about hooch.

Soon it was time for the Homecoming dance. Tulaplee's preparations began with the arrival of her father's chief henchman, a Lee Marvin look-alike with an undeniable overseer's air, who drove up from the Delta to hand-deliver a black velvet box containing the triple-strand pearl necklace that had been in the family for generations. It had the usual history centering around poker games, honor and dishonor, and houses in flames. The henchman arrived in a Tulip Enterprises, Inc. truck with a full gun rack in back. He delivered the heirloom into Tulaplee's hands, made arrangements to pick it up at nine the next morning, and repaired to the Rebel Motel for his vigil. If anything happened, Tulaplee was to call him at once.

I know what you're thinking, but it didn't happen. If this were a novel I could invent a Maupassant 'n' magnolia tragedy of errors starring a freaked-out good ole boy, but it isn't. Tulaplee did not lose the necklace, nobody got shot, and the henchman spent what was, for the Rebel Motel at least, a quiet night.

Here is what did happen:

Tulaplee arrived back from the dance fifteen minutes early and agreed to sit in the lounge with her date. As he lowered himself onto the sofa beside her, she gave a cry of despair.

'Oh! Ah left ma gloves in the car! Would you be an angel and run out and get 'em for me right quick?'

Hard-on with boy behind it rushes out door. Merciless cackle from depths of sofa. Tick-tock, tick-tock, tick-tock. Glove-bearer returns.

'Lookit all that ole black dirt on ma gloves!'

The boy began a stammering apology but Tulaplee cut him off and started laying into him for something that had happened at the dance. Shrieking, screeching, cawing she went, a Bird of Purgatory rending balls for breakfast.

I crept into the foyer just in time to witness the finale. The boy was coming apart; shaking, sweating, blubbering like a senile old man in the face of her unearthly rage.

'Langston Bob Treadwell, Ah banish you! You are banished! You are *gone*!'

'Tulaplee, Ah—'

Her head jerked up and her eyes widened to Theda Bara proportions.

'What's that? Are you talkin'? How come you're talkin'? Don't you know you can't talk anymore? You're banished! You can't talk if you're not there, and you are not *there*!' Raising her slim white arm, she pointed her taloned finger into his pasty face. 'Ah heahby poah acid on you! Ah melt you! You have ceased existin'! You're just a l'il ole grease spot on that rug! You are gone, Ah tell you, *gone*!'

She spun on her heel and stormed upstairs, her tulle skirts flouncing behind her. The dorm shook as she slammed her door. Just then the clock struck twelve.

'You have to go now, Langston,' I said. It sounded so inadequate.

The dorms remained open over the brief Thanksgiving holiday so I did not go home. Neither did the other out-of-state Southerners. In part our decision to stay put was based on practical considerations of limited time and holiday travel crowds, but only in part. The real reason was the subconscious Southern feeling that Thanksgiving is a Yankee holiday. Granny's generation was the last to say it out loud but the idea had not yet died.

Bres and the Grope were all having parent trouble, so they did not go home, either. We spent the day drinking in her apartment. The conversation centered almost exclusively on grants and freighters to Europe. With the Grope clustered worshipfully at her feet – they were inveterate floor-sitters – she held forth on the gentle art of separating philanthropists from their money. Despite her ivory tower rarefaction I detected a touch of the con artist in her makeup. Raised by an hysterical mother to be a belle, she had emerged from the fray with a bizarre gift for flirting with foundations. She was not greedy on a grandiose scale, wanting only enough to live a decently comfortable life of the mind, but she had a way of making herself everyone's favorite project. The late model car, for instance, was a demonstrator that had been given to her free by her brother-in-law, who had a Ford dealership. She never poormouthed, but rather presented herself as a gentlewoman in distress and let it be known that she was ready to receive her sponsors.

'Tell about the boy who went to Spain and never came back,' Vanny urged her.

This was Vanny's favorite story and she always requested it like a child who refuses to go to sleep until she hears a certain nursery rhyme recited in a certain way. It was about a graduate student in fine arts who went to Spain to catalogue the contents of the Escorial and never stopped. He was still at it after five years, and his grant had been renewed each year with a learned paper on some Philip II artifact – a sword, a vase, a wine goblet. He lived on two dollars a day and a Eurailpass, and when not cataloguing he rode around on trains getting to know 'the real people.' The journal he kept was the basis of some other grant he had just won.

All of Bres's stories involved someone who was writing an article, or sketching, or doing surveys in youth hostels or under bridges with a supporting cast of 'the real people.' That these same real people would have been designated immediately as 'trash' in the South was a reality the Grope chose to ignore, just as they chose to ignore their own thoroughly Southern orientation that lay just under the surface of their artsy exterior.

They were committed one hundred percent to *la vie de bohème*, but try as I might, I could not entirely share their enthusiasm. I liked the idea of living in Paris and wearing black turtleneck sweaters, but the more I heard about the joys of existing on rutabagas and stale bread dipped in wine, about the unadorned naturalness of squatting over a wire grate ('That's why Americans are constipated – they sit!'), and the bracing simplicity of a weekly sponge bath, the more bourgeois I felt myself becoming. When I boiled it down to the basics, I did not see how one could be a fully relaxed Lesbian without an American bathroom.

Bres was in a sexy mood that day. While we were in the kitchen making grilled cheese sandwiches, she asked me to spend the night with her.

'What about the anonymous phone calls?'

'They've stopped. Anyhow, it's different on a holiday, everybody has company then.'

I would have risked anything for that sleep of tangled legs, but I was scared. I was still not used to the Deep South's exquisite balance between hatred and hospitality. Making love in a ground-floor bedroom in Mississippi reminded me of *The Lady – Or the Tiger?* It would have been no more surprising to look up from Bres's twat and see a shotgun coming through the window than to see a smiling face saying, 'Hey, how y'all doin'?'

Because I expected death, that Thanksgiving night shines in my memory as a festival of lubricity. The old adage about danger enhancing sexuality is all too true, and the reason why Southerners are so horny. Much has changed now; liquor is in and racism, at least the blood-and-thunder kind, is out, but old-time religion is still flourishing and those black velvet nights are still ominous. I have a feeling that Mississippi is still the best place to be a consenting adult, and might even be our national G-spot. Just press Jackson and every woman in America will come.

The dorms closed over Christmas. I did not want to go home because I hated travel crowds, I could not afford the fare, and because there was no point to it. My family never paid much attention to Christmas except for eggnog. We had put up a few trees when I was very small but that was about it. Somehow the Yuletide spirit never seemed to penetrate the din made by the

Different Drummer Corps that marched back and forth across the parade grounds of our minds. Even Jensy was lukewarm about Christmas, considering it excessively festive and deficient in that bleak aura of sin she so enjoyed during Lent.

Bres could not go home because she had been declared officially dead. With one mother sitting Presbyterian *shivah* and the other yelling 'Hark the herald angels shit!' out the window at the carolers, there was no reason why we should not spend the Christmas holiday together. Neither of us particularly wanted to hang around the deserted campus for ten days, however, so Bres came up with a plan.

We'll visit the Darnay sisters. They own a motel near Vicksburg and make candy for a store in New Orleans. I have a standing invitation. I lived with them for four months when I was waiting for the Mary Margaret McChester Fund to come through.'

'What are they like?'

'In their fifties. They've been lovers since high school.'

'Sisters?'

'They're not blood sisters, and their name isn't really Darnay. It started years ago when they first moved to Vicksburg. They hired this gal to help with the candy-making, but she was a little simple and couldn't get their names straight. Instead of saying she was working for Miss Ella Darnell and Miss Pauline Naylor, she came out with "Darnay." Well, it spread through shacktown the way everything like that does, and before long all the colored thought that Ella and Pauline were sisters. The white people heard their maids talking about the Darnay sisters, so they picked it up, too. It made a good name for the motel, short and easy to remember, so they had the sign repainted, and now everybody calls them the Darnay sisters.'

She made a phone call that was received with Southern hosannas audible all the way across the room. Seated on the couch I heard, 'Y'all come right on down and stay as long as you want!' A grant from the Dixie Foundation.

We drove down to Vicksburg the next day. The Darnay Motel was actually a cluster of tourist cabins in a semicircle behind a larger house that served as home, office, and confectionary. Located on a back road in a small town some fifteen miles from the city, it was the kind of place that would not get many guests except in summer or during Civil War remembrance functions. There were no cars in front of the cabins.

As soon as we pulled up, the Darnay sisters spilled out of the house to greet us. I don't know what I was expecting – Colette and Missy, perhaps, or Radcliffe and Lady Una, but I was not expecting the Darnay sisters. That's exactly what they looked like: plump, rosy Southern maiden ladies in fingerwaves and print dresses who needed nothing but dead husbands to qualify as Ole Miss housemothers.

Never underestimate the power of Southern Lesbians to make just as much noise as any other Southern women. The Darnay sisters started talking simultaneously and we all surged into the house. My next surprise was their decor. My own ideal living room would have featured leather sofas and a ship's hatch coffee table. I sought this kind of solidity in the Darnay living room but found instead a furbelow factory in the grip of an imminent epiphany. Although the motel fronted on piney woods, they had a pink artificial Christmas tree. The furniture was covered in velour pastels that matched the Darnay bonbons: pink, yellow, and mint green, like Tulaplee's pencil. Everything else in the room was glass – tabletops, lamps, candlesticks, even the pictures on the wall were unframed sheets of glass bearing silhouettes of eighteenth-century figures chasing each other through gardens. Glass candy jars full of bonbons sat everywhere.

Looking into the kitchen, I saw a black woman stirring a huge kettle. The whole house smelled like hot sugar and boiling syrup. The bridge of my nose started to throb. I excused myself and went to the bathroom, and of course you know what I found: rosebuds of soap in glass jars, bath-oil balls in glass jars, book matches in glass jars, a toilet swathed in pink fur, a shower curtain with a valance, and hoop-skirted dolls concealing extra rolls of toilet paper.

I thought my first all-Lesbian social occasion would be marked by mutual awareness, a sense of freemasonry, some sort of verbal shorthand to indicate that we were all on the *qui vive*. I wanted silent acknowledgement, sly, clever allusions, and a little gruff humor. In short, I expected the Darnay sisters to be matey. That's what I expected. This is what I got:

When I returned to the living room, they were talking about some woman they knew who had refused to move from a condemned house.

'. . . and then the floor just opened up and swallowed huh,' said Miss Ella.

'She would have been killed if the cellar hadn't been flooded,' said Miss Pauline. 'The water was up to huh neck and she couldn't swim a stroke. It was just pitch black and there she was, just beside huhself with feah. She felt huhself startin' to drown, but just then an old chair floated by so she grabbed hold of it.'

The black woman shouted from the kitchen. 'It was de leaf f'um de dinin' room table, Miss Pauline.'

'Oh, that's right. So she floated ovah to the winda and tried to open it but she couldn't, it bein' stuck, you know what Ah mean, so she felt around in the darkness for somethin' to break it with and she found this old huntin' horn up on top of a chifforobe. It was an antique.'

'The chifforobe?' asked Bres.

'No, the huntin' horn. Her great-great-grandfather won it in England in 1820 in a race meet—'

'No'm, he dint win it, some dook give it to him when he was ober dar huntin' wid de Inglish peepuls and de dook's wife she fall off an' break her laig an' he carried her back to de big house an' de dook wuh so grateful he give him de horn.'

'Oh, that's right. But what was it he won? Ah just know he won somethin' . . . Ah declare, my memory is goin', it's just goin'. It's my time of life, Ah reckon. It's got to come to all of us someday.'

'Did she summon help by blowing the horn?' Bres asked.

'Oh, no, she didn't have the strength to get any sound out of it, she just broke the winda with it and started screamin' for somebody to rescue huh.'

'Screamed huhself hoarse,' said Miss Ella. 'But they finally came, and you know what? When they pulled huh outta there, huh hair had turned completely white.'

'Overnight,' sighed Miss Pauline.

At no time during our stay did our hostesses indicate by word or glance that the four of us had anything unusual in common. I suspected they were not Lesbians at all but merely partners in what the Victorians had called a 'Boston marriage' – an unconsummated relationship that never goes beyond hugging and kissing – but Bres said no. The woman who had seduced her when she was sixteen had known them for years and knew for a fact that they were full-fledged lovers.

They shared a room with twin beds and gave Bres and me another. We got in with each other a couple of times but it was not very satisfactory because I was afraid the sisters would hear us. *Glick-blick-sloosh* sounded exactly like the candy cauldron when it really got going, and they might think they had left the stove on and the latest batch was about to burn up.

Bres also said that they knew about her, and therefore about us, but I didn't believe it. I don't think they knew about themselves. Somewhere along the line they had actually become the Darnay sisters in their own minds.

16

Whatever the Darnay sisters did or did not do in bed, they had lived together most of their lives and were obviously happy. Driving back to Oxford after our visit with them, I was caught up in envious yearning. I wanted to be with Bres forever, but now I realized that 'forever,' at least that part of it that was my year at Ole Miss, was narrowing rapidly.

'It's January, almost a new semester,' I said with a frown. 'The year's half over.'

I was counting in scholar's fashion on a calendar divided into semesters and seasonal breaks. Having been in school for seventeen of my twenty-two years, it was now the way I measured time. September was the first month of the year and June was the last, and summer was a limbo to be spent working at a temporary job in what Bres and the Grope called 'the outside world.'

'June will be here before we know it,' I went on.

She reached for my hand and put it in her lap. 'As Babbitt said in the commencement speech, "Tempers fidgit."'

She was referring to an actual speech by a rich but ignorant alumnus whose attempt to say *Tempus fugit* had thrown the Classics Department into hysterics the previous year. But time did fly, and now it was no laughing matter.

'What's going to happen in June? I can't just leave you and go back to Washington.'

'I didn't expect you would,' she replied, squeezing her thighs around my hand. The car slowed for a second.

'But, Bres, I'm running out of money. I brought four hundred dollars with me from Washington, and now it's almost gone and I have no way of earning more. People on fellowships aren't allowed to work for the university, and there aren't any jobs in Oxford. Besides, fellowships aren't renewable. To stay at Ole Miss another year, I'd have to get a graduate assistantship, and they don't pay much more than fellowships. Even proctoring the dorm, it still wouldn't be enough. Anyhow, an assistantship wouldn't start until September, so that still leaves the summer to worry about.'

'Apply for a foundation grant,' she advised.

It was her answer to every problem, and I could not get anything more out of her. It was *finis* time. Three weeks after we returned to campus, it was final exam time as well, so I had to put my money worries aside for the moment and concentrate on racking up straight A's to keep the university fellowship I already had. I felt like a squirrel on a treadmill, but I told myself that this was the way academic life worked.

During exam week, Bres switched carrels so we could sit across the aisle from each other. One day a boy came in and spoke to the girl in front of me.

'Let's go eat.'

'But I'm not finished yet.'

'Aw, come on. All work and no play . . .'

'But—'

'Come *on*,' he insisted.

'Oh, okay.'

I wanted to holler 'Sit down!' I had heard 'All work and no play' all my life. Americans in general used it to hex intellectuals and well-behaved children, but specifically it was a corrective warning that men issued to women who were not malkins. It was closely related to cosmetic advertisements of the 'Go Crazy!' genre, whose enduring popularity indicated a great career on Madison Avenue for Aunt Nana, and to the plaintive inquiry, 'Whatcha lookin' so sad about?' that male strangers hurled at pensive women in airports and hotel lobbies. Any woman who worked half an hour overtime, or stopped by the podium to continue a discussion with a professor, was likely to hear 'All work and no play.' It was a declaration of war against female seriousness. Even Ralph had said it once. No matter how serious-minded a man is, the day will come when he decides he wants a good kid, and tag, you're it. Boiled down to its essence, heterosexual womanhood was Evelyn Cunningham slapping her knees in a Charleston.

Looking across at Bres as she wrote in Latin as rapidly as someone dashing off a letter, I felt that my spinster fantasy had come true. The musty library smells, the rattle of paper, the click of looseleaf rings were beloved talismans of school, of her, of us. I pictured us like this always, two women living a life of the mind, she a classicist like Edith Hamilton, and I . . . who?

I still had no idea what I wanted to do. In common with nearly everyone, I 'liked history,' but it occupied no particular place in my heart, it was simply the major I had fallen into after French fell in on me. Now, with a master's in sight, I was falling into a career as a history teacher, but I still did not want to teach. God knows, I did not want to teach. My hatred of watery moles made teaching in the grades out of the question, but a little bird told me that I was unfit for college teaching as well.

Like my love of uniforms, my love of reading and study stood alone, untainted by any personality traits that could conceivably make it pay off. Getting along in the groves of academe required a gift for manipulating people, a willingness to attend meetings, a tolerance for male hens, humility in the presence of important alumni like Billy Bo McAdoo the Popsicle King, a hungering and thirsting after petitions to sign, and an ability to keep one's mouth shut during earnest liberal debates about why so many former colonies fell apart the moment the British left.

If, by some miracle, I managed to skirt these pitfalls, all of which had my name written on them in big bold letters, there would still be the problem of handling students. As an only child, I was drawn exclusively to people older than myself; everyone younger symbolized the sibling rivals I might have had if Mama and Herb had gone back for seconds. I didn't hate them the way I hated watery moles, but I had a hard time *seeing* them. When you came down to it, the only school I was psychologically capable of teaching in was the studentless academy of my spinster fantasy.

What, then, could I do for a living that would enable Bres and me to remain together? I discussed it with her.

'Apply for a grant. You can drag out a doctorate for three years, and if you get a graduate assistantship as well, you'll be qualified to rent a Faculty Shack.'

'But why should I go for a doctorate in history if I don't want to teach?'

'Because it makes you eligible for a grant.'

Studying Aristotle had not diminished her gift for arguing in a circle whenever she got on her favorite subject. We went round it several times but I could not penetrate her blind spot. At twenty-eight she had perfected the arts of fellowship bumming and professional studenthood, and now she seemed content to let matters drift on: a grant here, a renewed assistantship there, a Faculty Shack, safety nets like the Darnay sisters, a gift car every few years, and enough left over for hooch. She claimed she intended to teach eventually and in fact had taught English for a year at an American military base in Germany, but she had looked on this job simply as a means of keeping afloat between grants. The grants had become her raison d'être.

She was doing what I had once resolved to do – stay in school as long as possible – but she had what it takes and I did not. I was a worrywart, and fellowship bumming requires the detached serenity of Buddha and the nervous system of a clam. Bres had them, plus something else that threw me for a loop when I heard about it. She was an expert poker player. Recently she had won three hundred dollars in the faculty floating game said to be in its fifth year. I hated to admit it even to myself but she was a bluffer.

She never lost her nerve and she had a way of making me feel déclassé whenever I gave way to worry. I gave way a lot because some of the things she did were incredible, like her income tax caper. Having neglected to file a return for the past two years, she got regular letters from the IRS, which she dropped unopened into the trash basket. The first time I saw her do it I went to pieces. 'Open it!' But all I got was a shrug. 'Why read it when I already know what it says?' *Finis.*

I did not understand how a woman so detached and blasé could be so electrifying in bed. When we made love she turned into a taut, quivering wire of sensation, but the rest of the time she was like an evanescent lamp of antiquity flickering somewhere beyond my reach. She eluded all my efforts to analyze her and remained an enigma, but I was too blinded by love and need to consider the possibility that there might have been something wrong with her. My only thought was to arrange things so that we could be together always.

Before I could arrange the distant future I had to arrange the immediate one. Bres had lined up another year at Ole Miss, so I had to do the same.

'I could get a job on campus,' I suggested. 'I type ninety words a minute.'

'Why do that when you can get a grant? Besides, that's a state job, and you're a niggah-lovin' Jew Communist, remember?'

She paused trenchantly, letting it sink in, then added, 'There's nothing you *can* do except apply for a grant.'

I felt checkmated. It was a familiar feeling; Herb always won our games but he never gloated over his victories. Bres, despite her serene expression, was gloating over hers. Somewhere in the back of my brain a tiny spark of anger flared, but it died for love. I had found the erudite spinster of my fantasy; to keep her I would even consent to coach field hockey.

'All right,' I said. 'I'll apply for a grant.'

Immensely pleased, she went to her vast file of Ford, Guggenheim, and Rockefeller material and gave me the applications.

The next day I took them up to my carrel and started filling them out. They were unbelievably officious. One of them asked for the titles of *all* the books ever read by the applicant, another asked for a detailed autobiography (Here it is, David!), and still another wanted to know what I planned to do for democracy. At least there would be one short answer.

At some point I became aware of a queasy feeling in my stomach. Maybe it was the bilious green paper of the form I was working on, but a better guess would be psychosomatic rebellion. I belched, wondering if I was going to throw up. Soon my mental block took the form of a splitting headache and a powerful thirst. Needing water, aspirins, and a break, I went downstairs.

Here we come to one of those but-for-a-nail situations that make people sit up all night arguing about Fate. Something was about to happen that would change my whole life. If the forms had not made me sick, I would not have gone downstairs. If I had not gone downstairs, I would not have run into Vanny, and if I had not run into Vanny, I would not have ended up in the reference room, because that was where she had left her Army surplus bag containing the aspirins I asked her for.

I was chewing on them when I noticed a book called *The*

Writer's Market on one of the reference shelves. I had never heard of it, and purely out of curiosity, I took it down to see what it was.

Would it have happened anyway, on some other day in some other library later on? Probably. But we can never be entirely sure, which is why we sit up all night arguing about Fate. I am sure of one thing: if I had never known Ann Hopkins, I would not have turned to the section on 'True Confessions,' and if I had not done that, I would not have read the first guideline. It said:

For the housewife with a high school education. First-person stories with sympathetic narrator, emotional impact, and strong reader identification. Stories may be about any subject of interest to the homebound woman: premarital and extramarital sexual temptation, sexual maladjustment in marriage, adultery, problem children, alcoholism, illness, accidents, religious crises, or the loss of a loved one. Upbeat ending essential. Some sadder-but-wiser okay. Narrator may sin but must feel guilty about it; no blithe spirits. No humor; our readers take life seriously. Length 3,000 to 5,000 words. Payment 5¢ per word on acceptance. Enclose SASE.

I remembered snatches of the confessions stories Ann used to pass around study hall; but I needed to refresh my memory – or 'study the market,' as I now knew it was called. I went to the campus newsstand and bought the issues they had and took them back up to my carrel. Pushing the grant applications aside, I opened the first magazine and began reading.

Two hours later I was finished in both senses of the word. My sick headache was gone but otherwise I felt like a veteran of the Hundred Years War. Had I not already known how malkins talked, I would not have believed lines like: 'Dear God, how can I face the children? A one-armed bandit stole my life before I could admit that I was addicted to gambling like a drug – yes, a drug!' Analyzing the stories, I discovered that many of them were close to being shaggy dog jokes. Whatever sin the narrator committed, it was seldom as bad as the titles and blurbs implied. For instance, 'I Spent the Night With My Husband's Best Friend' was about a misunderstanding over a delay caused by a snowstorm. 'They Called Me Locker Room Sal' was about a terrific girl and her steady boyfriend who were accidentally locked in their high school overnight; while there they found God and decided to wait for the church wedding her mother had planned instead of going through with the elopement they had planned.

What really mattered in all the stories was not what actually happened but what the heroine believed she had done, or what she seemed to have done in the eyes of other people. Once in a while a heroine went out and got plastered and fucked, but it was never worth it, never. Every plot was constructed on a solid foundation of free-floating female guilt.

The thought struck me that while I had never enjoyed reading true confessions, my whole life had prepared me for writing them. I should have gone to a crackerjack private school like Miss Porter's and then on to one of the Seven Sisters, but Fate had plunked me down in the shabby genteel class and sent me to public schools and a shitty college where I had met the kind of girls whose psychology I now needed to know. Thanks to Fate, I knew it.

I returned to the dorm and got out my typewriter. I spent the first hour doodling while I fixed my mind on Ann Hopkins, missions of mercy with Granny and Jensy, 'Help Me, Mr Anthony,' and El washing her fiancé's gummy socks. I sang 'The Curse of an Aching Heart.' I thought of Daughters drinking tea and talking about who was in the hospital, I thought of Mrs Bell talking about death, I reviewed all of Aunt Nana's gladsome tidings about nervous breakdowns. I sang 'In the Baggage Coach Ahead.' I thought about terrific girls who did it *for him* and of other terrific girls who would never do *that*. I sang 'Heaven Will Protect the Working Girl.' I told myself that having . . . a . . . baby . . . is . . . the . . . most . . . wonderful . . . experience . . . on . . . earth. I imagined a tricycle under the wheels of a truck and a small shoe lying in the road. I sang 'The Sunshine of Paradise Alley.' I devised a mantra, letting *malkinnnnnnnn* buzz through my brain until it gave me my title.

I Committed Adultery in a Diabetic Coma

Three hours later I had thirty-five hundred words. The next day I cut all my classes and stayed in my room to write a second story. I was in the process of arranging a meeting between Evelyn Cunningham and God, when my eye fell on my dog-eared copy of *Bérénice*. The pages were swollen from countless readings, their margins overgrown with a blue forest of notes and remarks. How odd that I should have found so much to comment on, I thought; it was such a simple story when you boiled it down to its essentials.

Jilted!
Tim did what he had to do, so I don't blame him. It was my fault for not being more understanding about his many responsibilities. The look on his face when he said, 'You're too selfish, Bernice,' still cuts through my heart, but with God's help I'll be able to pick up my life and go on.

I wrote THE END and mailed both stories to the first magazine in the market list, saying nothing to Bres. She thought I had been cloistered with the grant forms, so I let her think it and told her I had mailed them. I hated the stealth, but having heard her pan *Marjorie Morningstar*, which I loved, I could easily imagine what she would say about pulp magazine stories. It was a bridge I would cross if and when I came to it. If the stories did not sell there would still be time to apply for a grant.

Bres noticed that I was haunting the post office and teased me about it. It reminded her, she said, of the time she was stranded in Athens with fifteen dollars when the Arthur Bell Smallwood money arrived in the nick of time. Her good mood increased in direct proportion to my mounting anxiety over the mail. I tried to keep up an academic front but even my enthusiasm for my thesis had died. Finally I put it aside and wrote another story, 'My Baby Died While I Was Partying,' which I sent to another magazine.

Meanwhile, Tulaplee achieved her heart's desire that spring when the student newspaper named her Campus Cutie. They ran a picture of her in a bathing suit, standing on tiptoe at Biloxi Beach with foaming waves caressing her slim ankles. It reminded me of something but I could not think what it was until I noticed the scattered oyster shells on the sand in the background.

Tulaplee rising from the sea . . .

Tulaplee turning Langston Bob Treadwell into a grease spot like Circe turning men into swine . . .

Tulaplee sending boys on errands, the bring-me-three-of-something motif that runs through mythology and fairy tales . . .

She was a pagan goddess; hurling thunderbolts, casting spells, enraged one moment, seductive the next, sadistic beyond belief but endlessly fascinating. In short, Venus.

But that's not all she was. Oh, no. Ordinary American women strive for one Henry Adams image or the other, but Southern belles go for the jackpot. Beneath Tulaplee's photo was the personality profile she had given the reporter.

Favorite book: *The New Testament*

Favorite movie: *The Song of Bernadette*
Favorite song: 'Ave Maria'
Favorite hobby: babysitting
Ambition: motherhood

I folded the paper and looked at the clock in the coffeeshop. The mail was up by now so I hurried out to the post office. When I opened the door, my eye went to my box like a rifle shot and my stomach throbbed with anticipation as I made out that beautiful sight: the thin white slant of an envelope. I tried to read the return address as I worked the combination but the letter was turned the wrong way.

It was from the confession magazine. It contained a check for three hundred and fifty dollars and a note from the editor: '*Adultery' and 'Jilted' are great! Let us see more of your work.*

I walked out the door in a daze and sat down on the post office steps. I was a writer. It was as simple as that. I had been one all along. In high school, doing French translations, I had been a writer without even knowing it. But Herb had known it – '*You have an ear for music gone awry.*' Sound, melody, rhythm – I was a good dancer – and that odd certainty somewhere in my head when I *just knew* something was right or wrong without being able to explain how I knew. Herb was the same way. '*How do you know where to put your fingers?*' I used to ask him. '*I just know,*' he would say.

As soon as the first wave of ecstatic shock wore off, I thought of Bres. Now we could be together no matter what wandering scholarship came her way – I could do what I was going to do anywhere! I hurried off to find her and tell her the news, smiling as I imagined the lofty lecture on crass commercialism she would deliver. Well, she would deliver it over hooch, because I was going to treat us to a massive raid on Memphis. Besides, the Bernarr McFadden Fund sounded so much like one of her salt licks that she might eventually come to believe that I was a wandering scholar, too.

As expected, she was in her carrel. I caught her eye and waved her into the corridor. Smiling, she rose and came out. I rushed into speech.

'I didn't tell you before because I wanted to surprise you, but I've been writing true confessions and I sold two! Look, here's the check.'

She looked at it an unusually long time but she did not speak. When at last she raised her eyes, I saw that they were hideously flat. Something was happening to her face.

'Look,' I went on, 'here's a note from the editor. Read it.'

'No.'

'What's the matter?'

'How could you write those things?' she said contemptuously.

'It's money, I need it.'

'*I told you to get a grant!*'

It echoed in the hall, *grant-grant-grant*, and then went on its fading, spiraling way, leaving me alone with the pinched white face from which it had come.

'Bres—'

'Leave me alone. I'm busy.'

'Bres!' Panic-stricken, I grabbed her arm, but she threw off my hand.

'I'm tired of you.'

'Oh, my God . . . Bres—'

'Go away!'

She spun on her heel and returned to the carrel room. I was in such a frenzy to undo what I had done that I would have torn up the check had she come back out and demanded it. The need to push back time and start over was unbearable. Inchoate prayers flashed like epileptic discharges through my brain: *make it this time yesterday . . . make it ten minutes ago . . . take me back to before!*

I waited in the hall for almost an hour but she did not come out. Finally, I gave up and walked woodenly back to the dorm, the same way I walked home on my first day in college when I found I could not study French. Once again, a perfect femininity had been ripped away from me, and it had happened so fast I could not take it in.

Later that night I told myself that she hadn't meant it, that she would come to her senses and tell me she was sorry, and read my stories and laugh about them. Other people had lovers' quarrels, why should we be any different? It would be all right.

But it wasn't. The next day when I saw her on campus, she looked through me. I turned and walked after her, calling her name, but she gave no sign that she heard me. I waited for her outside the Classics Department, in the carrel room, in front of her house, but it was always the same.

'Bres—'

'Bres—'

'Bres—'

I thought of the times I had murmured her name to myself. Now I might as well have been talking to myself. She remained a frozen block of condemnation. Why? She had always been so disinterested in the actions of others, priding herself on her broad-mindedness, yet . . . *I told you to get a grant!* Did she need to control people, turn them into Grope members who would sit reverently at her feet and do her bidding? Did she want everybody to be a copy of her, living on grants and fellowships, so that her own mode of life would seem to be the norm? Or was it because *publish* was the foremost word in academia? There was no comparison between what Bres meant by publishing and the kind I had pulled off, yet I had been paid for writing . . .

My mind refused to entertain these thoughts for long. I could not imagine a jealous Bres, or a bad Bres of any kind. Instead, I turned to the Grope for advice. Vanny would not even speak to me. 'I don't know anything about it, she didn't say a word to me,

I haven't heard a thing,' she rattled nervously, sidling away from me as though I had a contagious disease. Sorella was equally unforthcoming, so I turned to the boys. I did not know how much they knew about our relationship, but I was beyond modesty.

'That's ole Bres for you,' Lucius sighed, after hearing my story. 'She's riding one of her wild hairs. That's why Vanny and Sorella won't talk to you. They're scared to death of her. She always gets mad at them if they don't get mad at her . . . at whoever she's mad at,' he amended carefully.

'You mean it's happened before?'

'Last year,' said Augustus. 'The Scottish woman. She was an exchange professor from the University of Edinburgh, 'bout thirty-five, real nice woman. She and Bres were thick, then they had a falling out.'

Something shriveled inside me. I knew there had been other women, but hearing about one made all of them unbearably real.

'About what?' I asked.

Augustus shrugged. 'Nobody ever found out. You wait for Bres to explain, you'll wait forever. The woman went back to Scotland and Bres started going down to New Orleans. Some girl from there came up to see her a few times last summer.'

'The one with the earrings,' said Lucius, placing his thumbs on his shoulders for measurement.

I saw the girl with the earrings a week later. She was about twenty, with an exotic New Orleans look that managed to combine an extremely short, shingled haircut with long, looping gypsy jewelry. She carried a suitcase affixed with decals from Sophie Newcombe, the sister school of Tulane, and she spent the spring break in Bres's apartment.

The dorms remained open for the holiday and Miz Arvella invited me to Easter Sunday dinner. I choked down leg of lamb and hot cross buns with her and the other housemothers, and threw them up later in my room.

I saw the girl from New Orleans again that week. Despite her emancipated air, she followed Bres around like a puppy. Passing them at the door of the Student Union, I heard the girl say 'Whatever you want' in a placating voice and skip to catch up with Bres, who strode on ahead as if she were alone. I opened my mouth to shout her name, intending to force her to listen to me even if I had to pin her to the wall, but suddenly a weak feeling swept over me and I broke out in a clammy sweat. I had eaten nothing and now it caught up with me and forced me into a chair in the television lounge. I was still sitting there when Bres and the girl emerged from the snack bar and walked out the door.

It was the last time I ever saw her. That night she was killed in a head-on crash on her way to Batesville. A pickup truck with a drunk at the wheel crossed the center line doing eighty and plowed into her car with such force that the engine was driven into the front seat. Bres and the other driver were dead when the troopers got there, and the girl from New Orleans died on the way to the hospital.

The Batesville road, known throughout the hooch-free state as the 'Malt Liquor Way.' My poor darling baby in her white cotton pants. Mississippi gave her to me, and Mississippi took her back.

The Grope came and got me and we went to Lucius's apartment, where we spent a stunned and helpless night. The next day, Bres's parents came up from the Gulf to make the arrangements. There was no funeral nor any kind of service; her remains were taken to Memphis for cremation, the ashes to be stored for the time being at the crematory until the family decided what to do with them. Lucius heard these details from a classics professor who had clashed with Bres's mother over the disposition of the ashes. He was coming up for a sabbatical in Athens and offered to take them with him and scatter them from some suitable literary or historical spot, but she would not hear of it.

Against the Grope's advice, I went down to Faculty Shacks while Bres's mother was cleaning out her apartment. The door was open and I saw a petite woman in her late fifties, with a towel tied carefully around the waist of her chic mint green linen dress, tossing books into a wheeled receptacle marked U. OF MISS. SANITATION DEPT.

I knocked on the jamb and she looked up. Searching her face, trying to find something of Bres in it, I found nothing. She was olive-skinned, with black eyes and a thin pursed mouth that indicated her French blood. *Mademoiselle Le Brès*, I thought.

'Yes?'

'I'm . . . I was Bres's friend,' I stammered. 'I wonder if I could have something of hers, a book, or—'

'Friend!' she snarled. 'Ah know what *that* means!'

She slammed the door in my face.

Lucius and Augustus tried to find the trash cart at the sanitation depot and salvage something for me, but they could not. Its contents were burned, too. I spent the following week in my room. Poor innocent Miz Arvella, to whom 'friend' had only one meaning, overflowed with sympathy and invitations to dinner, but I wanted nothing.

One night I heard a knock at my door and found Tulaplee holding a white pie carton with grease spots coming through.

'Ah brought you some barbecue from Grundy's. Ah just had some, it's real good.'

She set a place for me at my desk and smeared syrup on the biscuits while I took a few listless mouthfuls of the tangy steaming pork. After a few moments I put down my fork and looked at her.

'Where's your latest French exercise?'

'Oh, shoot, you can't fool with that ole thing now!'

'Yes, I can. It'll remind me of a happy time, when I was in high school.'

She relented and went and got the weekly translation, and I wrote it out for her.

Seconds after she left my room there was an altercation in the hallway. I heard one of the other girls say something indistinct, followed by a fluttery giggle. Suddenly there was a loud *crack!* and Tulaplee's screeching voice rang out.

'You shut your dirty mouth, you Gulfport trash!'

The other girl said, 'Oh . . .' and burst into tears. There was a scurrying sound of footsteps as she made for her room, then the dorm shook in the now-familiar fashion as Tulaplee slammed the door of hers.

When I emerged from the first stage of numb grief, I hurled myself into another more vigorous kind. I'm not sure why I did it; maybe to try and get killed in a drunken smash-up of my own, or shot in a Southern crime of passion, or simply to lose myself in dissipation. Whatever my motive, I went out and fucked my ass off. My partners were some men on campus who had been making eyes at me since September, whose initial interest had been further stimulated by my friendship with Bres. Nothing charms the male ego more than the prospect of converting a dyke, so when I played up to them, they saw nothing of the feverish despair that lay behind my flirting.

It's a miracle I did not get pregnant. I always inserted the diaphragm before leaving the dorm, but several times I was too drunk to remember to put in any jelly before the fucking started, and one night I removed the diaphragm when a man challenged me to fuck without it. 'Ah'm gonna give you sumpin that long, cool drink of water didn't have to give,' he promised, but it did not happen. All he gave me was a description of Bres that was more beautiful and fitting than he knew.

The last man I fucked was unconnected with the campus, and thus unaware of my relationship with Bres. His name was

Vardis and he owned the local tree-pruning firm that came up to rescue the dorm from a rotten oak that was about to fall in on it. He was in his early thirties and a special friend of Miz Arvella, being related in some way to her late husband's family.

From the conversation they had as he worked, I deduced that he lived in a room in town while keeping a wife and three children stashed away on a farm, where it was 'so much healthier for them.' Listening from my window, I could tell he had Miz Arvella convinced that Oxford was a smog-choked megapolis and he a devoted family man willing to suffer loneliness for the sake of his loved ones, whom he visited as often as possible but not nearly so often as he would like. Miz Arvella believed it but I did not. Vardis had the eyes, the smile, the walk of a dedicated slash hound, and like all slash hounds, he had figured out a way to lead a double life.

One thing led to another and we got together, ending up in a Memphis hotel near the bus station. Vardis stocked up on bourbon and beer and we drank boilermakers and fucked. His potency was effortless and endless, but somehow he wasn't *there*. He gasped out 'darlin' ' with each thrust, but his pale blue eyes were glazed and staring like the eyes of a man with an electrode wrapped around his cock; not making love but receiving shocks.

After the third fuck, while drinking my fifth boilermaker, I started crying. Most people are not in a position to realize it, but there is nothing sadder than being with one sex when you want to be with the other. I wanted Bres, but I wanted femaleness also. The sight of this naked man filled me with tearing pain; his hairy chest, his curveless trunk with no discernible waistline and the navel up so high, the tight flat nothingness of his buttocks, seemed like a mutation of the species.

Vardis sat down beside me and put his arm around my shaking shoulders.

'Honey . . . Honey? Whatsa matter? Ah say sumpin that hurt

your feelins? Don't cry so hard, darlin'. Ain't nothin' to cry
'bout, we're gonna have us a real good time this weekend. Ah
got plenny money and we gonna spend it all! Say, you want me
to buy you sumpin pretty? How's about that, huh? Look, tomorrow we'll go up to Lowenstein's and you can pick out a new
dress. Enythang you want. Then we'll go to the Peabody *Hotel*
for lunch! You like that? That sound good to you? That'll make
you feel better, sure as shootin'. Honey? Aw, darlin', if you don't
stop cryin' Ah'm gonna cry right along with you. You're just
tearin' the heart right outta me. Ah can't stand to see anybody
hurtin' like that—'

He broke off and sobbed. We sat there together on the edge
of the bed, weeping and drinking boilermakers. After a while he
began telling a story about Korea. Something about the timbre
of his voice made me stop crying and listen.

'Me and Quint Radley from Tupelo joined up together soon
as the news come. We was in the same outfit all 'long. The
night he got his was the coldest night Ah evva did see – Lord,
it was cold! Ain't right for a Miss'ippi boy to die in such cold,
but ole Quint did. The gooks come at us all of a sudden-like,
blowin' that bugle of theirs, 'cept it ain't pretty and clear like
our bugle. It's flat and tinny, the creepiest sound you evva
heard.'

He shuddered. The eyes that had not seen me as we fucked
now saw something else as he stared into the past. He drained
his glass and went on.

'Quint got separated from the rest of the squad somehow. Ah
don't rightly know what-all happened, but they got hold of
him. If they'd of killed him fair 'n' square it'd been one thang,
but . . .' His voice shook and he wiped his nose with the back of
his hand. 'They cut him open right down the middle, just like
you dress a pig. Craziest thang was, he was still alive when Ah
found him. His guts was hangin' out and startin' to freeze, and
he was still alive. Ah was 'bout to kill him myself to save him

sufferin' when he died. Ah carried him back to camp and by the time we got there, his guts was froze solid.'

His hand tightened on my shoulder. 'Next time, Ah got even for him. Ah killed me five gooks with a flame-thrower. Ah was spozed to take 'em prisoner but Ah dint . . .' He wiped the tears from his cheeks and crushed the empty beer can in his hand.

Rising, he walked unsteadily into the bathroom and returned with a long stream of toilet paper that he tore in half, giving one end to me. We both blew our noses.

'Ah know it's hard for a woman to unnerstand,' he went on, 'but when you fight together, eat together, sleep next to each other like we did . . . sumpin happens. It's like . . . well, Ah *loved* ole Quint. Ah don't mean nothin' funny or enythang,' he amended quickly, 'but like Ah say, he was the best friend Ah evva had.'

'I wish I could have met him,' I said.

He turned to me with an immensely pleased smile that made him seem very dear.

'Aw, you'd of liked ole Quint, Ah tell you! He was . . .' He paused inarticulately. 'What Ah mean to say is . . . It's like – well, he was a good ole boy.'

He sighed deeply. 'Ah feel better, don't you? You stopped cryin', dint you? Ah knew you would. Less have us another drink and lissen to the radio. Ah'll sing to you! How's 'bout that? J'know Ah could sing?'

He turned on a country station and sang along to 'I'm Throwing Rice at the Girl I Love' and 'One Has My Heart, the Other Has My Name.' He did sing well, and he had mastered Nashville's version of John McCormack's *larmes aux voix*. I cried a little more, but my tears were of a different kind now. He knew the words to all the songs the station played and sang steadily until two A.M., when he put his finger to his lips.

'They're signin' off,' he whispered reverently, 'here it comes.'

As the soaring notes of the national anthem filled the room,

I saw his Adam's apple move as he wiped away a tear. Unable to find anything else he liked on the radio, he mixed us two more boilermakers and began singing Civil War songs.

'*Oh, how proud you stood before me in your suit of gray, when you vowed to me and country ne'er to go astray . . .*' Suddenly he raised his head, his eyes taking on a fevered brightness.

'We coulda done it!' he cried. 'We coulda won! If only them simpleminded Nawth Ca'lina boys hadn't of shot ole Stonewall by mistake at Chancellorsville! And Gettysburg!' He turned to me with wild urgency. 'You know what happened at Gettysburg? Heah, Ah'll show you!'

He jumped up and, still naked as the day he was born, started moving furniture to make a mock-up battlefield for an illustrated lecture on military strategy. The Civil War being the most boring of all wars to women, I had no idea what he was talking about and would have fared no better had I been sober. A desk was the Yankees, a chair was Cemetery Ridge, and he was General Pickett. Backing up against one wall, he held out an imaginary sword and leapt forward.

'*Yeeeeeeaaaaayyyyyhhhhoooooo!*'

He, the chair, and a spindly table landed with a crash against the opposite wall. By some miracle he escaped both a broken neck and emasculation, but not the rage of our next-door neighbor.

'Hey! Wuss all 'at goddamn noise? Pussun cain't heah hisself think!'

'You ain't had a thought in your head since Hector was a pup!' Vardis yelled back.

'Sumbitch bastud!'

'Them's fightin' words! Ah'll kill him! Where's my knife?'

'Oh, please don't!' I screamed, sounding just like the distressed damsel in a melodrama.

He was rifling through his pockets for his knife when he passed out, falling backward in the direction of the bed and landing half on it. Groaning, he pulled himself up the rest of the way and sank into a drunken stupor.

I expected the manager to come knocking on the door to request quiet, but it was not that kind of hotel; either the police came or nobody did. I washed and dressed and sat down in the chair to wait for dawn. Gazing at Vardis's sprawled body and listening to him snort and fart, I found myself doing what Granny had recommended so often during my peer-problem days: looking for the good in people.

I could not deny that the man on the bed personified the worst aspects of the South. I had heard him cuss out the nigras in his work gang and seen them cringe from the pale blue fire flashing in his eyes. It was easy to imagine the rest. I had no doubt that him and ole Quint had whupped a few nigras in their boyhood forays, and I was even more sure that, driving along a lonely road on some black velvet night, they had spied a l'il nigra gal and slowed down. Technically they did not rape her, but only because they did not have to; she knew the path of least resistance was the way home. Afterwards, if they had it to spare, they gave her a quarter.

He had a clearly defined fighting side and woe to anyone who walked on it. He was entirely capable of killing, in a mob or alone, and if the Citizens Council's goon squad had firebombed Bres's house, he probably would have approved when he found out why. To his way of thinking, it would have been revenge for Quint's death at the hands of the Communists. The worst of the South? Yes, but also the best. There was no telling what he would do if he got riled, yet he had an underlying sweetness, an almost female tenderness, that had saved my life and sanity. He was that many-splendored thing called a good ole boy. He said grace, he said ma'am, and he loved his countries – both of them.

When dawn came, I wrote a note and left it on the night table:

I'm taking the bus back to Oxford. I can't see you anymore,
but I want you to know it's not because of anything you did or
said. I cried because somebody I loved died. Your kindness
helped me more than I can say. You're a gentleman.

I knew he would be parched when he woke up. Fetching a
can of beer from the cooler, I put it beside the note and, feeling
a little like Tosca, slipped silently from the room.

The spring dawn was gently pink and the air bore the vigorous tang of the river. I walked across the street to the station
and bought my ticket. Having an hour's wait, I was about to buy
a cup of coffee from a machine when suddenly I realized I was
hungry. I walked to a nearby diner and ordered a breakfast of
ham biscuits, grits, and gravy. When I had scraped the plate, I
ordered two doughnuts to eat with my coffee refill. Never,
before or since, has food tasted as good as it did that morning.

When I got back to campus, I threw away my unfinished thesis
and spent the remaining month of the year at Ole Miss writing
true confessions. Two more sold, so I now had seven hundred
dollars, more than I had started with back in September.

The year came to a close. Tulaplee left a few days early to go
to Europe with her parents, sending her maid and two of her
father's black employees up to campus to pack her winter
wardrobe and lug it back to the old plantation. They arrived in
a big truck and went to work. Some hours later a knock came at
my door. It was the maid, holding a huge, gaily wrapped box.

'Does you be Miss Flarnz King?'

I said I was.

'Miss Tulaplee, she say Ah's to give dis to you. She tell me to
tell you sumpin, too. She say, "Tell Miss Flarnz dat Ah fixed it
so nobody do huh duht."'

I frowned. 'She fixed it so nobody would do me dirt?'

'Yes'm. Dem huh verra wuhds.'

'Did she say anything else?'

'No'm.'

I thanked her and shut the door. The box contained a dusky blue cashmere knitted suit soft enough to pull through the proverbial ring. I had never owned anything like it in my life. The enclosed card said simply, *Merci beaucoup*, and underneath was a drawing of a tulip.

Do me dirt . . .

Suddenly I remembered Bres saying at Thanksgiving that the anonymous phone calls had stopped. The White Citizens Council . . . Tulaplee's father owned half the Delta . . . money . . . power . . . Tulip Enterprises, Inc. . . . Daddy's little girl.

A good ole boy and a Southern belle, two types who should have been my enemies, yet they had turned out to be my friends. One was a perfect gentleman and the other was a great lady.

The day I left was like a film running backwards. Mr Reece the cab driver took my luggage out as he had once taken it in, and Miz Arvella surged through the door in the opposite direction as she accompanied me down the walk. I was going to miss her and her thrice-told tales. She hugged me and gave me a box lunch she had prepared for me, and I got into the cab.

When the bus crossed into Tennessee, I turned around and looked back at the WELCOME TO MISSISSIPPI sign. Bres, Bres, rhymes with dress . . .

'You want a fellowship here? I'll fix it up.'

'No, not here. I'd like to see another part of the country.'

'What part did you have in mind?'

'The Deep South . . .'

'Well, how about the University of Mississippi? . . .'

'All right.'

How casual and happenstance it had been. As with my college

scholarship, I had grabbed the first graduate school offer that came my way without even bothering to apply for any others. It was one of the few ways I was like Mama; I had inherited her impatience. How much heartache I could have avoided if I had said no to Ralph's first suggestion and investigated some other schools. Did I wish I had said no?

No.

17

I had regained most of the weight I lost but not all of it, so the two champions of wholesomeness pounced the moment I walked in the door.

'Babe, you look lak sumpin de cat drag in! Dint dem pecker-woods feed you?'

'You're wasting away! You look consumptive!'

'Granny, you judge everybody by Lillian Russell.'

'I know bad lungs when I see them.'

'Since when are you interested in lungs? They're at the wrong end.'

'Doan you sass yo' big momma!'

'Cough into this handkerchief, I want to see what comes up.'

'Granny, would you like me to get a chest X-ray?'

'Doctors don't know anything.'

It went on like this for the rest of the evening. Mama gave me her shrewd look but said nothing, and Herb questioned me eagerly about William Faulkner. In short, a typical homecoming.

Herb was the only member of the household who recalled that I was supposed to return with a master's degree. Granny called graduate school 'going through college all over again,' Mama looked on it as some sort of extra inning or double-header, and Jensy was au courant only with divinity school.

'Did they write your degree in Latin?' Herb asked. 'I've always wanted to see one all in Latin.'

My heart turned over and I felt my throat tighten. The only thing that could save me from tears was an uproar, so I started one.

'I got bored with academic life, so I tore up my thesis and became a writer,' I said as flippantly as I could. 'I've sold several short stories to the true confessions magazines already. The first one was called "I Committed Adultery in a Diabetic Coma."'

That did it. Jensy's eyes rolled, Granny's hand fluttered to her heart, Mama chortled, 'Well, shit a brick,' Granny cried, 'Oh, Louise!' and whatever Herb said was lost in the ensuing chorus about trashy women and the devil's pencil. I wished Bres could have heard it; it surpassed any imitation I had ever done for her.

Not surprisingly, they all came around to my side. When I got Herb alone and explained to him how I felt about writing, his disappointment faded and a new enthusiasm took the place of the old one. A week later, when two checks forwarded from Mississippi arrived in the mail, practical-minded Granny sat up and took notice. Jensy went wherever Granny led, so descriptions of the red-hot tip on the devil's pencil ceased; and Mama, who had made no objections to begin with, repeated her 'Well, shit a brick.'

I treated them to the biggest roast of beef I could find and we had a festive celebration of my new career, complete with a new kind of table talk. Instead of polyps and clots and things that go splat at Colonial Beach, Granny and Jensy recalled all the diabetics they had ever nursed, describing in loving detail the sores that broke out on Mrs Ewing's legs and the time poor Mrs Warren gave herself an insulin shot without her glasses and pulled out a vein 'by the roots!' Herb, who had long since learned to eat silently and steadily through any conversation under the sun, did so.

For dessert we had Fudgsicles. Everybody had to eat them every day because Mama was saving the wrappers to send away for a full-color portrait of Mickey Mantle suitable for framing.

Having had a private room at Ole Miss for the first time in my life, I now found it hard to readjust to Granny as a roommate. There was also the problem of finding a quiet place to write. Where there was Granny, there was always a steady stream of people coming to call; and where there was Mama, there were noise and mess to an unparalleled degree.

It was time for me to live alone. I rented an efficiency apartment in the Mount Pleasant district near the library Herb had taken me to when I was little. Furnishing it was no problem; the attic of our house was full of Mrs Dabney's old stuff – the reason why I could not write in the attic – and our cupboards overflowed with the Bingo prizes Granny had collected over years of compulsive gambling. I took my pick of the toasters, coffeepots, dishes, and lamps stashed in various odd places – six iron skillets lay under the living room sofa – and promised to return for dinner each Sunday to eat my share of the Fudgsicles piled in the freezer.

My furniture smelled like the unguents Granny and Jensy had rubbed on Mrs Dabney's failing joints; I wrote on one of her sixteen card tables and piled my manuscript on an occasional table supported by a pug dog caryatid. I loved the apartment. The rent was seventy-five dollars a month, and if I bought more than ten dollars' worth of groceries at a time I needed a delivery boy to help me carry them home, so I managed to support myself.

I intended to write something better eventually but I kept at the confessions for the time being. Besides supporting me, they were the best possible training for a fledgling writer. The most important thing they taught me was how to

Capture your reader, let him not depart
From dull beginnings that refuse to start.

That's from Bres's translation of Horace's *Ars Poetica*. I ached for her. I spent that first winter crying myself to sleep, trapped in the futile litany of 'This time last year,' but when spring came and the first anniversary of her death passed, taking the unbearable phrase with it, I knew the worst was over.

Gradually I began to think about finding somebody else. I was not sure what I wanted. In my most objective moods I wondered if Lesbianism had been my ultimate exercise in non-conformity – after all, my different drummer could play anything – rather than a bona fide sexual preference. I knew that my real proclivity was swimming against the tide, yet I also knew that I had loved Bres. I was beginning to suspect that my real love was going to be my work, but I was young and horny as well as lonely, and I wanted somebody. The question was, who? Or more precisely, which?

Sometimes it seemed wiser to forget about 'Ole Miss' and go back to men. Several times I almost went up to my old campus to find Ralph; I would have enjoyed being in bed with him, but my psyche was not ready for a man. My affair with Bres had ended with such dizzying swiftness that I was left with an unfinished feeling about women, an 'overness' that I did not want. I needed to know more women as lovers before I could decide whether I was gay or straight, or both.

I'm sure Washington was full of Lesbians but I had no idea where they were. The only ones I could identify were the butches one saw in the dowdier sections of Georgetown around M Street, with combs and wallets in their back pockets, but they repelled me physically. The kind of women I found desirable were the kind who would never be taken for Lesbians by anybody, including me.

I knew there were such things as gay bars but I had no idea

where they were, either, so I haunted the museums and concerts, looking for certain 'signs.' These were still the days of the
pinkie ring signal, so I looked for pinkie rings. Very few women
wore them because everybody *knew* what they meant, but a
few women did. I tried to find significance in their unconventional habit, but given my family history, I was incapable of
finding significance in any unconventional habit. Besides, I
was put off by memories of the Tom Mix Clubs of my childhood. If I let myself look for pinkie rings, I would end up
looking for Lesbian lunch boxes, Lesbian Thermos jars, and
women who went around whispering, 'Hot Ralston for your
breakfast.'

Remembering the way Bres's eyes had widened with recognition the moment she knew for sure she would get me, I
looked for 'the look.' Any woman who really *sees* another
woman is giving out a signal whether she knows it or not. A
couple of times I thought I spotted the Lesbian look, but the
logical next step – inviting a possible to join you for an after-
concert cocktail – invariably foundered on the shoals of the
Nation's Capital. Given Washington's longstanding reputation
as the official city of lonely women, being seen drinking in
pairs was anathema to all Washington women, including me.

Then there was the security clearance problem. Anyone who
has an affair in Washington usually has it with a bureaucrat.
Writers make everybody nervous but we terrify Silly Service
workers. Our apartments always look like a front for something,
and no matter how carefully we tidy up for guests we always
seem to miss the note card that says, '*Margaret has to die soon.*'
We own the kind of books that spies use to construct codes, like
The Letters of Mme. de Sévigné, and we are the only people in
the world who write *oxymoron* in the margin of the Bible.
Manuscripts in the fridge in case of fire, Strunk's *Elements* in the
bathroom, the Laramie City Directory explained away with 'It
might come in handy,' all strike fear in the GS-7 heart. Nobody

really wants to sleep with a writer, but Silly Service workers won't even talk to us.

As they say in the soaps, I tried, God knows I tried, but I couldn't find a girl. What Lesbians need to get together is a cult atmosphere. Bres and I managed with no trouble because school is the biggest cult of all, but there were few other cults around in 1960. The Daughters of Bilitis had been launched in San Francisco but I didn't know about it, and even if I had, the name would have been an insurmountable stumbling block in my case. However, if they had had a Washington chapter, I don't need to tell you who would have joined it proudly as a matter of course without even knowing what it was. That would have solved all my problems because every dyke in Washington would have been up at the house.

I still made my Sunday treks. One afternoon when the table was set, I called down the cellar stairs to tell Jensy dinner was ready and got an uncharacteristic reply.

'Y'all go 'head without me. Ah got dat ole pain in my arm again.'

'You want me to bring your plate down?'

'No, babe, Ah ain't hungry jus' now.'

'I don't know what's wrong with her arm.' Granny sighed. 'It's always the left one. It starts in the shoulder and goes down. She says it's because she's left-handed and she must have strained something.'

'Why in the hell doesn't she go to a doctor instead of that crazy faith healer who speaks in tongues?' Mama demanded.

'Doctors don't know anything. I tried to get her to go to one but she refused.'

Herb and I exchanged 'our' look. Without Jensy feeding Granny lines, dinner proceeded in relative silence. Mama finished eating first, as usual, and lit a cigarette. Suddenly there was a crash below stairs.

'What was that?' we said in unison, and then we knew.

She was on the floor where she had fallen. Mama and I got there in time to hear the words 'Miss Lura' from lips that were going blue, but by the time Granny negotiated the steep cellar stairs, Jensy had died.

Granny groaned and started to sink down. Mama and I caught her and held her heavy swaying body between us. Her face was flaming. When Jensy's minister came in answer to Herb's summons, the doctor he brought with him had to treat Granny; her blood pressure was over two hundred. Not daring to let her walk upstairs to her room, we put her in Jensy's bed. When the undertaker's men came, she turned her head to the wall and sobbed the terrible sobs of an old lady as they put Jensy's body in the basket.

When they had gone, she recovered a little and insisted on holding court in Jensy's apartment, greeting the Lily of the Valley ladies whom the minister notified. We all sat in the small room and discussed the funeral plans.

The minister was almost white, with that fine-drawn look that Granny called 'good blood.' It was a Lee-Byrd-Randolph-Carver-Calhoun-Dandridge-Fairfax-Warfield-Oglethorpe-Devereaux look, and probably for good reason.

'I would take it kindly, and I know Sister Jensy would, if one of you-all would say a few words at the church service,' he enunciated carefully.

'Mr King would do that very well,' Granny said.

Herb nodded. 'I'll be happy to, sir.'

The minister made a little bow from the shoulders.

'I thank you, sir.'

It was a lovely moment, worthy of Versailles.

Herb gave us no indication of what he planned to say. I saw him look up a quotation in Bartlett's but he made no notes.

Jensy had a perfect fall day for her funeral. The church smelled of bay rum, Florida water, and sugary perfume. Several of our old neighbors from 1020 for whom Jensy had worked were there; Miss Inez and Miss Rose Shields, and Mr and Mrs Koustopolous. The eulogy was profuse, the kind Jensy always said she wanted. As I listened to the shouts and moans I wondered if Herb might be too much of an anticlimax. I glanced at him, but his face was as inscrutable as ever. In fact, he was the only member of the white delegation who did not look slightly uncomfortable.

The minister finished speaking.

'And now, brothers and sisters, Mr Herbert King is going to tell us about Sister Jensy.'

As Herb rose and went forward, a voice from the pew behind us whispered, 'Dat de scarf man.' He stepped into the pulpit and looked out over the church, his face still inscrutable yet somehow immeasurably sad. He began.

'A great lady has left us.'

A wordless stir went over the mourners, a sound of surprise expressed in slight shifting movements; stockings against stockings, hands against sleeves, worn soles against worn carpet. Beside me, Granny sighed and wiped her eyes. The word that she and Herb had argued about for years, the word that set his teeth on edge, he had uttered at last for Jensy.

He began telling Jensy stories, small, lighthearted, yet touching incidents that had occurred over the years, making himself the butt of them in a way that brought unforced smiles to black faces. I marveled at his deft touch; no white Southerner could have done it.

'You know, I was born in a country where "lady" is a title that a woman receives from her father or her husband. The word is always used with her name, as we use Miss and Mrs, so she is always instantly recognizable. When I first came to America, I was confused by the many definitions of "lady" I heard. Everyone spoke of ladies but no one seemed to be able to explain what a lady is.

'I remained confused for many years, until one Easter when I met Mrs Custis on her way to church. When I complimented her on her outfit, she said that although she bought a new dress every Easter, there was only one Easter outfit that she really wanted. I asked her what it was and she replied, "The Gospel armor."'

The audience made a sussurating sound of recognition, while in the loft, the choir mistress glanced at the organist and exchanged nods with him.

Herb went on. 'When Mrs Custis said that, I knew at long last what a lady was. In the words of the Spanish writer Cervantes, a lady is a woman who "is so resolved to be respected that she can make herself so even amidst an army of soldiers." That was surely Mrs Custis. I know she will have her armor, and I know she will wear it well.'

He stepped from the pulpit and walked back down the aisle. Mr Koustopolous wiped his eyes on his tie and the Misses Shields tore their last Kleenex in half so that each could blow her nose.

At a gesture from the minister, the mourners rose and the organist burst into the hymn that Herb had inspired.

> Stand up, stand up, for Jesus
> Stand in his strength alone
> The arm of flesh will fail you
> Ye dare not trust your own
> Put on the Gospel armor
> And watching unto prayer
> Where duty calls, or danger
> Be never wanting there

We left the church and got into the car. It was then that something happened I will never forget. Mama had only one gesture of affection and she rarely bestowed it, but she did now.

Balling her fist, she gave Herb a slow-motion left hook to the jaw.

'You did good,' she said.

He smiled at her. It was the sweetest smile I ever saw on a human face. I don't suppose I'll ever figure those two out.

When we got back home from the cemetery, Granny said, 'I never did like this house. I hate it now. I want to sell it and move back to the old place in Ballston.'

'What about Evelyn and Billy?' Mama asked.

'They can move back in with Aunt Nana.'

Herb and I exchanged glances. Only grief over Jensy could have made her give up her prize booty to the enemy so casually. Or perhaps Herb's eulogy had expanded her view of what a lady was, so that she no longer had to feed off Evelyn's femininity.

'And you,' Granny said, turning to me, 'have got no business living by yourself like a fallen woman when that great big house is just sitting over there waiting!'

I knew it was her way of asking me to live with them; she seemed to have aged ten years since Jensy died, and we were all silently but painfully aware that she did not have much time left. I had been wondering how I could broach the subject of moving in with them, but now she had done it for me in a way that salvaged my pride. Families composed of rugged individualists have to do things obliquely, and she knew it.

She sold the house, evicted Evelyn and Billy, and we moved into the old homestead. The first memorable event was the invitation Evelyn issued to Mama: 'Oh, Louise, I'm so glad you're back! I've been looking for somebody to have the Change of Life with, and you and I are exactly the same age!' I'll leave you to imagine Mama's reply.

Mama joined a local ladies' bowling team and quickly became its star. Discovering that the families of her teammates attended the matches to cheer them on, she insisted that Herb and I show up, too, so the three of us began going to the alley every Tuesday night, with me at the wheel. I thought I would never be able to drive again, but I had no choice: he wouldn't ride with her and she wouldn't ride with him, so it was up to me to transport us. In this, at least, I struck a happy medium, turning in a driving performance that fell somewhere between Herb's Last Post and Mama's Light Brigade.

He and I made a strange sight at the alley; neither of us understood the game and he never went anywhere without a three-piece suit and tie. The trophy tournament was especially memorable, with pins flying up every which way as Mama threw one crashing, deafening strike after another. Her team won and she, now captain of it, was interviewed by a reporter from a local throwaway shopping news. When asked about her family, Mama turned around and pointed dramatically at the stands.

'See those eggheads sitting up there like two bumps on a log?' Whereupon everybody turned around and stared at Herb and me.

Granny lost another friend when Aunt Nana died a few days before Christmas. Despite their sometime feud they had been very close, and we all noticed a change in Granny afterwards. Though she refused to admit it, she could no longer be left alone, so Evelyn or Aunt Charlotte always stayed with her whenever we had to be away from the house.

At last the day came when she had to enter a nursing home. The Daughters had one they liked so much they had virtually commandeered it, so we took her there. The rooms were what might be called almost-private, being separated by a plywood partition instead of a wall. This came in extremely handy, for Granny's next-door neighbor was a Mrs Benson, who had a thirty-year-old bachelor grandson named Fred.

Yes, you guessed it. She started matchmaking on her deathbed. Mrs Benson being equally eager to see Fred married, they joined forces in this their final battle, aided by the thin partition between them. Like two countesses of Monte Cristo, two prisoners of Zenda, they devised a system of knocks to signal each other on Fred's and my comings and goings. One knock meant, 'I just sent her to the coffeeshop,' and two meant, 'He's on his way.'

An aerodynamics engineer, Fred was the most colossal bore I have ever met, the John Glenn of the nursing home snack bar, whose measured, precise, mathematically perfect attempts to amuse me made Cheops look like a stand-up comic. I inadvertently encouraged him by laughing – at him – but incapable of discerning the difference, he soon believed himself to be the heir of Swift and Wilde. He told his grandmother I was charming, and she passed the intelligence along to mine.

'At last you're learning how to build up a man's ego,' Granny said happily.

She was convinced that my love life was launched. As things turned out, she was right. One day while I was sitting with her, she looked out the door and heaved a deep sigh.

'Look at those poor twisted women who love other women.'

'Where?'

'Across the hall,' she replied, gesturing weakly.

I peered into the room opposite and saw two women in their forties seated beside the bed of an old lady. Both were chic and soignée.

'The blond one is Mrs Kincaid's daughter. She told me all about it on the sun porch the other day. Her heart is just broken right in two. Ahhh! Thank the Lord I've been spared that.'

A nursing home is the best cult in town. If you can find one in which the Daughters are conducting guerilla theater and staging lie-ins, you can have anything you want, an-nee-thing. It was easy to devise errands to Mrs Kincaid. Soon I was going to the coffeeshop with the two women, and after a week or so they caught on. Arrangements were made for me to meet some of their friends.

Meanwhile, my first byline story appeared in print. I had written it some months before and sent it to a men's magazine under the pen name 'Ruding Upton King.' When the complimentary copy arrived I showed it to Granny. Immensely pleased, she gazed at the name for several minutes and then adjusted her bifocals and began reading the story.

Suddenly her smile faded and she handed the magazine back to me.

'Your grandfather was a perfect gentleman.'

I was glad the story arrived when it did, because she went down rapidly in the next couple of weeks. I stayed with her all the time now. One night while I sat with her, I happened to put my feet on the high frame of the hospital bed and let my skirt drop open. Weakly, Granny turned her head.

'Don't sit like that,' she rasped.

Obediently, I assumed one of the demure positions she had taught me and took her hand, holding it while she drifted off to sleep. Her breathing was regular but as I watched her, an odd change seemed to come over her features. She had a round face and a small nose and mouth, but now, in some inexplicable way, the roundness and smallness were going from her. Suddenly I remembered the old saying I had heard all my life: *You can always see the Indian blood in the end.*

As I jumped up and leaned over her, her breathing stopped.

After the funeral, the family sat around our kitchen table drinking coffee and talking about her.

'How old was Aunt Lura?' asked Billy Bosworth.

'God only knows,' Uncle Botetourt sighed. 'She lied to everybody about it.'

'That's a lady's privilege,' said Evelyn, 'and Aunt Lura was a lady to her fingertips.'

'No, she wasn't,' I said.

'Why, Florence! What a thing to say about your grandma!'

'She was something better than a lady, so was Jensy. They were viragoes.'

'What the hell is that?' asked Mama.

'The only V worth having,' I replied, smiling at Herb. My eyes filled as I remembered the night Bres defined the word for me. 'A virago is a woman of great stature, strength and courage who is not feminine in the conventional ways.'

'Shit, that's me!'

'The hell it is,' Uncle Botetourt grumbled. 'You're a slew-foot.'

'Shut your goddamn mouth! What the hell do you—'

'Oh, *please* don't start!' Aunt Charlotte wailed, pressing her palms to her temples.

'Listen, Gottapot, you don't know your ass from third base, but I run around with eggheads,' Mama said proudly. 'I heard so much about John Quincy Shitass from Big Egghead that I finally read *The Dynamite and the Virgin*. Now here comes Little Egghead that swallowed the dictionary to tell me something I've always wanted to know. I knew there was something different about me, but it's not because I'm a slewfoot, it's because I'm a *virago*!'

She had it painted on her bowling ball.

www.virago.co.uk

Virago

To find out more about Florence King and
other Virago authors, visit:
www.virago.co.uk

Visit the Virago website for:

- The Virago on-line book group

- News of author events and forthcoming titles

- Exclusive features and interviews with
  authors, including Margaret Atwood,
  Maya Angelou, Sarah Waters, Nina Bawden,
  Stella Duffy and Gillian Slovo

- Free extracts from a wide range of titles

- Discounts on new publications

- Competitions

- Exclusive signed copies

PLUS: subscribe to our free monthly newsletter

CASSANDRA AT THE WEDDING
Dorothy Baker

'I'm not, at heart, a jumper; it's not my sort of thing . . . I think I knew all the time I was sizing up the bridge that the strong possibility was I'd go home, attend my sister's wedding as invited, help hook-and-zip her into whatever she wore, take the bouquet while she received the ring, through the nose or on the finger, wherever she chose to receive it, and hold my peace when it became a question of speaking now or forever holding it.'

It is the hottest June on record and the longest day of the year. Cassandra Edwards – tormented, intelligent, mordantly witty – leaves her graduate studies and her Berkeley flat to drive through the scorching heat to her family's ranch. There they are all assembled: her philosopher father, smelling sweetly of five-star Hennessy; her kind, fussy grandmother; her beloved twin sister Judith, who is about to be married – unless Cassandra can help it.

'I – whose usual bed time is ten o'clock – stayed up all night reading that exquisite *Cassandra at the Wedding* – dazzled by the pyrotechnics of such an artist' Carson McCullers

THE FRIENDLY YOUNG LADIES

Mary Renault

Stifled by life with her bickering parents in a bleak Cornish village, Elsie Lane flees to London to find her sister Leonora who escaped eight years earlier.

But there are surprises in store for conventional Elsie: not only does Leo live on a houseboat, she writes Westerns for a living and shares her boat – and her bed – with the beautiful Helen.

Elsie's arrival is the first in a series of events that will set Leo and Helen's contented life spiralling away from cosy domesticity. Soon a handsome young doctor pays a visit, turning his attention from one 'friendly' young lady to the next and the delicate calm is broken – with results unforeseen by all.

Mary Renault wrote this delightfully provocative novel in 1943, partly in answer to the despair of Radclyffe Hall's *The Well of Loneliness*. The result is this stylish social comedy set in the 1930s.

'Undeniably charming' *New Yorker*

'Written with rare insight' *Boston Globe*

LOLLY WILLOWES

Sylvia Townsend Warner

'Witty, eerie, tender' John Updike

Lolly Willowes has endured twenty years of self-effacement as a maiden aunt when she decides to escape her extended family and move to a small Bedfordshire village. Here, happy and unfettered, she revels in a new existence, nagged only by a sense of a secret she has yet to discover. With her cat and the Devil, Lolly Willowes discovers that secret – witchcraft – and is finally free.

Deliciously wry and magical, *Lolly Willowes* is Sylvia Townsend Warner's piquant plea that single women should find liberty and civility, a theme later explored by Virginia Woolf in *A Room of One's Own*.

'She had a talent amounting to genius' Rosamond Lehmann

**You can order other Virago titles through our website: *www.virago.co.uk*
or by using the order form below**

☐	Cassandra at the Wedding	Dorothy Baker	£7.99
☐	The Friendly Young Ladies	Mary Renault	£8.99
☐	Lolly Willowes	Sylvia Townsend Warner	£7.99
☐	Mr Fortune's Maggot	Sylvia Townsend Warner	£7.99
☐	The Corner That Held Them	Sylvia Townsend Warner	£7.99
☐	Devoted Ladies	Molly Keane	£7.99

*The prices shown above are correct at time of going to press. However, the publishers
reserve the right to increase prices on covers from those previously advertised,
without further notice.*

Virago

Please allow for postage and packing: **Free UK delivery.**
Europe: add 25% of retail price; Rest of World: 45% of retail price.

To order any of the above or any other Virago titles, please call our credit
card orderline or fill in this coupon and send/fax it to:

Virago, PO Box 121, Kettering, Northants NN14 4ZQ
Fax: 01832 733076   Tel: 01832 737526
Email: aspenhouse@FSBDial.co.uk

☐ I enclose a UK bank cheque made payable to Virago for £ . . . .
☐ Please charge £ . . . . . . to my Visa/Access/Mastercard/Eurocard

Expiry Date   Switch Issue No.

NAME (BLOCK LETTERS please) . . . .

ADDRESS . . . .

. . . .

. . . .

Postcode . . . . Telephone . . . .

Signature . . . .

Please allow 28 days for delivery within the UK. Offer subject to price and availability.

Please do not send any further mailings from companies carefully selected by Virago ☐